OFFICE PROCEDURES AND TECHNOLOGY

First Edition

by Harry R. Moon, Curriculum Specialist
Materials for Business Education

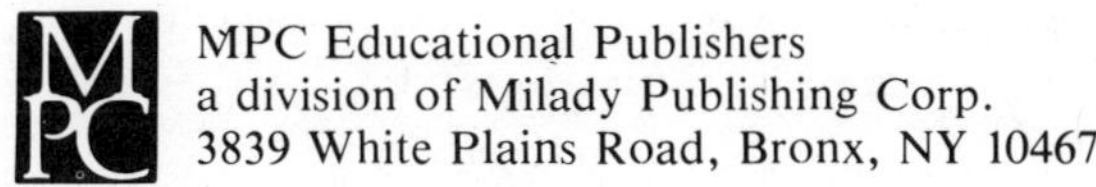
MPC Educational Publishers
a division of Milady Publishing Corp.
3839 White Plains Road, Bronx, NY 10467

Editor: Dr. Lois E. Frazier
Design Director: John Fornieri
Associate Designers: Pat Miret
Mark Stein
Illustrator: Shizuko Horii
Typographer: Barbara Cardillo

Bronx, N.Y.

Printed in the United States of America.

ISBN 0-87350-334-1

Acknowledgments

The author and the publisher of OFFICE PROCEDURES AND TECHNOLOGY take this opportunity to thank the following individuals and companies for their contributions to the textbook:

- Dr. Lois E. Frazier, Chairwoman of the Department of Business and Economics at Meredith College in Raleigh, NC, who edited the manuscript and advised the author.
- Mrs. Shizuko Horii, the artist who created the illustrations for the text.
- Bobbs-Merrill Educational Publishing for providing the plate of ***Speedwriting*** Shorthand, Regency Edition, ©1984, in Chapter 22.
- Mr. Rollie Cox, an instructor in the Business Division of the Madison Area Technical College in Madison, WI, who was a consultant on the electronic mail part of Chapter 10 and on the technology part of Chapter 11.
- Mr. Joseph Parker of Irmo, SC, who was a consultant on the data processing part of Chapter 10.
- Mrs. Doris Y. Gerber, former state supervisor of business education in the state of Washington, who was a consultant on Chapter 19.
- Ms Cheryl Baedke of the Milford Plaza Hotel (an affiliate of the Cox Hotel Corporation), who was a consultant on Chapter 18.
- Dr. Tony Bledsoe, a member of the faculty in the Department of Business and Economics at Meredith College in Raleigh, NC, who was a consultant on Chapter 25.
- Robert Garey, CPA, who was a consultant on the financial statements part of Chapter 12.
- The Reuben H. Donnelley Corporation for permitting the use of excerpts from the OFFICIAL AIRLINE GUIDE (OAG) in Chapter 18.
- Elvira Mezzanelli, the author's secretary, who prepared all the typewritten illustrations.

To The Student

OFFICE PROCEDURES AND TECHNOLOGY has been written to provide you with completely up-to-date information about the modern business office. The textbook includes complete, profusely illustrated information about such essential topics as:

Business communications
Human relations/Job attitude/Public relations
Basic office/secretarial skills and procedures
Office technology
Records management (including electronic storage and retrieval)
Reprographics
Planning business travel
Meeting/conference planning
Leadership
Management and supervision
Changing job roles

Careful, reflective study of the material in OFFICE PROCEDURES AND TECHNOLOGY will help you to have a complete understanding of the modern business office and the increasing role technology is playing in day-to-day business activities. You will also understand how the increased use of technology is changing (expanding and broadening) the job roles of office workers.

Each chapter in the text begins with a learning objective that will give you an overview of what you will know, do, think, and understand as a result of studying the chapter. A preview of new, job-related terminology that is introduced in the chapter follows the learning objective. Each chapter ends with review and discussion questions that will help you to recall the important information emphasized.

To help you to put the information in the textbook into a realistic, job-related perspective, a correlated workbook has been prepared that contains 41 projects. Those projects will help you to master subject matter and related skills.

The demand for management support (clerical and secretarial) workers is great in all types of businesses from the smallest rural offices to the largest international corporations all over the world! All of these organizations require the skills and understandings you are developing in this course.

Give your best efforts to this course, and it will pay you rich dividends in the months and years ahead!

Harry R. Moon

Table Of Contents

CHAPTER 1

The Image Created By The Office Worker

OBJECTIVE

After you have studied Chapter One you will understand how to:
- Express yourself with confidence
- Walk, stand, and sit with poise
- Dress and groom yourself to make a professional appearance
- Conduct yourself with confidence

JOB-RELATED VOCABULARY

Accessories—The secondary parts of an outfit or costume, such as jewelry, shoes, belt, gloves, and eyeglasses. They are the "extras" that add style and glamour to a basic outfit or costume.

Antiperspirant—A preparation that checks the flow of perspiration.

Deodorant—A preparation that **destroys or masks the odor** of perspiration.

Halitosis—The condition of having an offensive odor to one's breath.

Cologne—A pleasant smelling preparation to be applied to the body. Colognes are **light scents,** and they may be applied liberally.

Perfume—A pleasant smelling preparation to be applied to the body. Perfumes are **highly concentrated, long lasting** preparations, and they should be used sparingly.

Colleagues—Co-workers in a profession.

Propriety—Those actions and procedures that are considered to be socially acceptable.

Innovation—A new idea, method, or device.

Your image is the part of you that you project to others. Your image is projected **in**:
- The way you talk
- The way you walk, stand, and sit
- The way you dress and groom yourself
- The expression on your face
- The way you conduct yourself

The image you project as a business person determines to a great extent how people view the company for which you work. As an office worker, you have a responsibility to project a positive, businesslike, professional image for your company. Let's take a look at some of the ways you can do this.

The Way You Talk

How well you use the English language and the way you use your voice to convey your ideas to other people (particularly on the telephone) enable them to reach conclusions about you and about the company for which you work. This is fair enough since you are developing conclusions about other people and their firms in the same manner.

You will probably take a speech course while you are in school. If so, work diligently during the course to develop your speech to its highest potential. If you develop the following voice qualities, you will be using your voice well; and this ability will help you to create a more positive image for yourself and the company for which you work:

Voice Tone (mellow, pleasant to hear)

Volume (neither too loud nor too soft—well modulated)

Voice Control (not breathy and hurried, but relaxed and easy)

Grammatical Usage (clear, straightforward sentences that express thoughts concisely and that are free from slang and crudities)

The Way You Walk, Stand, And Sit

Very few characteristics indicate how a person feels about himself/herself like his/her carriage.

Always stand, sit, and walk "tall"; never slump over. When you are standing, keep your rib cage pulled in (not in an exaggerated manner), and keep your hips "tucked" under. Walk in a smooth, confident manner with your head balanced in the middle of your body and your chin parallel to the floor. Avoid swinging your hips from side to side as you walk. To sit correctly, sit on the edge of a chair and place your hands on the **seat** of the chair (not the arms) to push yourself back into sitting position. (When women are seated, they should avoid crossing their legs, particularly if they're wearing short skirts and sitting in a low chair.) When you want to rise from a sitting position, place your hands on the seat of the chair and push yourself forward to the edge of the chair. Then rise, putting your weight on whichever foot is closest to the chair, balancing your body as you step on the foot that is forward.

The Way You Dress And Groom Yourself

The way you dress and groom yourself not only affects the impression you make on others, but it affects your self-confidence (and thereby your competence) as well.

While there is considerable flexibility today in what is "right" for office wear, it is still important to coordinate, that is, to mix and match compatible colors, patterns, fabrics, and designs in your wardrobe. As a general rule, be somewhat conservative in what you wear to the office. Clothes and accessories that were designed specifically for "after five" wear are definitely out of place in the office. Be careful, too, about accessories that jangle and dangle; they can be a terrible distraction and an annoyance to other people. Colors, as long as the combination of them is in good taste, are "in." Wear them, and enjoy the fun of combining them creatively. When you purchase clothing for office wear, read the labels, watching for permanent press, drip dry, or easy-to-care-for fabrics. Buying them will save you both time and money in the care of your wardrobe.

Good grooming begins with keeping your body and your clothing perfectly clean. To be well groomed, you must shower or bathe every day. Washable clothes must be laundered after each wearing; other clothes must be cleaned and pressed regularly so they will be "crisp" looking and free from odors. Your shoes must be polished and in good repair. Your hands and nails, which must be clean at all times, need proper care. Your hair must be shampooed frequently and styled in a becoming (not exotic) way. Long hair must not be allowed to fly in a wild, disarranged manner. The daily use of an antiperspirant (to check the flow of perspiration) and a deodorant (to stop the smell of perspiration) is essential. In addition, teeth must be brushed thoroughly after each meal, and a mouthwash or breath mints should be used to check halitosis. In this enlightened day and age, there is absolutely no excuse for either body or breath odors.

A woman should wear makeup that is tastefully applied to accent her own natural beauty. Special glamour makeup techniques should be saved for those special (probably "after five") occasions where the lighting is suitable for them. Colognes and perfumes should be applied sparingly so the smell of them is not offensive to others in the office. Be sure that the scents of makeup, hair spray, and perfume are compatible.

Men should be clean shaven every day. If a man wears a beard or a mustache, it should be trimmed frequently so that it is appropriate for his facial features. A man might want to wear after-shave lotion and cologne, completing his facial grooming with an application of neutral or tinted talc. He, too, should be certain to use colognes and after-shaves sparingly to be sure the smell of them is not offensive. Men, too, need to be sure the scents of cologne, after-shave, and talc are compatible to avoid smelling like a walking flower garden!

The Expression On Your Face

It is possible to tell a great deal about how a person is feeling about life by observing the expression on his/her face. To this end, a pleasant, friendly, alert expression that seems to say "Good morning! How may I help you this morning?" before the words are actually spoken will do much to help you project a positive image for yourself and your company. Remember, the **look** of friendliness and the **act** of friendliness do much to convey that positive image!

The Way You Conduct Yourself

To work successfully with and for other people, it is necessary to develop positive attitudes about the way you conduct yourself, such as the following:

1. As soon as you start a new job, learn the names of your co-workers, and call them by name.
2. Observe company rules and regulations without exception. (Nothing will cause a new employee to start in the wrong direction on a new job like breaking company rules and regulations!)
3. When work assignments are being explained, listen carefully; and ask questions when you don't understand.
4. Do not be too eager to impress the people with whom you work. If you try to create the impression of extreme confidence and competence too soon, you will probably be interpreted by older employees as being smug and cocky. It is a far better plan to begin your association with your new colleagues with the attitude that you have much to learn and you hope they will help you to learn because you lack experience.

The way you conduct yourself should be based on consideration for other people and property. If you are in doubt about whether or not to proceed in certain situations, ask yourself these questions:

Is the action considerate?

Is the action appropriate?

If your answers to both of these questions are an honest "yes," you can proceed safely. If the answer to either one of the questions is "no," you should refrain from such conduct.

THE TRAINING OF THE GENERAL OFFICE WORKER

The fact that office technology is increasing rapidly in the United States makes it more important than ever before that potential office workers seek training that will enable them to develop skills, abilities, understandings, and procedures that will help them to be productive in today's complex, fast-changing business world. Furthermore, as an office worker, you must carry on a continuing training program that will enable you to keep pace with new office procedures introduced by technology, experimentation, and innovation.

Equally important to the office worker who seeks to grow with his/her job is an overall understanding of ever-changing business terminology, management functions, and the free enterprise system. It would seem, then, that a specialized education in business skills and procedures and a somewhat flexible liberal arts background would best prepare the beginning office worker for his/her place in the world of business.

FOR REVIEW AND DISCUSSION

1. Through what means do individuals project their image?
2. What specific speech qualities should you develop in order to use your voice to its best possible potential?
3. Explain how the way you walk, sit, and stand affects the image you project.
4. Explain the basics of appropriate dress and good grooming for business.
5. Explain some important points to remember about the way to conduct yourself in a business situation to project a positive image for yourself and your company.
6. What are the two key questions that you should ask yourself to determine whether or not you should proceed in certain business situations?
7. Describe the best type of training for a general office worker.

Turn to your workbook and complete Student Projects 1, 2, and 3.

CHAPTER 2

Developing An Effective Personality And A Positive Job Attitude

OBJECTIVE

After you have studied Chapter Two, you will understand how to cultivate pleasing personality traits and how to develop a plan for successful human relationships that will increase your chances for success on the job.

JOB-RELATED VOCABULARY

Inquisitive—Probing; wanting to examine or investigate.

Gushing—Making a very strong display of enthusiasm or emotion.

Affected—A manner assumed artificially or falsely.

Monopolizing—Controlling or commanding exclusively or totally.

Endearing—Making beloved or dear; making one the object of affection.

Integration—The incorporation of people into a group as equal participants.

Much has been written and spoken about what constitutes an effective personality. Basically, attention to the way you talk; the way you stand, walk, and sit; the way you dress and groom yourself; the expression on your face; and the way you conduct yourself (as described in Chapter One of this text) and the following factors are expressions of your personality. Each of these factors helps you to express your true self to other people.

- The way you act emotionally—the way you "handle" the varying situations of your daily life
- Your philosophy of life—the factors on which you base your life and plans; those things you consider to be essential requirements for a successful, happy, complete life
- Your versatility—your ability to adjust readily to ever-changing circumstances
- Your willingness to be helpful—your concern for the comfort and happiness of other people with whom you come in contact

These nine traits (five in Chapter One and four here) are the means by which you express your personality (or your "self"). They are the means by which other people develop an "image" of you as a person.

Pleasing Personality Traits

If you wish to be successful as an office worker, you must develop to the fullest possible extent various personality traits that will enable you to work with other people in a productive, harmonious way.

- Tact—Tact has been defined as the preservation of human dignity **under all circumstances.** It involves preserving the dignity of other people as well as your own dignity. The successful office worker must learn what to say, when to say it, and how to say it.
- Loyalty—This involves treating as confidential the affairs of the company for which you work and the activities of the people with whom you work. In addition, you will need to be prepared to defend to other people and other firms the objectives toward which your company is working.
- Compatibility—A person who is truly compatible finds joy in just being with people. Such a person recognizes that people differ from one another in appearance, in attitudes, in interests, and in abilities; and he/she makes allowances for those differences. A compatible person listens well, and he/she is easy to talk with.
- Poise (sometimes referred to as a person's "bearing")—It implies that the person is the master of himself/herself. He/she does not let distressing circumstances throw him/her into emotional turmoil. In a business situation, poise reflects the confidence a person has in himself/herself and in his/her company.
- Congeniality—It is the quality of finding genuine enjoyment and challenge in personal relations—in work, in people, in situations. The person who is truly congenial understands that problems are a part of daily life, and he/she does not expect everything and everyone to be perfect.
- Cooperativeness—Any office worker who is thinking clearly will understand that productivity is dependent on teamwork. He/she will cooperate with every member of the office "team" so the business can run more smoothly and more profitably. (Remember, a business must be profitable before the employees can receive increases in their salaries and fringe benefits.)
- Salesmanship—A good employee is sales minded. He/she is a good public relations representative for his/her company. He/she understands that the success of the company is directly related to its success in selling its products and its services. At every opportunity, the conscientious office worker "sells" his/her company in order to help it succeed.
- Dependability (or reliability)—It involves the willingness to do what needs to be done for the benefit of the company (and thereby to the benefit of the employee). It involves the willingness to accept additional responsibility, the willingness to meet special needs, and the willingness to exert extra efforts for special situations.

By mastering these eight personality qualities, you will be taking a giant step to a well-adjusted life. That, in turn, will help you to be a more effective office worker; and you will be able to work more harmoniously with your associates for the benefit of the company.

Annoying Personality Traits

Studies indicate certain personality traits that most people find irritating. As a prospective office worker desiring good relationships, you must search your own personality for indications of the following traits. If these traits exist in your personality, you must work diligently to replace them with pleasing, constructive personality traits.

Forcing people to buy
Bossy manner
Telling people to hurry
Gushing manner

Trying too hard to be funny
Idle gossip
Coughing in others' faces
Losing your temper
Telling petty lies
Being too inquisitive
Sarcasm
Habitually arguing
Noisy gum chewing
Giving unasked-for advice
Bragging about oneself
Coaxing others
Continually criticizing
Crowding to front of line
Spitting in public
Slapping people on the back
Sexy talk
Cheating in games
Looking glum
An affected manner
Talking loud in public
Baby talk
Using slang excessively
Monopolizing conversation
Disrespect toward older folks
Endearing names for casual acquaintances
Nagging others
Putting on airs
"Cutting up" to get attention

By ridding your personality of these undesirable traits and by replacing them with the pleasing personality traits discussed earlier in this chapter, you will be showing consideration for others. You will also be projecting your own image and the image of your company more positively.

A PLAN FOR SUCCESSFUL HUMAN RELATIONSHIPS

Human relations has been defined as: "the integration of people into a work situation in a way that motivates them to work together productively, cooperatively, and with economic, psychological, and social satisfactions." An analysis of this definition reveals several positive personality traits. First of all, people must **work together cooperatively** before anything worthwhile can occur. As a result of working together cooperatively, they are able to produce; and, as a result of their productivity, they are able to earn a paycheck and to have the social and emotional satisfactions that accompany a job well done. Human relations has also been described as simply: "the art of getting along with other people, keeping their loyalty and goodwill."

Basic Human Needs

Whatever your definition of human relations, the fulfillment of the following six basic human needs is essential to treating people as separate, important personalities. Understanding these needs will enable you to work more effectively at getting and keeping the loyalty of other people.

- **The Need to Belong**—We all want to feel that we are a part of what is going on and not an outsider.
- **The Need to Be Needed**—Whether we want to admit it or not, we all want someone to count on us to "produce" either on the job or in a social situation.
- **The Need to Contribute**—Most people recognize a sincere need to supply something that is of benefit to someone else.
- **The Need for Recognition**—We all seek acknowledgment in some form (praise, financial reward, advancement, additional responsibility, friendliness) from our superiors, our colleagues, our families, and our friends.
- **The Need for Security**—In order to be happy, successful people, we all must have the "I can do this" feeling that comes from self-confidence that is related to past success.
- **The Need for Flexibility**—We all need to know that the rules and procedures governing our lives make allowances for changing circumstances and individual differences that permit growth.

By helping other people to fulfill the six basic human needs in their own lives, we are well on our way to developing better human relationships; and we will be helping other people to live healthier, happier, more confident lives.

Human Relations Personally Applied

Unfortunately, understanding the preceding six basic human needs is not enough. Here are some steps you can take to build better relationships with others:

- Develop Empathy—Empathy is the ability to "see" situations objectively from the other person's point of view. If you develop your ability to empathize, you approach situations from a point of view that will make them easier and more positive for the people with whom you live and work.
- Become Objective—Objectivity is seeing things from the "What is best for everyone concerned?" point of view instead of from the "How will this affect me?" point of view. Becoming objective permits working out circumstances to everyone's satisfaction rather than frustrating many individuals to satisfy a few.
- Be Tolerant—Learn to accept people's basic shortcomings, to be tolerant of people with ideas different from your own and with a philosophy of life different from yours. You live in a world filled with many wonderful ideas, attitudes, and traditions contributed by a wide variety of people. Think of how much you can gain by sharing these ideas, attitudes, and traditions.
- Show Appreciation—By showing appreciation for the efforts of other people and by praising them when they have performed well, you are helping other people to cope more effectively with daily life. More than that, appreciation and praise help to create within everyone the desire to do more work and to be more effective.
- Be Understanding—Learn all you can about what makes a dynamic, successful personality. Develop an understanding of what motivates other people. As you do this, you will be preparing yourself to live more creatively, more productively, and more realistically with them.

If each of us practiced with the deepest kind of sincerity the personality and human relations concepts discussed in this chapter, think of how our person-to-person relationships would benefit!

FOR REVIEW AND DISCUSSION

1. Explain briefly the nine factors that express personality.
2. Explain briefly the eight personality traits that are essential to success in business (or elsewhere).
3. Name some annoying personality traits.
4. Explain the two definitions of human relations discussed in Chapter Two.
5. Discuss the six basic human needs that have been identified in this chapter.
6. Discuss the steps each of us can take to build better relationships with other people.

Turn to your workbook and complete Student Projects 4 and 5.

CHAPTER 3

Becoming A Part Of The Office Team

OBJECTIVE

By studying Chapter Three you will learn to understand a job, a company, and the people with whom you will work. You will also understand how to become a more efficient worker.

JOB-RELATED VOCABULARY

Specifications—Detailed plans or proposals for doing something.

Adherence—Steady and faithful compliance with something.

Communicate—To make known—such as to make known an idea or a thought.

Anticipate—To give **advance** thought, discussion, or treatment to something.

Appropriate—That which is suitable, compatible, or fitting.

Endeavors—Strives to reach or achieve a certain level or position.

Morale—The mental and emotional attitudes of individuals.

Work in a business office must be a team effort if the business is to prosper. Each person who works for the company is a part of the company "team," and he/she must take responsibility for the "position" he/she plays on the team! The failure of one worker to take his/her position on the team seriously and responsibly will cause a breakdown in the total structure of the business operation, and it will have an adverse effect on everyone who works for the company.

UNDERSTANDING YOUR JOB

The way you get started on a new job will have a great deal to do with how well you will be "accepted" by your new colleagues and, to some degree, how successful you will be on the job. Here are some suggestions that will help you to make a good start:

1. Use Office Manual
   Many companies have an office manual that contains, among other things, a job analysis, a job description, or job specifications from which you can determine the full extent of the responsibility your job entails.
2. Listen to Instructions
   Listen carefully as the people from whom you are getting job directions explain the procedures to be followed. If you don't understand something they tell you, don't be afraid to ask questions. (Many times someone will be assigned to train you. Other times, you will be "on your own" to do the job the best way you can with very little direction.)
3. Consult Files
   If you are assigned a project with very little direction, you can sometimes get ideas about format, styles to be followed, and requirements of the job by consulting the files for jobs of a similar type.

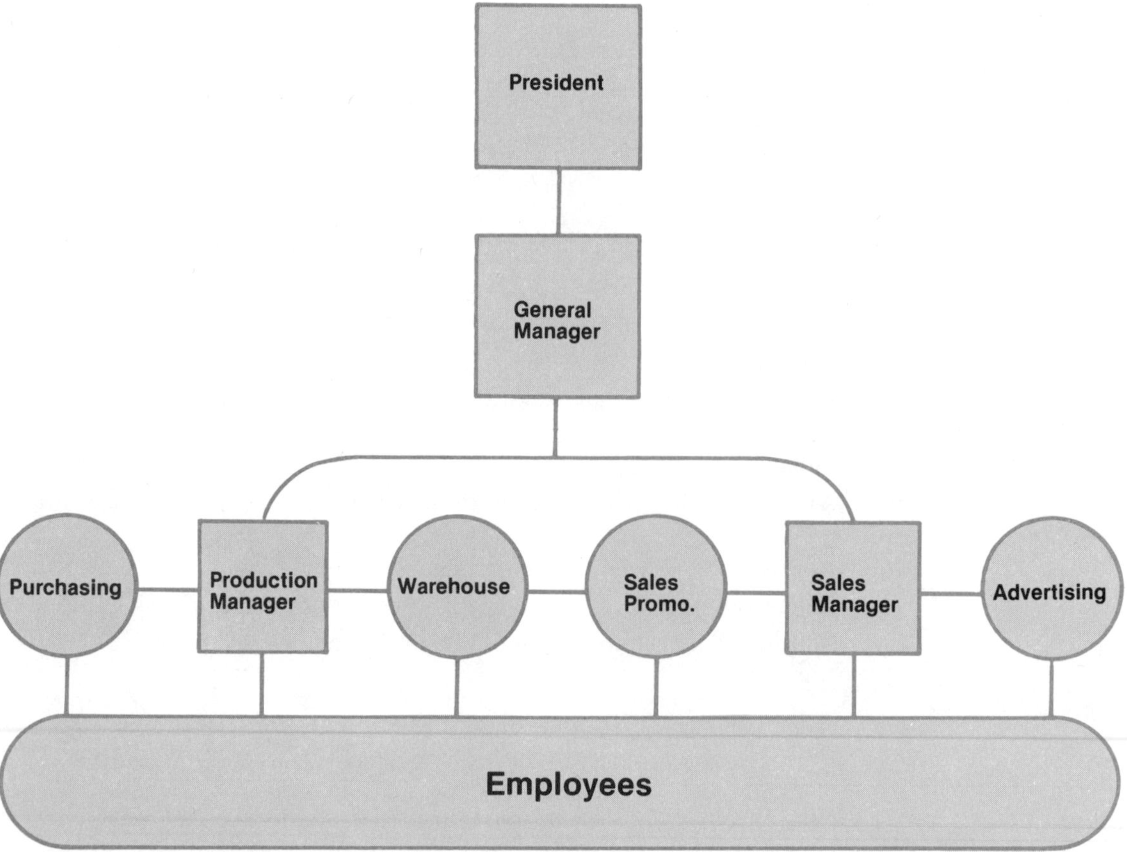

Fig. 1. The line positions, represented by the rectangles, make the decisions and formulate the policy. The staff positions, represented by the circles, advise and service the line organization.

4. Study Organization Charts
   It is essential to learn early in your employment how the lines of authority run within your company. Find out who gives the orders and how the chain of command works until the directions get to you. It is equally important to know to whom you are expected to pass the chain of command. Strict adherence to lines of authority is essential for business harmony. A line-and-staff organization chart is shown on page 10 of this text to give you some idea about lines of authority.
5. Communicate
   The ability to communicate your ideas to other people so they understand what you are trying to do is important. Many new employees who have great potential fail miserably here. How can people within a company function for the benefit of the company if they can't communicate their ideas to one another in an effective way?
6. Be Alert for Improvements
   By being alert, you will soon become aware of situations within your organization that can be improved. Your company will want your suggestions, and you will want to take the initiative in assuming the responsibility to do what should be done in the best way. Your alertness is evidenced by your ability to anticipate requirements and your ability to meet them.
7. Check Accuracy
   Be certain of the accuracy of every statement you make before you make it. If you make a series of statements that prove to be inaccurate, other employees will begin to question your judgment and doubt your sincerity.

Observing these suggestions will help you to get started on a new job in a positive manner.

UNDERSTANDING YOUR COMPANY

During your first few months on a new job you will be constantly learning about the company, its products and/or services, its customers, and its method of doing business. Read all company literature so you will be well informed about those functions. A clear understanding of the company organization, products, services, and customers will help you to feel like "a member of the team"; and it will help you to do a more efficient job as an employee because you will be well informed.

Many companies have office manuals that explain company regulations and procedures. In addition, office manuals often give detailed explanations about how certain types of jobs are to be done. By studying such a manual carefully, you will be learning about company procedures and preferences. This information will help to make you seem more efficient in the eyes of your co-workers and your superiors. It will also enable you to establish a reputation as an "interested, enthusiastic" employee—an enviable reputation with any company!

As an employee of any company you will want to grow in your knowledge about and understanding of the company. You can keep informed by listening carefully to what you are told, by observing the trends of the company as reflected in the work for which you are responsible, and by studying the company "house organ" (employees' newspaper) for indications of growth and shifts in product or service emphasis. When you become aware of changes, you will want to be able to make the appropriate shifts in your own job emphasis and in your overall thinking to help the company to prosper in its new endeavors, too.

UNDERSTANDING YOUR CO-WORKERS

The best way to influence your co-workers in a positive manner is to be considerate and thoughtful of them as people and to be a **contributing, productive** member of the office "team." (People soon get tired of dragging someone else's weight along with their own.) Here are some thoughts about dealing with other people in a thoughtful, considerate way:

- Avoid interrupting other people at work. When it is necessary to interrupt someone, always inquire about whether he/she is able to talk with you at that time.
- Don't get the reputation of "bearing tales." If you have a criticism of another employee, take it directly to him/her in a helpful, constructive manner.
- Learn to work cooperatively with other employees. Nobody can do everything himself/herself.
- Learn to keep your emotions under control. Try to keep circumstances from getting to the "boiling" point. Handle difficult-to-cope-with situations as they arise in a tactful, cooperative way.
- Keep the confidences of your co-workers. Everyone soon learns to distrust a person who talks too much.
- Try to develop a pleasant, easy-to-like personality. Put a smile on your face. (You will be surprised how this attitude will bring a positive response in others.)

Current research has revealed some thoughts about the way workers feel and act. By studying these suggestions and by putting the ideas into practice, you will be relating more creatively with your co-workers. In addition, you will be displaying the kind of thinking that indicates management ability to your superiors.

- People like to be treated courteously. Most people will recognize that someone has to be "in charge" in a working situation, but they want that person to be considerate and thoughtful.
- People do not like to be dominated or threatened. When people work under negative psychological pressure and an "or else" threat, morale breaks down; and rebellion is encouraged.
- People like to feel useful, and they like to receive recognition. The intelligent supervisor is the one who praises even small contributions made by his/her workers. By doing so, he/she helps the worker enjoy a sense of personal satisfaction in his/her work.
- People like to be informed about things that affect them. Change can be a threat to a person's sense of security. By keeping workers informed about things that affect them, the supervisor is reassuring them; and he/she is contributing to their sense of worth. In addition, he/she is avoiding the problem of broken morale.
- People like to feel that they "belong" to the group. Most people feel that the atmosphere created by the "every person for himself/herself" approach is risky, uneasy, and lonely. Belonging to the group and cooperating with the group gives the worker a sense of security, which takes uneasy pressure off the individual.
- People like to have a chance to express themselves. By weighing the opinions of his/her workers on any major issue, the supervisor makes it easier for them to feel a part of the decision-making process and to accept the final decision.

- People like to be treated fairly. Experience indicates that workers who are loyal to the company and who give their best efforts for the company want to receive a full share of the company's benefits, including a fair salary. In addition, workers will have more respect for co-workers who are willing to stand beside them at a time of stress.

OFFICE EFFICIENCY

Another quality that will help the "team" effort and will permit the company to operate more productively is office efficiency. The following suggestions will enable you to do your job with a minimum of stress, and they will help your co-workers to function more productively, too:

- Do the most important work first. (Doing this will make you seem more efficient.)
- Do complicated tasks in a step-by-step manner. (Breaking difficult tasks into steps provides you with a periodic measurement of what you have accomplished.)
- Give every task (even small, uncomplicated tasks) your complete attention.
- Insofar as possible, complete one job before you start another.
- Pursue every detail until the entire job has been completed.
- Before you start a job, be sure you understand what is to be accomplished and how it is to be done. Ask questions if there is something you do not understand.
- As you work, try to discover more efficient ways to perform your job.
- Arrange your work materials in a way that will make them easy to use.
- Use office supplies wisely. Do not waste pencils, stationery, paper clips, and carbon paper. Money saved here means additional profits for the company (and additional benefits for the employees).
- Keep your desk clear except for the materials with which you are working at the moment. (A cluttered, disorganized work area sometimes indicates a disorganized, confused person.)
- Double check all of your work for accuracy. Doing so will ensure more efficient handling of the job as it moves from place to place within the company. (Remember: "Time saved is money earned!")
- Always keep your immediate superior informed about what you are doing. In that way, he/she can plan for the total operation of the department and/or the company more realistically.
- Take special care to keep office equipment assigned to you clean and in top operating condition. Doing so will enable you to work more efficiently and to produce better results.

FOR REVIEW AND DISCUSSION

1. What are some steps a new office employee can take to understand his/her new job?
2. Describe how a new employee in an office can learn about the company, its products and/or services, its methods of doing business, and its regulations and procedures.
3. Why is it important for an employee to learn all he/she can about the company for which he/she works?
4. Explain how a new employee can relate to his/her co-workers as a thoughtful, considerate, productive person.
5. Discuss the ideas that current research has revealed about how employees feel and act.
6. What steps can a new office employee take to be efficient on the job?

Turn to your workbook and complete Student Project 6.

CHAPTER 4

Your Future As An Office Worker

OBJECTIVE

In Chapter Four you will learn about the factors upon which job success is based and about the factors that make employees of a company promotable.

JOB-RELATED VOCABULARY

Explicit—Plainness; without difficulty in interpretation; fully visible.

Impartial—Not biased.

Motivation—A need or a desire that causes a person to take action of some type.

Dignity—Esteem or worthiness.

Substantial—Satisfying or important.

Effectively—Efficiently; with purpose.

It has been said that business is the cornerstone of our country. If that is true—and it seems that it is—there should be unlimited opportunity for office workers who have developed excellent job skills and effective personalities and who apply both to their jobs.

YOUR JOB FUTURE

Your future on any job is dependent upon the success you have with the work you are doing. From that point of view, you should examine the factors that enable a person to be successful in the business world.

Success in business is based on achieving results, accepting responsibility, earning a profit, and upon company and employee growth. However, this is not to imply that business people who are successful are easily defined, explicit types. Perhaps the following discussion of characteristics usually found in successful business people is the easiest way to understand success in business.

- The motivation to develop a plan in careful, logical detail and to implement the plan to get the desired results
- The willingness to accept the responsibility for decisions and actions
- The ability to see the entire business picture (finance, production, marketing, management) and not just the limited part of the business for which you are responsible. By developing this ability you begin to see the need (and the means) to control costs in order to earn a profit.
- The ability to get people to work together calmly and happily
- The ability to make decisions based upon careful and impartial study and analysis
- The ability to evaluate the results of decisions made and to determine if those decisions have borne effective results

How many of the preceding success-oriented characteristics do you possess? As a prospective business person, you should work diligently at developing each of them!

SUPERVISORS AND THE WORKERS THEY SUPERVISE

Most people who work in business look forward to the time when they will have management or supervisory responsibilities. Those responsibilities come as a result of successful experiences on the job, excellent skills, and continued study and growth.

In Chapter Three of this text, you studied the results of research showing how workers feel and act. The person who wants supervisory responsibility must learn to focus on the personality of the worker, the worker's needs, and the work to be completed.

If you would move "up the ladder" to a position of supervision and leadership, you should understand the procedures that are considered effective in working with employees. Thousands of articles have been written on the subject of relationships with employees. From those articles, the following points seem to be essential:

- **Employees prefer to be treated as individuals.** A person-to-person conversation with capable employees to learn about their hopes and their plans for the future and to clarify their ambitions seems to do more for the employees' self-image than expensive plans to develop "team spirit" or even profit-sharing plans.
- **Employees like to know that their superiors have confidence in them.** They want to feel sure that superiors will recognize their worth and will give the employees credit for original, productive ideas. All employees want to be free of the fear motivation of the "yes man."
- **Employees respond to praise.** A good supervisor finds situations that he/she can praise in order to encourage employees. If criticism is necessary, it is much more effective if the person criticizing emphasizes the facts and avoids belittling comments about people involved. The supervisor should always follow any criticism with suggestions for improvement.
- **The use of humor with employees helps to create a pleasant working atmosphere.** This does not mean to imply that, to be successful, a supervisor must be able to "laugh off" any problem. It does mean to

imply, though, that the supervisor or leader who can inject humor into a situation takes some of the "sting" from even the harshest problem. By using humor creatively, the supervisor preserves the dignity of the workers and his/her own dignity as well.

- **Good supervisors deal with specific points.** Employees should be told specifically what to observe and what to do rather than to "observe what is happening in the office" and to "keep busy." Directions to employees should be given in clear, straightforward language; and employees should be encouraged to ask questions if they do not understand.
- **Employees prefer a supervisor who has a positive manner.** It is an old concept, but it is true: "An enthusiastic supervisor creates enthusiasm in his/her workers." The creative supervisor is a teacher and a leader. He/she inspires workers to be loyal to the supervisor and the organization. In a time of stress where some form of discipline may be necessary for an employee, the supervisor who has a positive manner tries to help his/her employee by using the situation to strengthen the employee's personality in order to help him/her meet future problems more adequately.

Anyone who chooses to supervise other workers will be most successful if he/she thinks in terms of helping others to grow and to solve their problems instead of dominating them. This can best be done by a supervisor who has a high level of maturity and who sets a positive example for employees by his/her own actions.

BEING PROMOTABLE

Much has been written about qualities that make a worker promotable. Whatever circumstances prompt promotion of a worker, he/she should be evaluated for promotion. A formalized rating system can be used if it meets the following criteria:

- The structure of the rating system must be constructive rather than critical. (It should be designed to help the employee to grow and progress.)
- The qualities to be rated should deal with reactions to job-related tasks and impersonal situations.
- Ratings should be based on past performance of the employee, not on what he/she may be able to do in the future.
- Only those persons who know the employee well (under a wide scope of conditions) should be asked to rate him/her.
- Each employee should be rated by at least three different people. (Each of us is unconsciously conditioned by our total experiences in such a way that we cannot—no matter how hard we try—be entirely impartial. Therefore, a rating by more than one person provides a greater chance for fairness.)

Here are the types of characteristics on which people are usually rated:

- Physical and emotional characteristics
- Appearance
- Conversation ability
- Ability to deal with others
- Mental efficiency
- Attitude toward self
- Moral traits (honesty, dependability)
- Conduct on the job

Take a few minutes to think about your own personal characteristics as they relate to the above list. What is the ratio of positive traits you possess to traits that need improvement in your own personality? What steps can you take to improve those traits that need improvement?

To ensure yourself of a substantial place in the world of business, you will want to learn all you can about yourself as well as the way to work effectively with other people.

FOR REVIEW AND DISCUSSION

1. Upon what factors is success in business dependent?
2. Discuss the types of characteristics often found in successful business people.
3. Discuss the factors that enable supervisors to deal more effectively with employees.
4. What are the criteria for a good rating system for employees?
5. What are the types of characteristics on which employees are usually rated? Discuss each one briefly.

Turn to your workbook and complete Student Project 7.

CHAPTER 5

Business Communications

OBJECTIVE

After you study Chapter Five you will understand how to type a letter in the full-block and the modified-block letter styles with the primary and secondary parts of a business letter. You will also understand when to use a No. 6 and a No. 10 envelope and how to address those envelopes correctly. In addition, you will have a clear understanding of how to write eight types of business letters; you will understand the functions of and the procedures for interoffice memorandums and news releases, and you will understand effective procedures for oral communications.

JOB-RELATED VOCABULARY

Addressee—A person to whom something is addressed.

Elite Type—Typewriter type providing 12 spaces to the inch (horizontally).

Pica Type—Typewriter type providing 10 spaces to the inch (horizontally).

Composing—The act of creating something.

Sequence—A succession of related parts put together in progressive order.

Acknowledging—Recognizing the validity of something.

Alternate—Something that takes the place of something else. Example—An alternate solution (a solution that takes the place of another).

Tactful—Having the ability to do and say those things that are both fitting and considerate in order to maintain good relationships with others.

Factually—That which is based upon the facts or actuality (reality).

Vague—Not clearly expressed.

Concise—Brief and to the point; free from flowery language.

Confidential—Private or secret in nature.

Letters and memorandums are an important part of business because they are the means by which businesses communicate with their customers and other business firms. Therefore, they deserve considerable attention if communications are to be as effective as possible.

Business people produce letters from shorthand dictation, machine dictation, or handwritten rough drafts; or they compose their own letters. This chapter is concerned with handwritten rough drafts or self-composed letters. Transcription of letters from shorthand or from machine dictation will be discussed in Chapter 22 (Dictation/Transcription and the Secretary).

BUSINESS LETTER STYLES

There are seven essential parts of a business letter which must appear in all business letters:

1. The date
2. The inside address
3. The salutation
4. The body of the letter
5. The complimentary close
6. The signature line
7. The reference initials

In this chapter, you will find the two most frequently used business letter styles: the full-block style and the modified-block style.

Full-Block Letter Style

This letter style is frequently used in business offices because of the placement of the seven essential parts at the left margin (see Fig. 2). It is particularly popular in word processing centers that use a standard format for all letters. Here are some guidelines for typing a letter in full block style:

1. Type the date two lines below the last line on the letterhead blocked at the left margin.
2. The blank lines left between the date and the inside address may be adjusted so the letter will be centered on the page. If the letter you are typing is a long one, you will allow four lines (the minimum) between the date and the inside address. If you are typing a short letter, you will allow more space between the date and the inside address.
3. The inside address is blocked against the left margin, and it is always at least three lines in length. If you have an address with only a person's name and the city, state, and zip code, type the name on the first line, the city name on the second line, with the name of the state and the zip code on the third line.
4. Space twice between the inside address and the salutation (or greeting). Type the salutation blocked against the left margin; and, when using mixed punctuation, follow it with a colon.
5. Space twice between the salutation and the body of the letter. Type paragraphs blocked against the left margin. Space twice after each paragraph.
6. The complimentary close is typed two lines below the last paragraph in the body of the letter, and it is blocked against the left margin. When mixed punctuation is used, the complimentary close is followed by a comma.
7. Space four times (minimum) after the complimentary close, and type the signature line blocked against the left margin. The signature consists of the full name of the person who will sign the letter (typed as he/she will sign it) followed by his/her title. If either the name or the title is extremely long, type the name on one line and the title under the name on the next line.
8. Space twice after the signature line and type the reference initials of the typist only (in small letters). There is one exception to this rule about reference initials. When the letter is prepared (or dictated) by one person, but will be signed by another person, type the initials of the person who prepared the letter first (usually in caps), followed by a colon (no space before or after the colon); then type the initials of the typist. Example: HM:ld

MGC

MORGAN GLASS CORPORATION
4675 West Market Street
Greensboro, NC 27408-1925

March 28, 19--

Ms Susan D. Pelter, Vice President
Camden Glass Corporation
516 Columbia Boulevard
Camden, NJ 08101

Dear Ms Pelter:

This is an example of a letter typed in the full block style. It is easy for the typist to type this letter neatly and accurately.

The full block style saves time and energy when you have many letters to type. Many typists and executives prefer this style.

Practice typing this letter until you can prepare a neat, attractive business letter. Pay attention to spelling and punctuation. Retyping a letter is far better than mailing it with glaring mistakes and poor corrections.

Sincerely yours,

Helen D. Thomas

Helen D. Thomas, President

em

Fig 2. Full-block letter with mixed punctuation

Modified Block Letter Style

This letter style permits some relief from the rigid straightness of the full-block letter style (see Fig. 3). Here are some guidelines for typing a letter in the modified-block (semi-block) style:

1. The date is usually typed two lines below the last line on the letterhead, beginning exactly in the center of the page. As an option, the date is sometimes centered; or it can be typed blocked at the **right** margin (the last figure in the date ends at the right margin).
2. Again, the number of spaces between the date and the inside address will vary with the length of the letter. The minimum number of lines is four, but you might need to leave as many as ten or twelve blank lines between the date and the inside address of a short letter.
3. The inside address is blocked against the left margin. It is always at least three lines long.
4. Space twice between the inside address and the salutation (or greeting). Type the salutation blocked at the left margin; and, when using mixed punctuation, follow it with a colon.
5. Space twice between the salutation and the body of the letter. The first line of each paragraph in the body of a letter typed modified-block style may be indented five spaces or blocked at the left margin.
6. The complimentary close is typed two lines below the last line in the body of the letter. It begins exactly in the center of the page (in line with the date).
7. Space four times (minimum) after the complimentary close and type the signature line, beginning exactly in the center of the page (in line with the date and the complimentary close). The signature line may be expanded to two lines if necessary.
8. Space twice after the signature line and type the reference initials of the typist only at the left margin in small letters. Again, the exception to this rule explained on page 20 (number 8) could apply.

MGC

MORGAN GLASS CORPORATION
4675 West Market Street
Greensboro, NC 27408-1925

March 28, 19--

Ms Nancy C. Hart
1625 Temple Street
Philadelphia, PA 19130

Dear Ms Hart:

This is an example of a letter typed in the modified block style. It has an attractive appearance, and many companies prefer this style.

The difference between this style and the full block style is that the date, complimentary close, and signature line begin exactly in the center of the page instead of at the left margin. On this particular letter, the paragraphs are indented five spaces also.

Many office workers who are not concerned with mass production favor this style, because it is not so severe as the full-block style letter.

Sincerely yours,

Wilma C. Conover

Wilma C. Conover
Personnel Department

em

Fig. 3. Modified-block letter with mixed punctuation

Secondary Parts Of A Business Letter

The secondary parts of a business letter are so called because they need not appear on every letter. As you study each of the secondary parts of a business letter, look at Figs. 4 and 5. They illustrate the placement of the secondary parts on the full-block and modified-block letter styles. Here are the secondary parts of a business letter listed in the order in which they appear on a letter:

1. **Attention Line**—When a letter is addressed to a company, an attention line is sometimes used to direct it to a particular person within the company. The attention line may be centered two lines below the inside address. However, it is frequently blocked at the left margin and underscored. Two lines are left after the attention line before the salutation is typed. (Caution: Even though the attention line directs the letter to a particular person, the letter is still addressed to a company, so the salutation is still "Gentlemen" or "Ladies and Gentlemen.")
2. **Subject Line**—In order to make the contents of a letter easier to identify, a subject line is sometimes used. The subject line may be typed at the left margin two lines below the salutation or centered two lines below the salutation. It is either typed in all caps or typed with initial caps and underscored. Two lines are left after the subject line before the body of the letter is typed.
3. **Company Signature Line**—The company signature line is sometimes typed in all caps two lines below the complimentary close of a business letter. The company name is typed as it appears on the letterhead. (The purpose of the company signature line is to identify the company to the reader of the letter once again before he/she finishes reading the letter.) Four lines (minimum) are left after the company signature line; then the signature and title of the person who will sign the letter are typed.
4. **Enclosure Notation**—When brochures, checks, and other items are to be placed in the envelope with the letter, an enclosure notation is blocked at the left margin on the line below the reference initials. The proper notation is usually either "Enclosure" or "Enclosures." However, **sometimes** the enclosures are listed as follows:

```
Enclosures:  Purchase Order
             Report
             Check
```

5. **Carbon Copy Notation**—When a carbon copy (or a machine-made facsimile copy) of a letter is being sent to a person other than the person to whom the letter is addressed, a carbon copy notation must appear on the original of the letter. If there is no enclosure notation, the carbon copy notation is typed on the line below the reference initials. If there is an enclosure notation, the carbon copy notation is typed on the line below the enclosure notation. (Double space in both instances if there is room.) The form for a carbon copy notation is as follows:

```
cc  Ms T. C. Hunt
    Mr. Howard Mendez
    Mrs. Sidney Weller
             or
    Copy to Ms C. L. Bradon
```

There would seldom be a time when **all** the secondary parts of a business letter would appear on one letter.

Fig. 4. Full-block letter with mixed punctuation showing secondary parts

April 10, 19--

Bellmont Glass Company
111 East Hanover Street
Indianapolis, IN 46204

Attention: Ms Doris Lang

Gentlemen:

Subject: Secondary Parts of a Business Letter

This is an example of a letter typed in the full block style, showing the secondary parts of a business letter.

On this particular letter, the date, the attention line, and the subject line are blocked at the left margin and underscored. (The attention line and the subject line may also be centered and underscored.) Notice, too, that the typist spaced twice between the last line of the inside address and the attention line and between the attention line and the salutation. In addition, the typist spaced twice between the salutation and the subject line and between the subject line and the body of the letter.

The company signature line is typed two lines below the complimentary close in all caps, and it is blocked against the left margin. The enclosure notation is typed on the line below the reference initials, and the carbon copy notation is typed on the line below the enclosure notation. (Double space after both the reference initials and the enclosure notation if there is room.)

Sincerely yours,

ROBERTS & WILLIAMS

C. D. King

C. D. King, Vice P

em

Enclosure

cc Mr. R. S. King
Mr. D. L. Thom

April 12, 19--

Orange County Manufacturing Corporation
4814 Harbor Boulevard
Anaheim, CA 92805

Attention: Mr. C. R. Strawn

Gentlemen:

Subject: Secondary Parts of a Business Letter

This is an example of a letter typed in the modified block style, showing the secondary parts of a business letter.

On this particular letter, the date starts at the center of the page. The attention line and the subject line are centered and underscored. (The attention line and the subject line may also be blocked at the left margin and underscored.) Notice the spacing between the inside address and the attention line and between the attention line and the salutation. Notice also the spacing between the salutation and the subject line and between the subject line and the body of the letter.

The company signature line is typed two lines below the complimentary close in all caps, and it begins in the center of the page in line with the date. Also notice that the signature line begins in the center of the page in line with the date, the complimentary close, and the company signature line. Notice the form used for the enclosure notation on this letter. Also notice the placement of the enclosure notation and the carbon copy notation. (Double space after both the reference initials and the enclosure notation if there is room.)

Sincerely yours,

ROBERTS & WILLIAMS, INCORPORATED

June B. Smith

June B. Smith, Esq.
Corporate Counsel

em

Enclosures: Check 1511
Voucher 14B

Copy to Mr. R. D. Simon

Fig. 5. Modified-block letter with mixed punctuation showing secondary parts

6. **Blind Carbon Copy Notations**—Occasionally a carbon or photocopy of a letter is sent to someone, and the person who wrote the letter doesn't want the addressee to know that anyone else is getting a copy. In that case, the original and the carbon copies of the letter being typed are removed from the typewriter. The carbon copies (without the letterhead copy) are then reinserted into the typewriter; and the carbon copy notation is typed on the carbon copies only, one inch down from the top of the page and blocked at the left margin. (See Fig. 6.) The blind carbon copy notation can also be placed at the bottom of the page in the position of the regular carbon copy notation.

bcc Ms R. L. Teller
Mr. T. D. Livingston
Ms K. L. Morton

August 1, 19--

Mr. R. D. Thomas, President
Crosier Restaurant Supply Company
1839 Peachtree Road, Northeast
Atlanta, GA 30308

Dear Mr. Thomas:

This is an example of a letter that has been typed with a blind carbon copy notation. In this particular letter, the original or letterhead copy is removed after the entire letter has been typed. The carbon copies of the letter are then reinserted into the typewriter, and the blind carbon copy notation is typed, blocked against the left margin, one inch from the top of the letter.

The blind carbon copy notation is used when the person who writes the letter does not want the addressee (the person to whom the letter is addressed) to know that anyone else is receiving a copy of the letter.

Sincerely yours,

Helen D. Thomas, President

em

Fig. 6. Letter with a blind carbon copy notation

Envelopes Because envelopes will carry the important letters your company will be sending, they should be prepared with as much care as the letters themselves.

A No. 10 envelope is 9½ inches from side to side x 4⅛ inches from top to bottom. It is always used for a two-page letter or a letter with enclosures, and it may be used for a one-page business letter also.

A No. 6 envelope is 6½ inches from side to side x 3⅝ inches from top to bottom. A No. 6 envelope is used for a personal letter, or it can be used for a one-page business letter.

Mail is being sorted at the post office by an automatic scanning device with more and more frequency. Eventually the United States Postal Service expects to have most mail read/coded/sorted/cancelled automatically at regional "sorting stations" where mail will be processed at the rate of 30,000 letters an hour. (It has been estimated that by sorting mail automatically, 23,000 fewer employees might be needed!) In order for automatic sorting to work efficiently, business firms must prepare all mail in a format that the automatic equipment can "read." Here are the guidelines suggested by the United States Postal Service for addressing mail for automatic sorting:

1. Type all envelope addresses in the blocked format (even **left** margin).
2. Capitalize **everything** in the address.
3. Eliminate **all** punctuation in the address.
4. Use the standard two-letter state code instead of the spelled name of the state.
5. The last line of the address must contain the city, state code, and zip code and it must not exceed 22 digits. The digits should be distributed so they will not exceed the following limits:

Allowance for city name	13**
Space between city and state	1
Allowance for state code	2
Space between state code and zip code	1†
Allowance for zip code	5††
	22

** If the city name contains more than 13 digits, you must use the approved code for that city that is shown in the "Abbreviations Section" of the NATIONAL ZIP CODE DIRECTORY (or in Customer Service Publication 59).

† When the nine-digit zip code is used, the space between the state code and the zip code is expanded to two to five spaces. (Two spaces are suggested by the author.)

†† When the nine-digit zip code is used, the space allowance for the zip code is expanded to nine.

6. All addresses must be properly placed on the envelope so they can be "read" by the automatic equipment:

No. 10 Envelope

Type the address 12 to 14 lines from the top of the envelope and four inches (48 spaces elite type, 45 spaces pica type) from the left edge of the envelope.

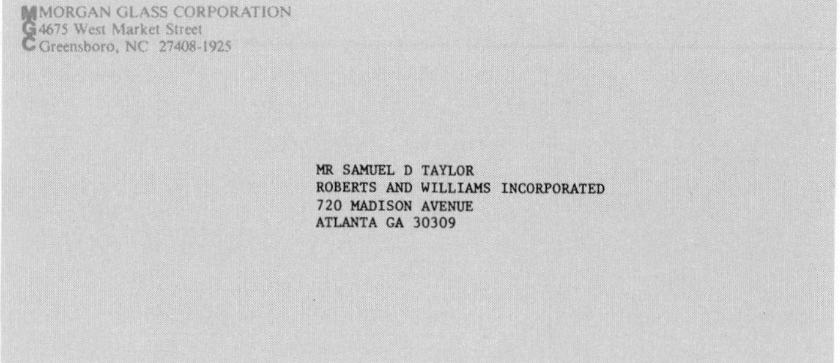

Fig. 7. Properly addressed No. 10 envelope with a printed return address

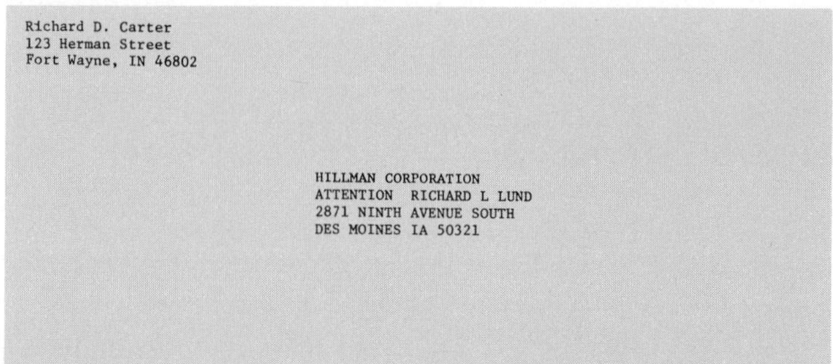

Fig. 8. Properly addressed No. 10 envelope with a typed return address

No. 6 Envelope

Type the address 12 lines (2 inches) from the top of the envelope and 25 spaces, pica type, or 30 spaces, elite type, from the left edge of the envelope.

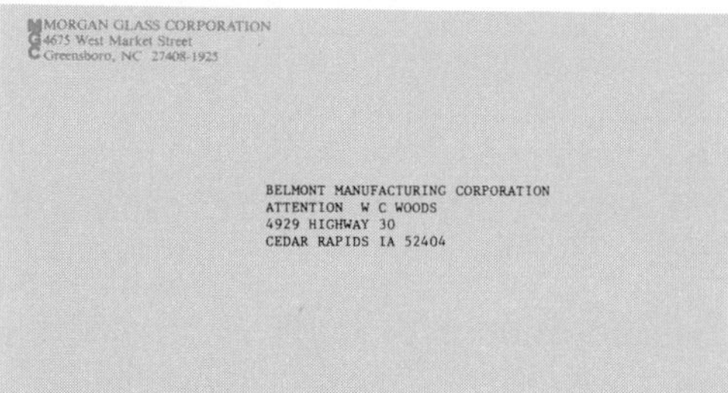

Fig. 9. Properly addressed No. 6 envelope with a printed return address

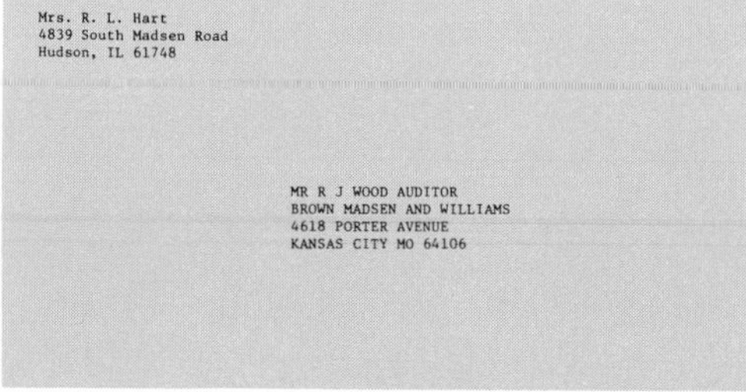

Fig. 10. Properly addressed No. 6 envelope with a typed return address

7. When an address contains the notation "personal" or "confidential," type the notation **two lines below the return address and three spaces from the left edge of the envelope in all capitals.**
8. When a special mailing procedure (such as SPECIAL DELIVERY or REGISTERED MAIL) is used, **type the notation in the upper right-hand corner of the envelope immediately below the area where the stamp will be placed. Type the notation nine lines from the top of the envelope in all capitals. Be sure the notation ends at least one-half inch from the right edge of the envelope.**
9. When an address contains an "ATTENTION" line, it should be typed as a second line of the address. The "ATTENTION" line may also be typed two lines below the return address.
10. On business envelopes, the return address is usually printed. If it is not, type the return address in the upper left-hand corner of the envelope three lines from the top and three spaces from the left edge of the envelope. The return address is single spaced, and no titles of respect are used except "Mrs." (Study Figs. 8 and 10.)

USING THE NINE-DIGIT ZIP CODE

Soon the United States Postal Service anticipates using nine-digit zip codes that will enable automatic scanning devices to sort mail down to the mailing addresses on each individual letter carrier's route. This additional sorting capability will mean that mail will move from arrival at the destination post office to delivery to the addressee in a much shorter period of time. The preceding suggestions for addressing mail for automatic sorting will still apply except for the following changes:

1. Leave **two to five spaces** between the last character of the state code and the first digit of the zip code. (The author suggests two spaces.)
   NEW YORK NY 10467
2. Use the existing five-digit zip code **followed by a hyphen** (no space before or after the hyphen).
   NEW YORK NY 10467-
3. Add the four new digits.
   NEW YORK NY 10467-1234

To accommodate the nine-digit zip code, the maximum number of digits in the last line of the address will be expanded from 22 digits to 27 digits (the hyphen and four additional digits).

What do the new numbers mean?

Just as the current five-digit zip code designates a particular geographic location, the new numbers will serve a similar purpose, but they will represent two even smaller geographical areas. The **first two** new numbers will identify a specific **sector,** which can be several blocks or a group of streets, large buildings, or a small geographical area. The **last two** numbers divide sectors into even smaller areas called **segments.** A segment can be one side of a city block or both sides of a particular street, one floor in a large building, a cluster of mailboxes, one post office box or a group of boxes, or other similar **limited** geographical locations.

MGC MORGAN GLASS CORPORATION
4675 West Market Street
Greensboro, NC 27408-1925

MS JOAN T HOLTON
CONTINENTAL PLAZA HOTEL
909 NORTH MICHIGAN AVENUE
CHICAGO IL 60611-8106

Fig. 11. Properly addressed No. 10 envelope with the nine-digit zip code

Folding Letters The following illustrations show the correct way to fold letters so they will fit a No. 10 envelope and a No. 6 envelope.

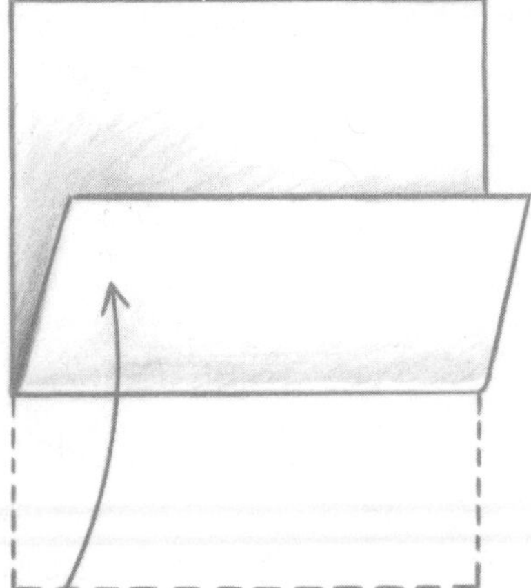

Fig. 12. No. 10 envelope
Place the letter on the desk face up and fold slightly less than one third of the letter up.

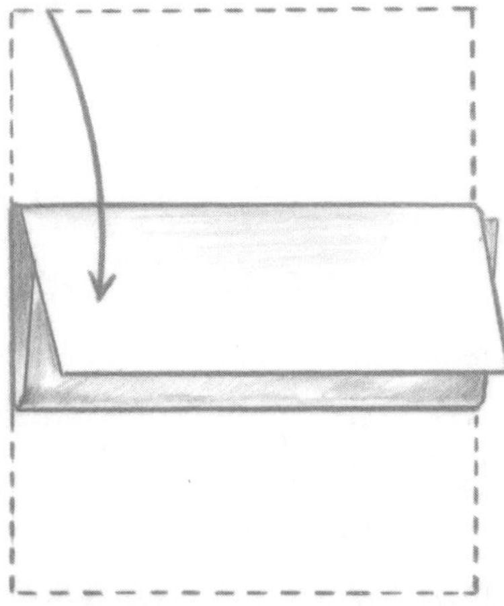

Fold the top of the letter down to within ½ inch of the bottom fold.

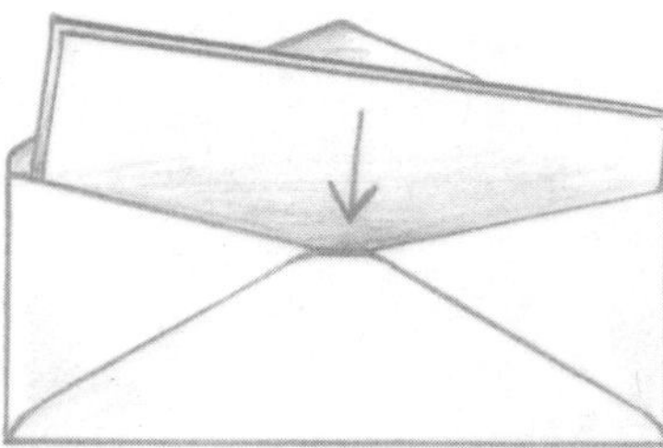

Insert the letter in the envelope with the ***final crease toward the bottom.***

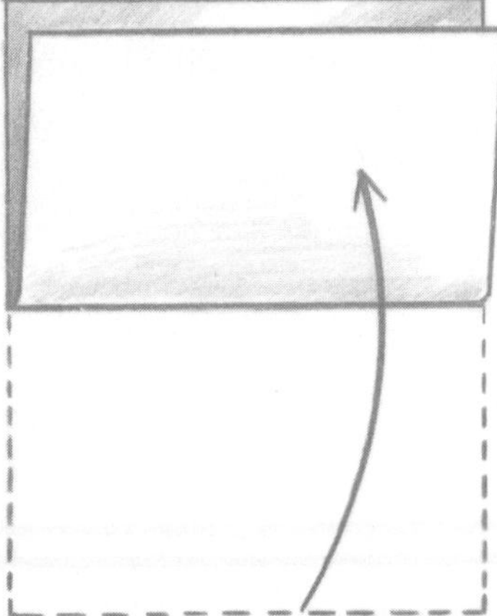

Fig. 13. No. 6 envelope
Place the letter on the desk face up and fold the bottom up to ½ inch from the top.

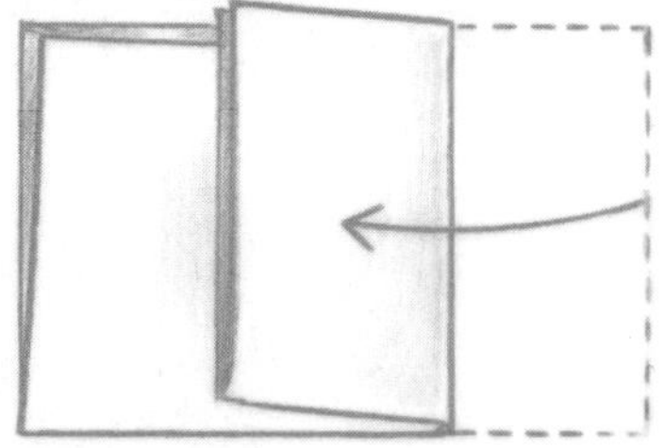

Fold the right third of the letter to the left.

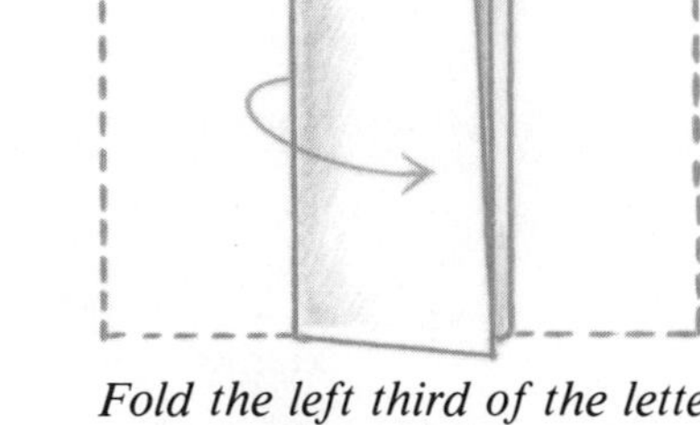

Fold the left third of the letter to ½ inch from the previous crease.

Insert the letter in the envelope with the ***final crease toward the bottom.***

TWO-LETTER STATE CODES

The United States Post Office suggests the use of two-letter state codes when addressing mail. The codes actually speed the processing and handling of the mail because they are "read" by an automatic scanning device. A properly typed address, using the state codes, looks like the following:

SUMMIT MANUFACTURING COMPANY
37 MARSHALL STREET
GREENFIELD MA 01301

Note: The state codes are always typed in capital letters without periods or spaces.

Here is a list of the two-letter state codes:

Alabama	AL	Montana	MT
Alaska	AK	Nebraska	NE
Arizona	AZ	Nevada	NV
Arkansas	AR	New Hampshire	NH
California	CA	New Jersey	NJ
Colorado	CO	New Mexico	NM
Connecticut	CT	New York	NY
Delaware	DE	North Carolina	NC
District of Columbia	DC	North Dakota	ND
Florida	FL	Ohio	OH
Georgia	GA	Oklahoma	OK
Hawaii	HI	Oregon	OR
Idaho	ID	Pennsylvania	PA
Illinois	IL	Puerto Rico	PR
Indiana	IN	Rhode Island	RI
Iowa	IA	South Carolina	SC
Kansas	KS	South Dakota	SD
Kentucky	KY	Tennessee	TN
Louisiana	LA	Texas	TX
Maine	ME	Utah	UT
Maryland	MD	Vermont	VT
Massachusetts	MA	Virginia	VA
Michigan	MI	Washington	WA
Minnesota	MN	West Virginia	WV
Mississippi	MS	Wisconsin	WI
Missouri	MO	Wyoming	WY

Presenting Letters For Signature

Once letters have been typed, they should be presented to the person who will sign them (if he/she is different from the typist). Present a letter for signature by inserting the original, the copy, and the enclosures (if any) under the flap of the envelope with the addressed side of the envelope at the back (see Fig. 14). (Note: Some typists prefer to present a letter for signature with the **addressed side** of the envelope **in front** so the person who is signing the letter can see immediately that the envelope is addressed correctly.) After the letters have been signed, they should be returned to the typist, who will fold them, insert them in envelopes, and place them in the outgoing mail basket. The carbon copies will be put in the file basket, or they will be prepared for distribution.

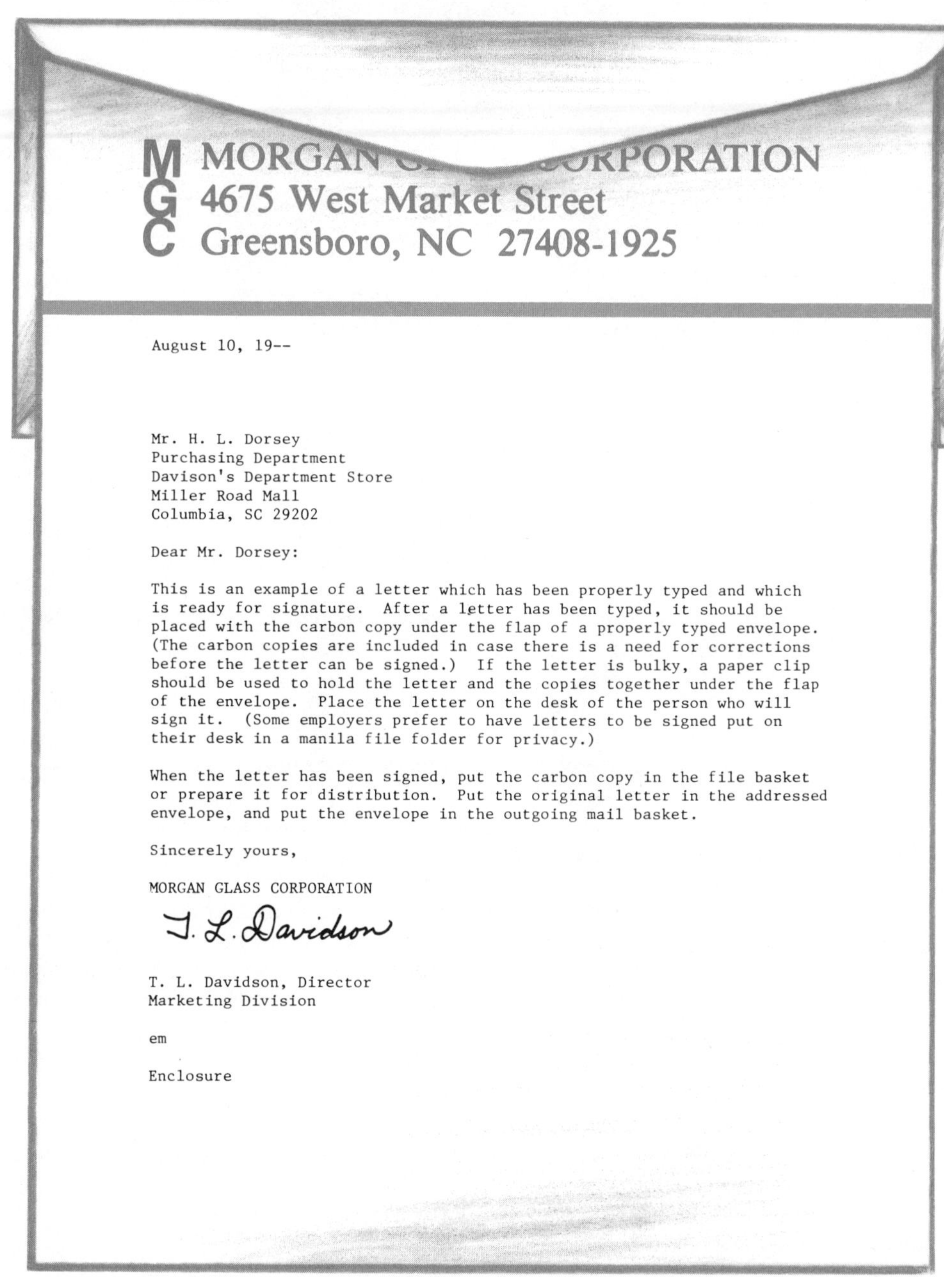

MGC MORGAN GLASS CORPORATION
4675 West Market Street
Greensboro, NC 27408-1925

August 10, 19--

Mr. H. L. Dorsey
Purchasing Department
Davison's Department Store
Miller Road Mall
Columbia, SC 29202

Dear Mr. Dorsey:

This is an example of a letter which has been properly typed and which is ready for signature. After a letter has been typed, it should be placed with the carbon copy under the flap of a properly typed envelope. (The carbon copies are included in case there is a need for corrections before the letter can be signed.) If the letter is bulky, a paper clip should be used to hold the letter and the copies together under the flap of the envelope. Place the letter on the desk of the person who will sign it. (Some employers prefer to have letters to be signed put on their desk in a manila file folder for privacy.)

When the letter has been signed, put the carbon copy in the file basket or prepare it for distribution. Put the original letter in the addressed envelope, and put the envelope in the outgoing mail basket.

Sincerely yours,

MORGAN GLASS CORPORATION

T. L. Davidson

T. L. Davidson, Director
Marketing Division

em

Enclosure

Fig. 14. A letter prepared for presentation

THE BASIC CONTENTS OF SUCCESSFUL LETTERS

When writing business letters, you should make the tone of your writing warm and friendly. Keep in mind that many of the people to whom you will write business letters will never see anyone from your company in person. The impression these people will have of your company will be determined by the tone of the letters you write on behalf of the company. For that reason, it is essential that you write warm, friendly, well-planned letters.

Although much has been written about how to judge a good business letter, the best measure of a good business letter is the fact that the letter gets action. A good business letter is a letter that will influence the reader to act in a way the sender suggests. From that point of view, a good business letter must meet the following tests:

Attractiveness—The letter must be neat and placed well so as to encourage the addressee to read. If it is not, the addressee might not even try to understand its message.

Completeness—The letter must say all that is necessary so the reader will know what he/she is to think, how he/she is to feel, or how he/she is to act.

Conciseness—While the letter must be complete, it must also say what is necessary in a minimum number of words. Excessively wordy letters are uninteresting to read.

Clearness—Try to look at your letters from the addressee's point of view. Will he/she understand what you are saying? Your responsibility is to make each sentence so clear that the reader could not possibly misinterpret.

Courteousness—Always be sure your letters imply an interest in serving the needs of the addressee. One way to do this is to use the personal pronoun "you" instead of "I." (*You will receive*. . . instead of *I will send*. . .)

If a letter meets these five tests, the possibility that it will get a positive response from the addressee is greatly increased.

COMPOSING YOUR OWN LETTERS

In addition to the letters that will be given to you in handwritten form or in typed or rough form to type for your employer, you will sometimes be handed letters by your superiors and told to answer them, using your own signature. Often such letters will contain a handwritten notation such as "O.K.—ship on open account" or "article available in 30 days" to give you some guidance in answering the letter.

Preparing To Write Letters

The key to success in composing letters is planning and organization. When you have been given a composing assignment, try following these steps:

1. Read the incoming letter (if one is available). Ask yourself: What does the writer need? How can I serve his/her needs best?
2. If the writer has asked questions, decide on answers to the questions. Collect data you will need to give complete answers and verify them.
3. In order to help you to organize the points you want, make notes in logical sequence. Keep these notes before you as you compose the letter.

On August 15, the Morgan Glass Corporation received the following letter from Ms Louise Chambers of Bennett Restaurant Supply Company of Atlanta, Georgia. (See Fig. 15.)

Bennett Restaurant Supply Company
1671 International Boulevard
Atlanta, Georgia 30309

August 10, 19--

Order Department
Morgan Glass Corporation
4675 West Market Street
Greensboro, NC 27408

Gentlemen:

On July 15, I ordered a shipment of 50 dozen glass dessert plates and 25 dozen Hansford white wine glasses to be delivered to Atlanta on or before August 1. I ordered these items to be used during a special promotion of restaurant ware to be held during the last three weeks in August. Your acknowledgment of the order (dated July 20) indicated that the order would be shipped in plenty of time to arrive here by August 1.

Today is August 10, and I still have not received the shipment. I need this glassware desperately to supply my customers during the special promotion I mentioned. Can you tell me if the order has been shipped and when I may expect to receive it?

Please handle this matter immediately. As you can readily understand, it is absolutely essential for me to be able to supply my customers promptly.

Sincerely yours,

BENNETT RESTAURANT SUPPLY COMPANY

Louise C. Chambers

Louise C. Chambers
Purchasing Department

em

Fig. 15. A letter from Bennett Restaurant Supply Company

Karl Thomas, an employee in the Order Department of Morgan Glass Corporation, was given the letter to answer. Here are the notes he made before writing an answer to Ms Chambers' letter (see Fig. 16).

The following letter is the one Karl Thomas composed as the result of his notes. Notice how easily Karl progressed from the original letter to his answer, because he had organized his thoughts. (See Fig. 17.)

1. On vacation the last two weeks of July -- not explained

2. Shipment to be made today -- August 13

3. Extra 10% discount if bill is paid by E.O.M.-- delay our fault

Fig. 16. Karl Thomas' notes about the letter from Bennett Restaurant Supply Company

MORGAN GLASS CORPORATION
4675 West Market Street
Greensboro, NC 27408-1925

st 13, 19--

ouise C. Chambers
hasing Department
ett Restaurant Supply Company
International Boulevard
nta, GA 30309

Ms Chambers:

You have my sincere apologies on behalf of the Morgan Glass Corporation for the delay in your order of July 15 for 50 dozen glass dessert plates and 25 dozen Hansford white wine glasses to be shipped to arrive in Atlanta by August 1.

At the time your order was acknowledged, you should have been told that our entire operation would be closed during the last two weeks in July, making delivery to you by August 1 impossible.

I have just checked with our Shipping Department, and your order is on our dock ready to be shipped today. You should receive it within five days.

Because you have been inconvenienced by this delay, we shall allow you another 10 percent discount on your invoice if it is paid by the end of the month.

Thank you for your continued patronage.

Sincerely yours,

MORGAN GLASS CORPORATION

Karl R. Thomas

Karl R. Thomas
Order Department

em

Fig. 17. Karl Thomas' answer to the letter from Bennett Restaurant Supply

Composing Letters

Here are some letters you might be asked to compose in the course of doing your job:

- Letters to go with some item being sent (transmittal letters)
- Business-social letters
- Letters making a request for something
- Letters explaining delays
- Letters indicating that you have received something
- Letters making, changing, or acknowledging appointments
- Letters referring a matter to someone else
- Letters to follow up meetings, assignments, and shipments

Whenever you write a letter of any type, determine what course of action is called for in the letter, then PLAN (including making notes) carefully how you will get the message across to the reader in clear, concise terms.

Here are some suggestions for writing the various types of letters mentioned in the preceding paragraph.

Transmittal Letters

When you write letters to go with some item being sent (transmittal letters):

1. Tell what is being sent, how it is being sent, when it is being sent, and why it is being sent.
2. Make it clear to the reader what he/she is to do.
3. Be sure to list the enclosures in the letter, and be sure they are actually sent.

> Enclosed are two copies of our contract for building your office building. Please sign both copies; and return them to us in the enclosed business-reply envelope by Tuesday, June 10.

Fig. 18

Business-Social Letters

When you write business-social letters:

1. Use simple, sincere-sounding words. Don't be too flowery.
2. Make the letter (or note) brief and to the point without being curt.

> I sincerely appreciate your thoughtful invitation to attend the monthly dinner meeting of the Executive Forum on Tuesday, May 12. Unfortunately, I shall be in Los Angeles on company business during that week. I do hope you will invite me again.

Fig. 19

Letters Requesting Something

When you write letters making a request for something:

1. Give complete details without making the letter too long.
2. If it will help the reader to understand the reason for your request, explain briefly how you will use the article or the information you are requesting.

Would you please send me 25 copies of your firm's annual report for use in my investment club. If you will send me a statement, I shall be glad to pay for the annual reports.

Fig. 20

Letters Explaining a Delay

When you write letters explaining a delay:

1. Explain (briefly) why the delay is necessary. (Don't try to "cover up.")
2. Do not make a promise your company can't fulfill.
3. Do not give confidential information when explaining the reason for a delay.
4. If possible, try to give a date when the information, or shipment, will be sent.

Thank you for reminding us that we still must ship 40 cartons of shoes, Stock No. 14807B, to complete your order of June 15.

Our factory and shipping departments have been closed during the past two weeks for employee vacations. Production will begin again on July 10, and we should be able to ship the remainder of your order by July 17.

Fig. 21

Letters Acknowledging Receipt of Something

When you write letters indicating that you have received something:

1. Acknowledge the receipt promptly.
2. Indicate what was received—package, letter, purchase order.
3. Don't commit the company to anything that would be difficult to fulfill.

We have received the papers relating to the sale of the real estate at 1201 Short Hills Road to Mr. and Mrs. Richard D. Harmon. As soon as Mr. Davis has processed the papers, we shall return them to you.

Fig. 22

Letters Concerning Appointments

When you write letters making, changing, or acknowledging appointments:

1. Include all the information that is necessary, such as the date, the time, the location, and what is to be discussed.
2. When it is necessary to cancel an appointment, be tactful; and be sure to give a reason. Where possible, suggest alternative dates.

```
An important business meeting makes it necessary
for me to be out of town all next week.  I expect
to return to my office on Monday, February 10.

Will it be possible for me to meet with you on
that date at 10:00 a.m. instead of Friday,
February 7?  Unless I hear from you to the
contrary, I shall expect to see you on
February 10.
```

Fig. 23

Referral Letters

When you write letters referring a matter to someone else:

1. If you refer a letter to a branch office or another division, attach a copy of your letter to the letter being referred.
2. Indicate to the reader that his/her request is being handled promptly.
3. If it is necessary to refer someone to a company other than your own, give the complete address of the company and, where possible, the name of a person to contact.

```
Thank you for your letter of October 10 and for
your generous order for cosmetics.

All our cosmetic sales are handled by our regional
sales offices.  Therefore, I am referring your
letter and your order to Mr. Sam Levine, Manager
of our St. Louis office, which serves your area,
at 7421 Harper Boulevard, St. Louis, MO 63115.
I feel certain you will be hearing from Mr. Levine
soon.
```

Fig. 24

Follow-Up Letters

When you write follow-up letters:

1. Develop a usable system that will remind you to follow up.
2. Be extremely tactful; don't scold.

```
The check you indicated was enclosed with your
letter of September 10 was not included.  Would
you please send it to us in the enclosed business-
reply envelope.
```

Fig. 25

In addition to these basic types of letters, your job might also require you to write the following types of letters, which are more complex:

- Letters making adjustments
- Letters regarding collections

Adjustment and Collection Letters

Here are some suggestions for writing adjustment and collection letters.

When you write adjustment letters:

1. Explain the mistake factually (and briefly).
2. Explain the adjustment in specific terms. (Try to make the adjustment the reader wants.)
3. Restore confidence in your company.

> After a careful investigation, I discovered that the cartons containing the floors for Stock No. 41864 Garden Shed and the cartons containing the reinforcement kits for the same garden shed were incorrectly marked. For that reason and because the cartons are exactly the same size, we sent you the reinforcement kit instead of the floor kit.
>
> The floor kit will be delivered to your home on Monday afternoon, April 12. You may keep the reinforcement kit without additional charge.
>
> I feel sure you will be pleased with the sturdy floor for your garden shed. However, if for any reason you are not completely satisfied with it, we shall refund your money promptly.

Fig. 26

When you write collection letters:

1. Indicate the amount due.
2. Request payment.
3. Appeal for prompt, specific action.
4. Avoid vague threats.

> Is it possible that you have overlooked a past-due bill? Our records indicate that the amount of $43.67 has been outstanding on your account with us for forty-five days.
>
> Will you please use the enclosed business-reply envelope to send us your check for $43.67 today!

Fig. 27

THE FUNCTION OF THE OFFICE MEMORANDUM

An office memorandum is an informal written communication that is used within a company. The office memorandum can be used for the following purposes:

1. To keep employees of a company informed about what is happening within the company
2. To set responsibility for actions
3. To notify employees about new policies and decisions

Office memos should be written in clear, concise language that everyone who will read them will understand. A one-page memo is far more effective than a two-page memo. Memos should be typed with a single spacing (use a 60-space line) with double spacing between paragraphs and three **blank** spaces (space four times) after the heading. Figure 28 shows an office memorandum typed on a printed memo form.

Figure 29 shows an office memorandum typed on plain white paper. This type of memorandum would be used if a preprinted form was not available. (The directions for typing memos are included in the illustrations.)

An interoffice memorandum that is confidential in nature is sent in a sealed envelope with the name of the person to whom it is going typed on the outside of the envelope.

THE NEWS RELEASE

The most newsworthy press release will lose some of its attention-getting power at the editor's desk if it is not typed properly. A news release must provide the information it is intended to convey in clear, straightforward language and in a neatly typed format. Here are some guidelines for preparing a news release:

1. Type the words **News Release** (spread) at the left margin beginning on line 10 (1½-inch top margin).
2. Type the name and complete address of the person who will verify the facts in the news release ten lines from the top, beginning in the center of the page. After a double space, type the release date in line with the name and address of the person who will verify the facts in the release.
3. Type the suggested title for the news release in all caps and centered on the page, a triple space after the release date. The title should "tell the story at a glance."
4. Type the body of the news release a triple space after the suggested title. Start with the "dateline" (the city in which the release is being made and the date of the release).
5. Use a 5- or 6-inch typing line on a news release.
6. Be positive the typing is accurate. (Otherwise, editors will question the reliability of the news content.)
7. Keep the news release to one typewritten page. A one-page release has a better chance of getting and holding the attention of the editor than a long, rambling release.

Figure 30 shows a news release prepared according to the preceding guidelines.

Fig. 28. Office memorandum on pre-printed form

MEMORANDUM

TO: Mr. L. K. Vernon **DATE:** July 20, 19--

FROM: Samuel Taylor **SUBJECT:** Office Memorandums

This is an example of an office memorandum typed on a preprinted form. Notice that the heading has been filled in opposite the printed guides. The complete heading is followed by three blank lines before the message begins. The body of the memorandum is usually typed with a 60-space line, and it is single spaced.

An office memorandum is used to keep employees of a company informed about what is happening within the company, to set responsibility for actions, or to notify employees about new policies and decisions. The message in the memo should be written in clear, concise, easy-to-understand language. A one-page memo is much more effective than a two-page memo. When you are writing an office memo, say only what needs to be said.

Ordinarily, an office memorandum is not signed. However, sometimes the
person who writes it
heading to indicate
The secretary or cle
ordinarily types his
last line of the mes
typed on the line be

em
cc Mr. R. L. King

M E M O R A N D U M

TO: Mr. L. K. Vernon

FROM: Samuel Taylor

DATE: July 21, 19--

SUBJECT: Office Memorandums

This is an example of an office memorandum created at the typewriter. It is used if no preprinted office memorandum is available.

The heading, MEMORANDUM, is centered and spread on the 13 line of a sheet of plain white paper 8½ by 11 inches. Each letter of the heading is underlined. After a triple space, the guides TO, FROM, DATE, and SUBJECT are typed blocked against the left margin. The names, date, and subject are typed opposite the appropriate guides 11 spaces from the left margin. (Set the tab stop.) Leave three blank lines after the complete heading, and begin the message. The message is single spaced with double spacing between the paragraphs.

Ordinarily, an office memorandum is not signed. However, sometimes the person who writes it initials the memo beside his/her typewritten name in the heading to indicate that he/she has read it. The secretary or the office clerk who types the memo for the person who writes it places his/her initials in small letters two spaces below the last line of the message. The carbon copy notation, if one is used, is typed on the line below the reference initials.

em
cc Mr. R. L. King

Fig. 29. Office memorandum prepared at the typewriter

N E W S R E L E A S E

From Richard L. Sherman
Roberts & Williams, Incorporated
720 Madison Avenue
Atlanta, GA 30309

Release July 30, 19--

PREPARING A NEWS RELEASE

ATLANTA, July 30---A news release helps an editor to determine the facts about a particular story. If a news release is to get proper attention from the editor, it must present information in a clear, straightforward manner; and it must be presented in a neatly typed format. If it is not, the editor will have cause to question the reliability of the news it contains. Here are some guidelines for preparing a news release:

1. The words NEWS RELEASE should be typed (spread and underlined) at the left margin beginning on line 10.

2. The name and complete address of the preson who will verify the facts in the news release should be typed 10 lines from the top, beginning in the center of the page. After a double space, type the release date in line with the name and address of the person who will verify the facts in the release.

3. Leave three blank lines after the release date and type the suggested title for the news release in all caps and centered on the page. The suggested title should "tell the story at a glance."

4. Leave three blank lines after the suggested title and type the body of the news release. Start with the "dateline." (The city in which the release is being made and the date of the release.)

5. Use a 5- or 6-inch typing line.

6. Be positive the typing is accurate. (Otherwise, editors will question the reliability of the news content.)

7. Keep the news release to one typewritten page. A one-page release holds the attention of the editor better than a long, rambling release.

Fig. 30. Sample news release

COMMUNICATING ORALLY

The important point to remember about conversing with your colleagues and business associates is that they will be judging your company and your effectiveness as an employee of the company by what you say and how you say it (as well as by what you do and how you do it). If you are always careful to speak clearly and to use precise language, people will understand what you mean.

Effective Use Of Your Voice

Your voice reflects the quality of your physical and mental health. If you are extremely tired or extremely angry, for example, those circumstances are reflected in your voice. Sometimes people have difficulty concentrating on **what** is being said because they are concentrating on **how** it is being said. In a business situation, it is extremely important for people to understand what is being said, so you must become aware of your voice and the effect it has on other people.

> Do you speak too softly? too loudly? too rapidly? too slowly? Is the pitch of your voice too high or too low? Does your voice sound strained (harsh or raspy)?

If you will learn to use your voice correctly, you will produce a pleasing, businesslike voice that will help you to communicate with other people efficiently and effectively.

Pronunciation

Remember, too, that the pronunciation of words differs from region to region. Experts have suggested that words should be pronounced the way they are most readily understood and accepted in the office where you work and in the community where you live. However, if you work and live in a community that is in a different part of the country from where you grew up, it may be difficult for you to adopt the speech of the new area immediately. In fact, if you try to imitate the speech of the new area, you might sound unnatural and affected. Most people will be tolerant of differences in pronunciation. If you are not certain about the pronunciation of a word, look it up in the dictionary; and practice saying the word aloud until you are comfortable with the way it is pronounced.

Enunciation

Enunciation has to do with the precision with which you pronounce every syllable of a word. If you learn to enunciate clearly, you will always be understood (the goal of effective oral and written communications). Two enemies of clear enunciation are:

1. Running words together
   Say: Did you eat?
   Instead of: Geeat?
2. Failure to sound every syllable in a word
   Say: Winning (win/ing)
   Instead of: Winin

Some words in the English language are similar in appearance and pronunciation but different in meaning. If these words are not enunciated clearly, the listener may not be able to understand what you are saying, and your meaning may be misunderstood.
The following words are examples:

affect	irrelevant	where
effect	irreverent	were
cease	statue	while
seize	stature	wile
	statute	wild

Slang

There is no place in business communications for slang. (Slang is made up of new words or meanings that are popular for a short period of time—"guy," "babe," "diggin' it," "right on," "hangin' in there.") Slang expressions do not express exact, precise, meanings; and they are contrary to good English usage. Make a point of eliminating slang from your written and oral communications.

Clear Expression

A businessperson who speaks clearly and who conveys to his/her listener exactly what he/she intends to say paves the way for efficient and productive business transactions. Keep in mind that the speaker hasn't communicated effectively until the listener has understood. As you speak, make a point of organizing your thoughts, speaking distinctly, and using words that express exact, clear meanings.

FOR REVIEW AND DISCUSSION

1. With a brief illustration, show the placement of the seven essential parts of a business letter on the:
   A. full-block letter style
   B. modified-block letter style
2. Explain the five secondary parts of a business letter.
3. A. When is a No. 10 envelope used?
   B. When is a No. 6 envelope used?
4. Take two sheets of paper 8½ x 11 inches and show how a letter should be folded for a No. 10 envelope and a No. 6 envelope.
5. Explain the five tests of a good business letter.
6. Explain a good three-step procedure to follow when you are preparing to write a business letter.
7. What are the points to remember when you write a letter explaining a delay?
8. What is the purpose of an office memorandum?
9. Explain the essentials of preparing a news release that will get the desired attention from editors.
10. How does your voice reflect the quality of your physical and mental health?
11. How should a businessperson handle the differences in pronunciation of words from region to region?
12. What is enunciation? What are the two enemies of enunciation?
13. Why should slang expressions be avoided in business communications?
14. What factors help to assure clear expression?

Turn to your workbook and complete Student Projects 8, 9, 10, and 11.

CHAPTER 6

Incoming Mail

OBJECTIVE

After you have studied Chapter Six, you will understand the procedures for processing incoming mail, including:

- Recognizing important mail
- Handling routine mail
- Dating incoming mail
- Annotating the mail
- Routing and referring the mail
- Preparing follow-up
- Handling the mail register
- Digesting the mail

JOB-RELATED VOCABULARY

Annotating—Furnishing explanatory notes or comments. (Annotating the mail—furnishing explanatory notes or comments on an incoming letter, invoice, or statement.)

Digesting—Making a short summary of something. (Digesting the mail—making a short summary of the contents of the mail.)

Disposition—To make final placement of something. (Disposition of the mail—the final placement of the mail with individuals and departments after it has been sorted.)

The daily mail is the lifeblood of most businesses. Therefore, it is essential that each day's mail is processed in a speedy, efficient manner so the orders and requests it brings can be handled promptly. In addition, efficient handling of the incoming mail helps the company executives to use their time to the best advantage.

PROCESSING INCOMING MAIL

As soon as the mail bags are delivered to the mail room, the mail room staff will sort the mail by departments and deliver the mail promptly. (In smaller companies, where there is no separate mail room, the mail may be brought directly to your desk by a letter carrier.) At any rate, when the mail arrives in your department, it becomes the responsibility of someone in the department—perhaps you—to sort the mail and to deliver it within the department to the people who will be responsible for answering it.

You will need certain supplies efficiently arranged so that you can process the mail easily. These supplies include:

- An envelope opener
- A date stamp and ink pad (or a mechanical time stamp)
- Cellophane tape (for mending)
- A stapler and paper clips
- Pencils
- A sorting tray

Mail Processing Supplies

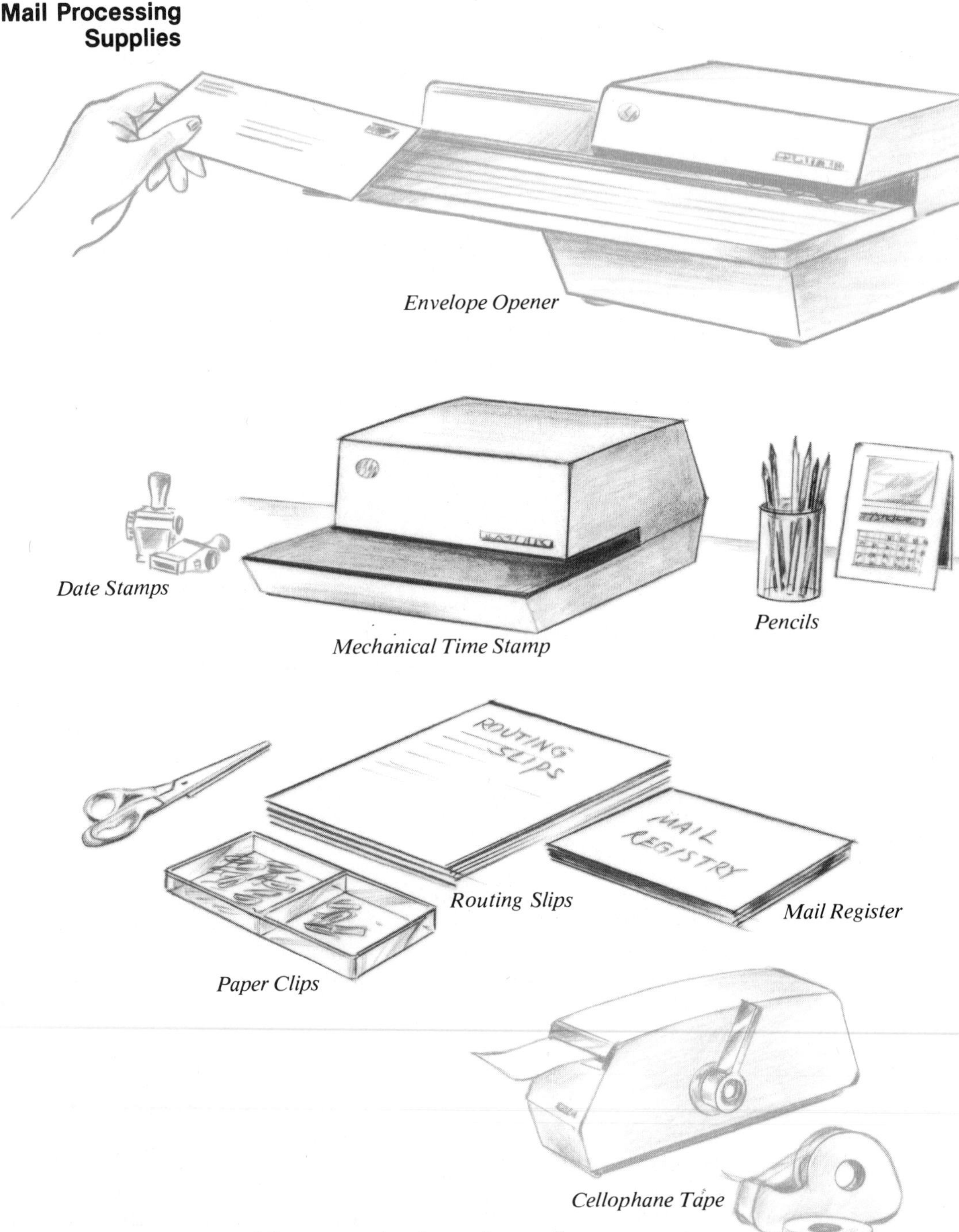

Fig. 31. Supplies needed for processing incoming mail

Once you have your supplies arranged, you will start your processing by sorting the mail for your department. First, sort the mail into groups indicated by the person in the department who will handle that particular piece of mail. Next, sort each person's mail (starting with the top executive in the department) into two piles:

Important Mail (such as letters, orders, remittances, invoices)
Routine Mail (such as periodicals and advertising)

Recognizing Important Mail

As you gain experience in your job, you will soon come to recognize by the sender's name or address that mail which is IMPORTANT. Mail that is sent by Registered Mail, Certified Mail, MAILGRAM®, or Parcel Post can be considered to be IMPORTANT.

Place the stack of important mail to your left with the flaps up and the top edges to the right, and open this mail first. (In some larger offices, the mail will have been slit open by an electric letter opener in the mail room.) If the full address of the sender does not appear on the letter, invoice, or order that is inside the envelope, staple the envelope to it (in case additional follow-up is required). Attach enclosures sent in the envelope to the letter with a paper clip. Date the mail in the upper right-hand corner with the current day's date. As a general rule, you will not open mail marked "Personal" or "Confidential." However, **sometimes** an executive asks his/her assistant to open **all** mail that is delivered to the office.

If you should open mail marked "Personal" or "Confidential" by mistake, reseal the envelope with cellophane tape. Then write "Opened by mistake" on the envelope and sign your name.

Place the important mail in a file folder bearing the name of the person in the department who is to receive it. (By doing this, you will protect the contents of the mail from the prying eyes of those people who are not involved with it!) Place the file folder on the desk of the person who should get it.

Handling Routine Mail

Once you have sorted and opened the important mail and put it on the desks of the people who will answer it, you are ready to sort the routine mail. (By handling the important mail first, you will seem more efficient; and the people in your department who handle the mail will get a "head start" on answering the important mail while you are sorting the routine mail.) First, sort the periodicals—newspapers, magazines, newsletters—into a separate pile because they are usually more bulky and more difficult to handle than letters. Next, open the other routine mail. Start with a stack of envelopes at your left, with flaps up and the top edges to the right. Then open the envelopes, staple the envelope to the back of the letter or brochure if the contents of the envelope do not contain the complete address of the sender. Attach any enclosures to the mailing piece with a paper clip. Date the mail with the current day's date in the upper right-hand corner.

Never throw away advertising mail, considering it "junk" mail. The people in your department will want to know what is happening in the "direct mail" business. Reviewing the "direct mail" that comes into the office is one way to do this.

Dating Incoming Mail

There are several important reasons why incoming mail should be stamped with the date it is received at your office (as mentioned in the preceding mail-sorting procedures).

1. A letter may be delivered to you that does not contain a date. Therefore, the only clue to the date of the letter would be the date it was received at your office or, perhaps, the date in the postmark if it is legible.
2. The date provides the motivation to answer the letter promptly if an answer is required. A letter sent by your company is an opportunity to build goodwill. However, if you delay too long in preparing your answer, the opportunity for building goodwill is greatly diminished.
3. The letter may contain a request that must be filled by a certain date to be valuable to the writer. If you date the incoming mail, you have a record (sometimes for your own protection) that the letter may have arrived too late to fill the request.
4. Your date on a letter furnishes you with a record of the date you received the letter.

SPECIAL MAIL PROCESSES

The following mail processes may not be a part of your daily processing procedure. However, you should know about them in case the person for whom you work requests them or in case you encounter them in the course of your work. The special mail processes include:

- Annotating the mail
- Routing and referring the mail
- Preparing follow-up
- Handling the mail register
- Digesting the mail

Annotating The Mail

At some time you might work for an executive whose flow of mail is tremendous. After he/she gets to know you and to feel confident of your ability, he/she may ask you to help answer the mail by annotating the mail before he/she sees it. The following steps are necessary to annotate the mail:

1. Read the letter carefully. Watch for important facts. If necessary, make appropriate notations on your calendar.
2. On the second reading, underline the **key words** that tell what the letter is about. (Do not underline too many words. That practice is confusing!)
3. Write notations in the margin of the letter that will be helpful to the person who will answer it. For example, something may be mentioned in an incoming letter that has been handled by previous correspondence. In that case, you would attach a copy of the letter handling the situation to the letter you are processing; and you would make the notation "see attached letter" in the margin next to the reference to that situation that had already been handled.

Figure 32 shows an incoming letter that has been properly annotated.

OHIO HOME PRODUCTS DISTRIBUTORS
2317 Jamesville Road
Warren, OH 44482

March 17, 19--

Advertising Department
Morgan Glass Corporation
4675 West Market Street
Greensboro, NC 27408

Gentlemen:

On March 15, I received a packet of advertising materials from your company, including some of the products we shall feature in our spring and summer catalog. In the packet are three glossy prints of water goblets (Stock Nos. 9811-7, 9811-8, 9811-9). The accompanying description applies to Stock No. 9811-7 only. I have no description for the other two stock numbers. Also it looks to me, after studying the pictures carefully, as if all three of the goblets are exactly the same.

Please send me a description of each of the goblets so I can list them accurately in my catalog. In addition, I shall need your suggested list price for each of the goblets.

The 19-- summer season promises to be an outstanding one in this area as there seems to be considerable money available. That should mean excellent sales for our glassware line.

Sincerely yours,

Henry A. Shell

Henry A. Shell, General Manager

em

9811-7
nexpensive
9811-8
medium price
9811-9
expensive
ch goblet
different
the quality
the glass)

outward appearance exactly the same

Send price list showing three options

Fig. 32. A letter that has been annotated

Routing And Referring The Mail

Sometimes as you process the mail, you will realize that a letter should be read not only by the executive to whom it is addressed but by some of his/her business associates as well. In that case, you would attach a routing slip to the letter and check the names of the people who should receive it. As each person reads the letter, he/she writes the date the letter was received and the date it was passed along to the next person on the list whose name was checked. If you want the letter to be returned to you, type your own name at the end of the list.

If the mail being routed is confidential in nature, it should be placed in an interoffice envelope; and the routing slip should be stapled to the outside of the envelope. Figure 33 shows an interoffice envelope with a routing slip on it.

Figure 34 shows a routing slip that has been checked to indicate who should receive the attached mail. Notice that W. Conover and M. Mendez have received the mail and have passed it on to the next person indicated.

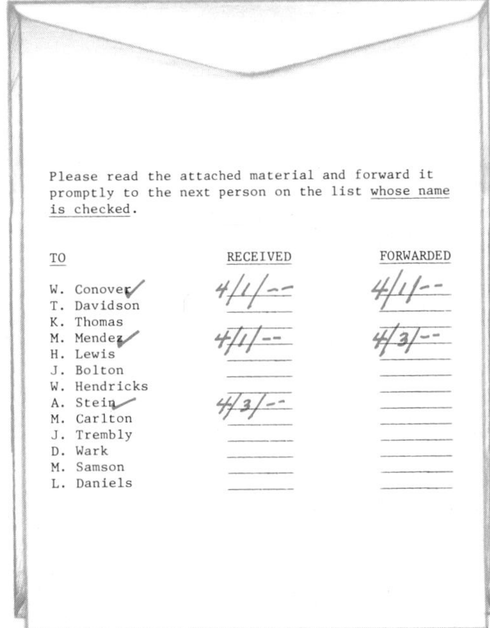

Please read the attached material and forward it promptly to the next person on the list whose name is checked.

TO	RECEIVED	FORWARDED
W. Conover ✓	4/1/--	4/1/--
T. Davidson		
K. Thomas		
M. Mendez ✓	4/1/--	4/3/--
H. Lewis		
J. Bolton		
W. Hendricks		
A. Stein ✓	4/3/--	
M. Carlton		
J. Trembly		
D. Wark		
M. Samson		
L. Daniels		

Fig. 33. An interoffice envelope with a routing slip attached

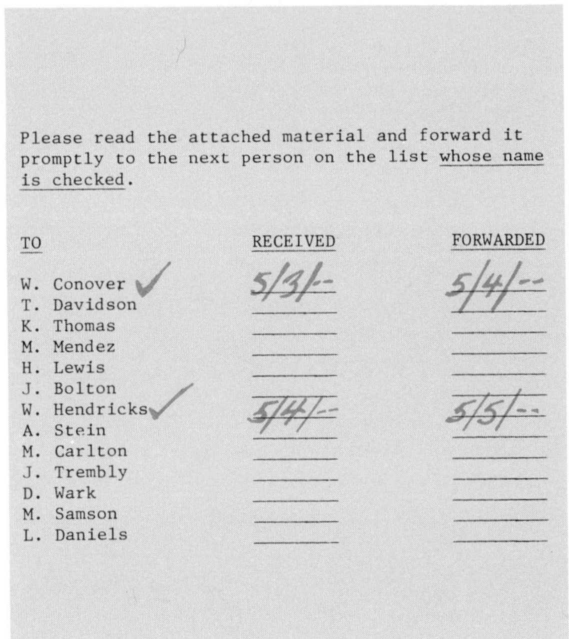

Please read the attached material and forward it promptly to the next person on the list whose name is checked.

TO	RECEIVED	FORWARDED
W. Conover ✓	5/3/--	5/4/--
T. Davidson		
K. Thomas		
M. Mendez		
H. Lewis		
J. Bolton		
W. Hendricks ✓	5/4/--	5/5/--
A. Stein		
M. Carlton		
J. Trembly		
D. Wark		
M. Samson		
L. Daniels		

Fig. 34. A routing slip

Executives frequently refer mail and other important business papers to their assistants and associates for handling. Usually a referral slip is attached to an item being referred to someone else. If the company for which you work does not have a referral slip, you may want to design one similar to the example shown in Fig. 35 and duplicate it. A referral slip saves the person doing the referring the need to dictate a memo explaining what is wanted.

Whenever you refer important business papers to someone else, be sure to make a record of the referral so you can follow up at a later time. Failure to make such a record may cause you to lose track of some valuable business papers. The record of the referral should include the following information:

- The date the referral was made
- The name of the person to whom it was sent

- The subject of the referral
- The action to be taken
- The date on which you expect to follow up if a follow-up is necessary

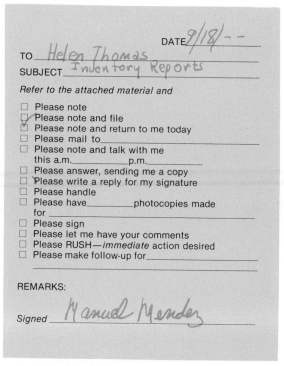

DATE 9/18/- -

TO Helen Thomas

SUBJECT Inventory Reports

Refer to the attached material and

☐ Please note
☑ Please note and file
☐ Please note and return to me today
☐ Please mail to____________
☐ Please note and talk with me this a.m.________p.m.________
☐ Please answer, sending me a copy
☐ Please write a reply for my signature
☐ Please handle
☐ Please have________photocopies made for____________
☐ Please sign
☐ Please let me have your comments
☐ Please RUSH—*immediate* action desired
☐ Please make follow-up for____________

REMARKS:

Signed Manuel Mendez

Fig. 35. A referral slip

Preparing Follow-Up

There are times when mail requires follow-up:

- When additional mail related to the matter will follow
- When action other than a routine answer is required
- When a piece of mail must be answered on a certain date or within a certain time period

When such situations exist, follow these procedures:

1. Determine the date on which the action should be completed.
2. On your desk calendar, make a notation on the date you select that will remind you to take action.
3. If you are expecting additional mail about the matter, note that on your desk calendar on the approximate date you expect the mail. Also, notify the Mail Department so they can be watching for the mail.

Handling The Mail Register

In some offices, the person who sorts the mail for each department keeps a Mail Register in which he/she enters the receipt and disposition of all Registered, Certified, Special Delivery, or Insured mail. Many office workers have indicated that the Mail Register has been a "lifesaver" in keeping track of important mail. It should be emphasized that a Mail Register is the most beneficial when a large amount of special (Registered, Certified, Special Delivery) mail is received. Figure 36 shows a Mail Register kept by the Advertising Department of Morgan Glass Corporation.

DEPARTMENT Advertising

MAIL REGISTER

RECEIVED		FROM	DATED	ADDRESSED	DESCRIPTION	REFERRED	
DATE	TIME	NAME/ADDRESS		TO	(Type of Mail)	TO	DATE
7/10/--	1 PM	Prudential Ins. Co. Newark, NJ	7/8	Mr. Mendez	Registered	Legal Dept.	7/10
7/13/--	10 AM	Garden State China Trenton, NJ	7/10	Mr. Davidson	Special Delivery	—	—
7/22/--	11 AM	Howard J. Dalton Phoenix, AZ	7/18	Mr. Bolton	Insured Mail	—	—
7/24/--	2 PM	Juanita Saunders Philadelphia, PA	7/21	Mr. Daniels	Special Delivery	Mr. Lewis Accounting	7/28

Fig. 36. Mail Register kept by the Advertising Department at Morgan Glass Corporation

Digesting The Mail

Sometimes it is necessary for a business person to be out of his/her office for a long period of time on company business. In such a situation, the person might request that someone (usually his/her secretary) take time to "digest" (make a summary) of the daily mail. The "digest" can be mailed to the person who is traveling at his/her hotel, or it can be reported to him/her when he/she calls the office. Ordinarily, only letters, reports, and telegrams are included in the digest. Advertising materials and periodicals are not usually included. Figure 37 shows a digest of Ms Helen Lewis' mail for April 20.

It is very important to remember that mail-handling procedures vary greatly from office to office. This chapter has presented the basic mail-handling procedures that are followed in some offices. To be successful as an office worker, you must be able to adapt your own understanding to the needs of the office.

DIGEST OF INCOMING MAIL

For Helen Lewis

April 20, 19--

DATE OF MAIL	FROM	DESCRIPTION
4/16	Stein & Woodman	Suggested copy for July advertisement in HOME LIFE magazine
4/16	Howard/Noeboff Agency	Adjustment for advertising mistakes in three catalog advertisements they did for us
4/18	Sutton Wholesale Raleigh, NC	Request for advertising copy and an illustration for Bar Ware Set 91178-1
4/19	Business and Professional Women--Greensboro Club	Invoice for current dues and notice of a Board of Directors' meeting April 24, 7 p.m., Holiday Inn Four Seasons

Fig. 37. Digest of incoming mail addressed to Helen Lewis

FOR REVIEW AND DISCUSSION

1. What supplies will be needed to process incoming mail?
2. After mail has been sorted into groups indicated by the people in the department who will handle the mail, what is the next suggested sorting procedure?
3. How is mail dated as it is sorted, and why is dating incoming mail an important procedure?
4. Name and describe briefly the five special mail processes.

Turn to your workbook and complete Student Projects 12 and 13.

CHAPTER 7

Outgoing Mail And Shipping Services

OBJECTIVE

After you have studied Chapter Seven, you will understand the regulations and procedures for handling outgoing mail and for shipping services, including:

- Classes of domestic mail • General Delivery
- Official and free mail • Change of address
- Mixed classes of mail • Postal money orders
- Mail by the blind or handicapped • Freight
- Special mail services • International mail
- Forwarding mail • Processing outgoing mail
- Undeliverable mail • Business reply mail
- Remailing returned mail • Direct mail
- Bills of lading

JOB-RELATED VOCABULARY

Periodically—With a fixed interval between (every two weeks, every month, every calendar quarter).

Transient Rate—A special rate for individuals mailing a newspaper or part of a newspaper. (When newspaper publishers mail newspapers in bulk lots, they pay a different rate based upon: destination, amount of advertising included in the newspaper, and the number of pages in the newspaper.)

Physical Impairment—A bodily condition that diminishes one's strength or one's ability to function completely.

Nonnegotiable—Cannot be transferred from one person to another.

Denominations—Values such as money values. (Example: stamped envelopes.)

Dispatched—To be sent out—particularly to be sent out rapidly and efficiently.

Affix—To fasten or to attach physically (to attach a stamp to a letter).

Endorse—To write an official title or inscription on something. (To endorse a piece of mail second class would be to write or print the words, SECOND CLASS MAIL, on it.)

Appropriate—Suitable for or designed for that purpose.

Payee—A person to whom money is paid or is to be paid.

Aerogram—Airmail forms in international (Postal Union) mail.

Receptive—Able or inclined to receive ideas.

Perishable Food—Food that is likely to spoil if it is not properly cared for.

Consignee—A person to whom something is shipped or formally delivered.

Cargo—Goods or merchandise conveyed in a shipment.

Expertise—Special skill or knowledge in a particular subject or in a particular field.

In Chapter Six of this textbook, the incoming mail was described as the "lifeblood" of a business. Outgoing mail can be described as the "lifeblood" of a business, too, because it helps to generate interest in the company's products and services. In addition, the outgoing mail enables business people to handle the millions of details that are a part of every business in an efficient way and to build goodwill for the company.

Shipping services, too, play a dynamic role in today's business because it is through the use of a variety of shipping services that most companies distribute their products.

POSTAL REGULATIONS AND PROCEDURES

The final authority as far as postal regulations are concerned is the POSTAL MANUAL. The POSTAL MANUAL explains the services offered by the United States Postal Service; and it describes the rates, fees, and conditions under which these services are available. A copy of the POSTAL MANUAL can be ordered from the Superintendent of Documents, Washington, DC 20402. As changes are made, revised and new pages of the manual are sent to the people who order it.

DOMESTIC MAIL

Domestic mail is defined as mail that is transmitted within, among, and between the United States, its territories and possessions, Army-Air Force post offices (APO), Navy post offices (FPO), and mail delivered to the United Nations in New York City.

Classes Of Domestic Mail

First-Class Mail—consists of letters in any form, postal cards, business-reply mail, and material partly in written form such as invoices and checks. Pieces of mail less than 3½ inches wide by 5 inches long are not accepted for mailing by the post office.

Second-Class Mail—consists of printed newspapers and periodicals. Publishers and news agencies can get second-class rates if they file the proper form available at the local post office and if they pay the required fee and comply with the regulations. Second-class mail must bear a notice that it is second class, and it must be mailed in bulk lots periodically.

Newspapers and periodicals sent unsealed by the **general public** are sent at a Transient Rate.

Controlled Circulation Publications—are publications of 24 or more pages containing up to 75 percent advertising that are circulated free (or mainly free) by industry.

Third-Class Mail—consists of mailable matter that cannot be classed as first- or second-class mail and that is less than **16 ounces** in weight. Third-class mail that is **sealed** must bear the notation: THIRD CLASS.

Fourth-Class Mail (or Parcel Post)—consists of mailable matter not in first, second, or third class with a **weight of 16 ounces or more.** Rates for parcel post are scaled by the weight of the parcel and the distance it is to travel. By sealing either third- or fourth-class mail, the sender **implies** that the mail may be opened for inspection even if the mail does not contain the endorsement: MAY BE OPENED FOR POSTAL INSPECTION.

There are both weight **and size** limitations to parcel post according to the postal zone to which the parcel is traveling.

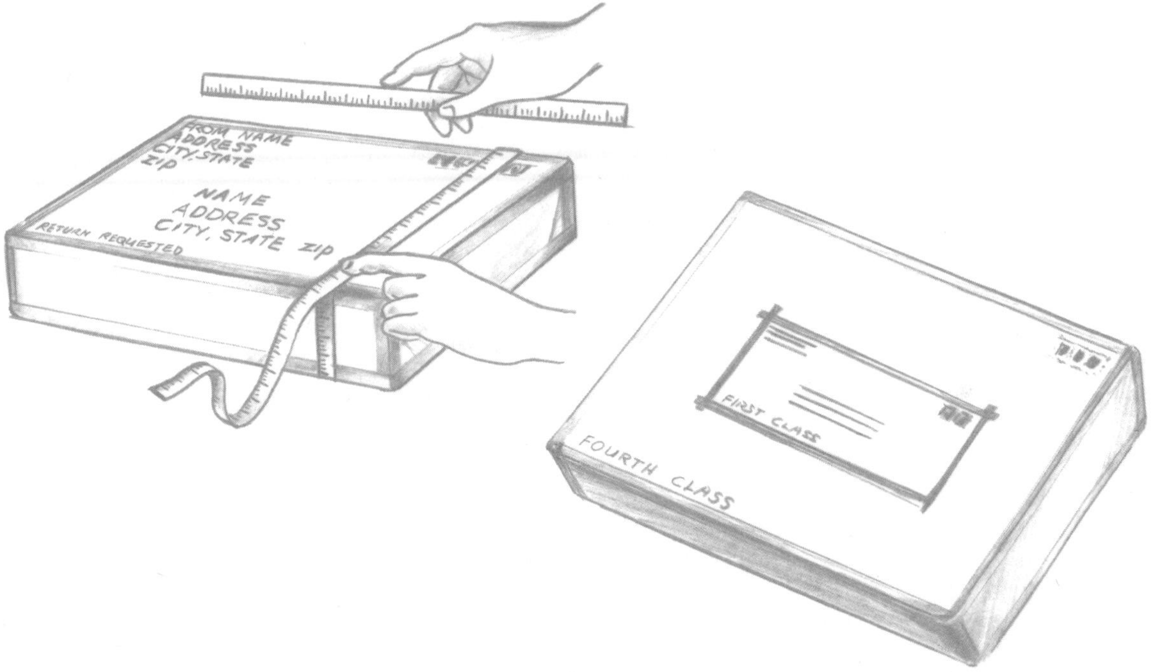

Fig. 38. A package properly wrapped and addressed for mailing. To determine the size of a parcel, measure the longest side to get the length; measure the distance around the parcel at its thickest part to get the girth; and add the two figures together.

Special Fourth-Class Rate—consists of books, manuscripts, printed music, objective test materials, sound recordings, 16 mm films (or narrower)—materials that were in the **former mail classification,** EDUCATIONAL MATERIALS RATE. The package must be marked SPECIAL FOURTH-CLASS RATE, and the contents must be named.

Library Rate—applies to materials sent to or from libraries, schools and certain nonprofit organizations that are approved by the United States Postal Service. Packages may be sealed, and they **must** be marked LIBRARY RATE.

Priority Mail—consists of first-class mail **weighing more than 12 ounces.** The charge for Priority Mail is determined by the weight of the material being mailed and the postal zone to which it is addressed. The maximum weight for Priority Mail is 70 pounds.

Airmail—Since domestic mail is routinely transported by air, Airmail now applies only to foreign mail.

Official and Free Mail—is of three types:

- **Franked Mail**—Only a few people have the privilege of using the frank: the Vice President of the United States, members and members-elect of Congress, Resident Commissioners, the Secretary of the Senate, the Sergeant-at-Arms of the Senate, and elected members of the House of Representatives and the Senate. A piece of franked mail must contain the seal or facsimile signature of the person authorized to use it in place of the stamp and the words PUBLIC DOCUMENT/OFFICIAL BUSINESS on the return address side.

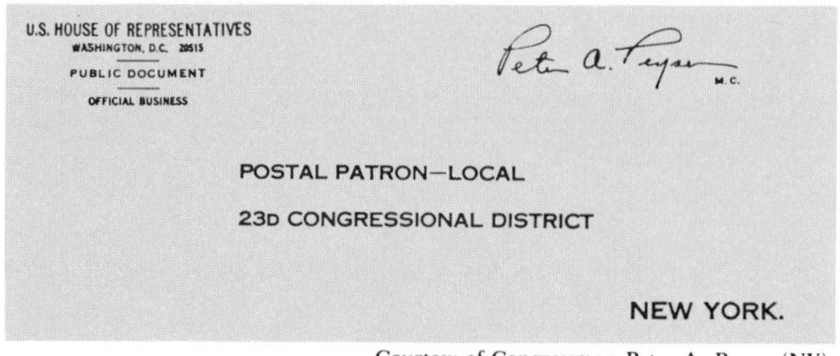

Courtesy of Congressman Peter A. Peyser (NY)

Fig. 39. A franked envelope

- **Penalty Mail**—consists of mail concerning official United States Government business. Penalty mail travels in penalty envelopes or under penalty labels.

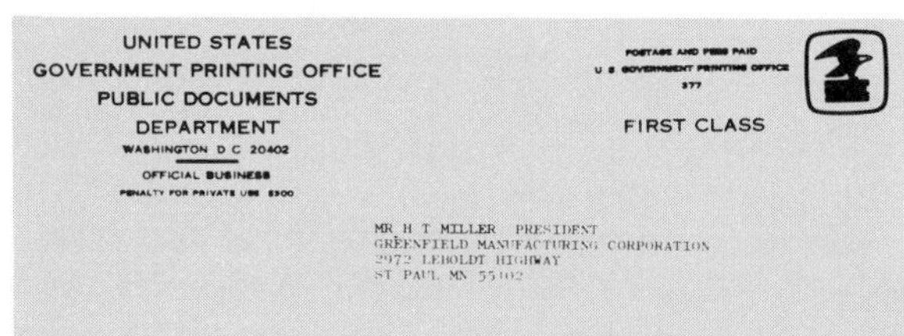

Fig. 40. A penalty imprint that can be used only on official U.S. Government mail

- **Free Mail**—consists of mail addressed to the Register of Copyrights, census mail, immigration and naturalization service mail, and absentee ballot envelopes for members of the Armed Forces that can be sent without postage by the general public. **Such mail must travel in a penalty envelope or under a penalty label.**

Mixed Classes of Mail

Sometimes it is important to have two pieces of mail of different classes arrive at their destination at the same time. EXAMPLE: A first-class letter may be attached to the outside of a fourth-class package, or it may be enclosed in the package. When a first-class letter is **attached** to a fourth-class package, the correct postage is affixed to each part separately. When a first-class letter is **enclosed** in the package, the postage is computed on each part separately, but it is affixed together on the outside of the package. In addition, the words FIRST-CLASS MAIL ENCLOSED must be typed, stamped, or written above the address and below the postage. Mixed-class mail is handled as mail in which the bulk portion of the package or envelope falls, not as first-class mail.

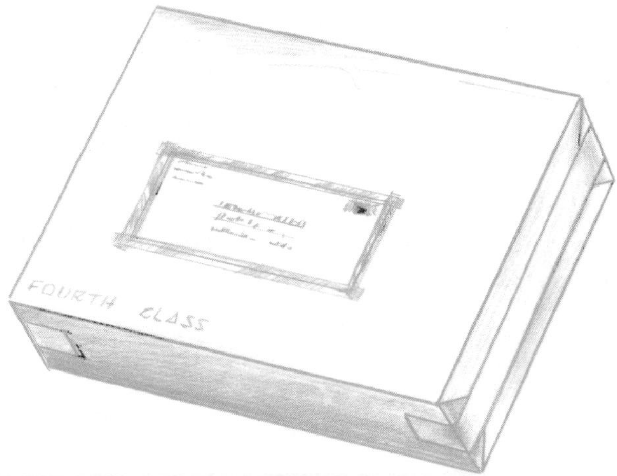

Fig. 41. A package with a letter attached

Mail by the Blind or Handicapped
Unsealed letters sent **by** a blind person or **by** a person having a physical impairment that is in raised characters or in 14 point (approximately 3/16 inch) or larger type or in the form of sound recordings can be mailed free. Such letters must be endorsed FREE MATTER FOR THE BLIND OR HANDICAPPED in place of the stamp. (Note: This regulation applies only to mail sent **by**—not to—a blind or handicapped person, and it applies only to letters.)

Special Mail Services

Registered Mail
First-class mail may be registered for its full value. The fee charged is based on the full or actual value. The fee is less if the sender has private insurance that will accept part of the liability in case of loss. Registered mail must be tightly sealed along the edges (not with transparent tape), and it must bear the complete address of both the sender and the addressee. The sender must take mail to be registered to the registry window at the post office, where a postal clerk will inspect it and compute the fee. Because it is mail containing material of special value, Registered Mail is carefully monitored from the time it is mailed at the original post office until it reaches the addressee.

Insured Mail
Third- and fourth-class mail and Priority Mail containing third- and fourth-class matter may be insured up to $400. The mail to be insured must be taken to the post office, where a clerk prepares a receipt for the insurance, stamps the mail INSURED, and writes the receipt number on the mail. (If the mail is insured for $15 or less, no receipt is issued.) After placing the regular and insured postage on the mail, the clerk gives the sender a receipt to keep. If the mail is lost or damaged, the post office will reimburse the sender the **actual value** of the damaged or lost item up to the amount of insurance taken upon presentation of the receipt and a claim for loss or damage. (Note: The post office of the sender and the post office of the addressee work together on processing the claim.)

Return Receipt
Whenever the post office accepts registered or insured mail for delivery, the sender is furnished with a receipt. For an additional fee, the sender can get a return receipt, which is legal evidence that the registered or insured mail was actually received by the addressee.

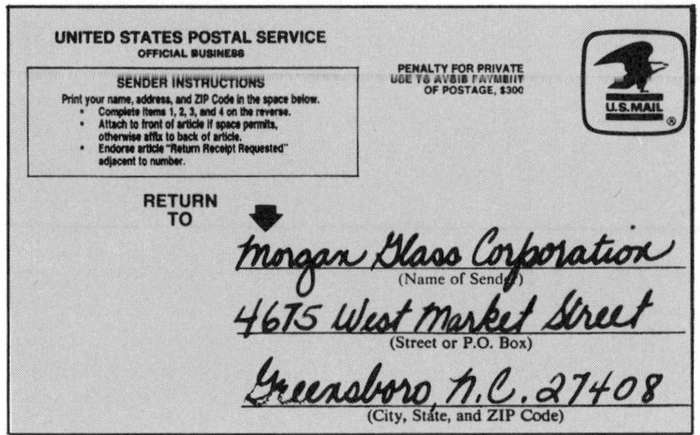

UNITED STATES POSTAL SERVICE
OFFICIAL BUSINESS

SENDER INSTRUCTIONS
Print your name, address, and ZIP Code in the space below.
- Complete items 1, 2, 3, and 4 on the reverse.
- Attach to front of article if space permits, otherwise affix to back of article.
- Endorse article "Return Receipt Requested" adjacent to number.

PENALTY FOR PRIVATE USE TO AVOID PAYMENT OF POSTAGE, $300

U.S.MAIL

RETURN TO

Morgan Glass Corporation
(Name of Sender)
4675 West Market Street
(Street or P.O. Box)
Greensboro, N.C. 27408
(City, State, and ZIP Code)

Fig. 42 (Part 1)

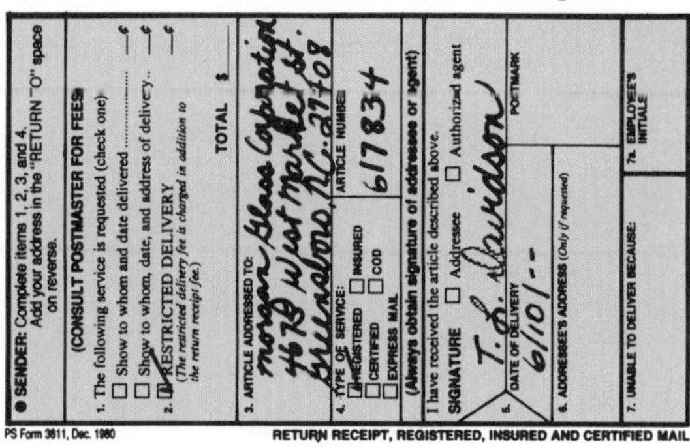

● SENDER: Complete items 1, 2, 3, and 4. Add your address in the "RETURN TO" space on reverse.
(CONSULT POSTMASTER FOR FEES)
1. The following service is requested (check one).
☐ Show to whom and date delivered .... ¢
☐ Show to whom, date, and address of delivery.. ¢
2. ☒ RESTRICTED DELIVERY (The restricted delivery fee is charged in addition to the return receipt fee.) ¢
TOTAL $
3. ARTICLE ADDRESSED TO: Morgan Glass Corporation 4675 West Market St. Greensboro, N.C. 27408
4. TYPE OF SERVICE: ☒ REGISTERED ☐ INSURED ☐ CERTIFIED ☐ COD ☐ EXPRESS MAIL
ARTICLE NUMBER 617834
(Always obtain signature of addressee or agent)
I have received the article described above.
SIGNATURE ☐ Addressee ☐ Authorized agent
T. L. Davidson
5. DATE OF DELIVERY 6/10/--
POSTMARK
6. ADDRESSEE'S ADDRESS (Only if requested)
7. UNABLE TO DELIVER BECAUSE:
7a. EMPLOYEE'S INITIALS
PS Form 3811, Dec. 1980
RETURN RECEIPT, REGISTERED, INSURED AND CERTIFIED MAIL

Fig. 43 (Part 2). A Return Receipt indicating that the mail is to be delivered only to the addressee

Restricted Delivery

For an additional fee, the sender may request that COD, registered, and certified mail or mail that has been insured for more than $15 be delivered only to the addressee. If the sender also wants a return receipt as proof that the mail was delivered only to the addressee, he/she completes a form supplied by the post office and pastes it on the back of the mail. At delivery, the letter carrier removes the card, obtains the addressee's signature, fills in the information required, and mails the card to the sender. When this service is used, the face of the mail must bear the words RETURN RECEIPT REQUESTED.

COD

Merchandise may be sent **Collect on Delivery** if the shipment is based on a bona fide order or on an agreement made with the addressee by the mailer. The sender prepays the postage on the shipment and the COD fees, but they may be included in the amount to be collected from the addressee (value of merchandise plus postage and COD charges), or the addressee may pay the amount of the merchandise plus the fee for a money order to return the amount collected to the sender. The maximum amount collectible on one parcel is $400.

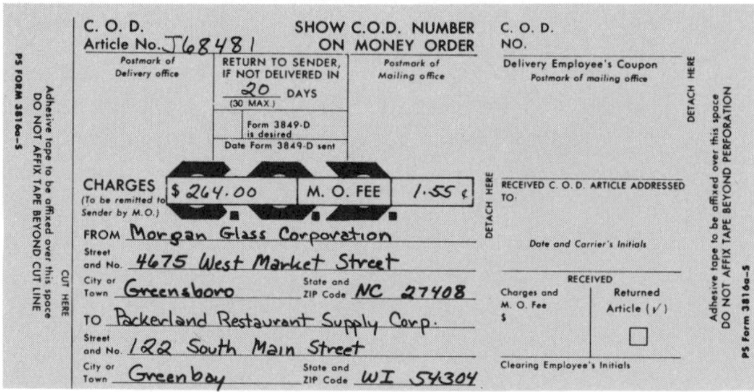

PS FORM 3816a–S
Adhesive tape to be affixed over this space
DO NOT AFFIX TAPE BEYOND CUT LINE
CUT HERE

C. O. D.
Article No. J68481
SHOW C.O.D. NUMBER ON MONEY ORDER
Postmark of Delivery office
RETURN TO SENDER, IF NOT DELIVERED IN 20 DAYS (30 MAX.)
Form 3849-D is desired
Date Form 3849-D sent
Postmark of Mailing office
CHARGES (To be remitted to Sender by M.O.) $ 264.00
M. O. FEE 1.55 ¢
FROM Morgan Glass Corporation
Street and No. 4675 West Market Street
City or Town Greensboro
State and ZIP Code NC 27408
TO Packerland Restaurant Supply Corp.
Street and No. 122 South Main Street
City or Town Greenbay
State and ZIP Code WI 54304

DETACH HERE

C. O. D. NO.
Delivery Employee's Coupon
Postmark of mailing office
DETACH HERE
RECEIVED C. O. D. ARTICLE ADDRESSED TO:
Date and Carrier's Initials
RECEIVED
Charges and M. O. Fee $
Returned Article (✓) ☐
Clearing Employee's Initials

Adhesive tape to be affixed over this space
DO NOT AFFIX TAPE BEYOND PERFORATION
PS Form 3816a–S

Fig. 44. COD Forms completed by the sender

Certificate of Mailing

For the postage required to send the piece of mail, the sender can obtain a Certificate of Mailing that is proof that a piece of mail was taken to the post office for dispatching. The sender fills in a Certificate of Mailing (available at the post office) with the name and complete address of the sender and the name and complete address of the addressee for **each piece of mail** on which he/she wishes to obtain a Certificate of Mailing and pastes a stamp in the place indicated. The sender hands both the mail and the Certificate of Mailing to the postal clerk at the post office, who cancels the stamp on the certificate and returns the certificate to the sender. This certificate provides the sender with proof of having mailed something of value to the addressee without going to the extra expense of registering, insuring, or certifying the mail. (No insurance or proof of delivery is provided with a Certificate of Mailing.)

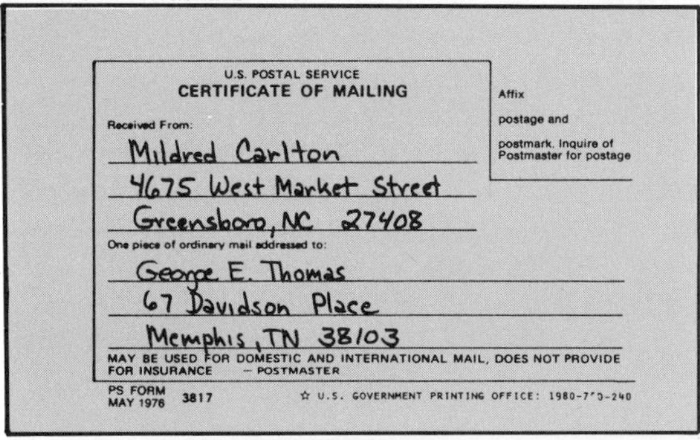
U.S. POSTAL SERVICE
CERTIFICATE OF MAILING

Affix postage and postmark. Inquire of Postmaster for postage

Received From:
Mildred Carlton
4675 West Market Street
Greensboro, NC 27408

One piece of ordinary mail addressed to:
George E. Thomas
67 Davidson Place
Memphis, TN 38103

MAY BE USED FOR DOMESTIC AND INTERNATIONAL MAIL, DOES NOT PROVIDE FOR INSURANCE — POSTMASTER

PS FORM 3817 MAY 1976 ☆ U.S. GOVERNMENT PRINTING OFFICE: 1980-7'0-240

Fig. 45. A Certificate of Mailing that has been properly completed

Special Delivery

Special Delivery Mail is given immediate delivery at the destination post office. Mail is delivered immediately after it arrives by a Special Delivery messenger (within prescribed hours and to points within certain limits of the post office). Mail must be marked SPECIAL DELIVERY above the address, and an extra fee must be paid for this service. Do not send Special Delivery Mail to post office box addresses or military installations (APO, FPO).

Special Handling

Special Handling permits third- and fourth-class mail to receive preferential handling in both dispatching and transportation. However, parcels do not receive special delivery at their destination city. An extra fee must be paid for special handling, and the parcel must be clearly marked SPECIAL HANDLING.

Certified Mail

Airmail or first-class mail that has no real value (a letter, a bill, a non-negotiable bond) may be certified for a fee. Certified Mail provides the sender with a means of checking on the delivery of a letter; it provides official evidence of mailing; and it is sometimes used to give a piece of mail the appearance of importance or urgency. The sender completes a receipt for Certified Mail and attaches the gummed end of the receipt to the letter. When the letter is delivered, the receipt is detached and returned to the sender with the postmark of the city where the letter was delivered and the date of delivery. For an additional fee, the sender can request delivery only to the addressee.

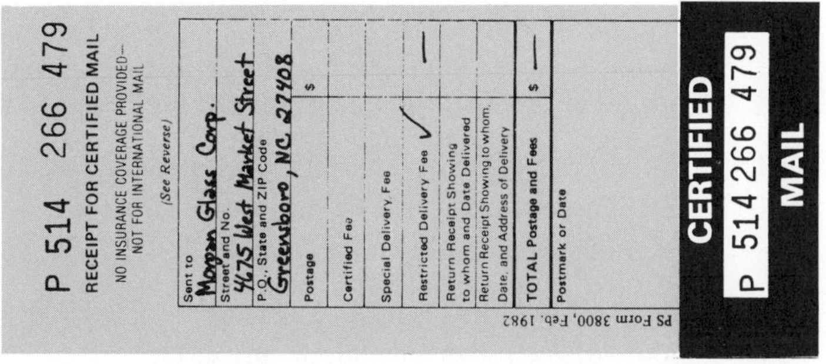
P 514 266 479
RECEIPT FOR CERTIFIED MAIL
NO INSURANCE COVERAGE PROVIDED— NOT FOR INTERNATIONAL MAIL
(See Reverse)

Sent to: Morgan Glass Corp.
Street and No.: 4675 West Market Street
P.O., State and ZIP Code: Greensboro, NC 27408
Postage: $
Certified Fee:
Special Delivery Fee:
Restricted Delivery Fee: ✓
Return Receipt Showing to whom and Date Delivered:
Return Receipt Showing to whom, Date, and Address of Delivery:
TOTAL Postage and Fees: $ —
Postmark or Date:

PS Form 3800, Feb. 1982

CERTIFIED
P 514 266 479
MAIL

Fig. 46. A properly completed Receipt for Certified Mail

Express Mail

There are four types of Express Mail services available through the United States Postal Service:

- Express Mail Next Day Service
- Express Mail Same Day Airport Service
- Express Mail Custom Designed Service
- Express Mail International Service

Express Mail Next Day Service **guarantees** to get a package to its destination by 10 a.m. the following business day, or the sender can get the entire mailing fee refunded. Here is how Express Mail service works:

Express Mail Next Day Service

1. Express Mail must be at the receiving post office by 5 p.m.
2. Anything up to 70 pounds (that is not dangerous or perishable) may be mailed.
3. The United States Postal Service **guarantees** to get the package to the destination Express Mail Post Office by 10 a.m. the next **business day.**
4. For a small additional fee, the United States Postal Service will **deliver the package directly to the addressee** by 3 p.m. (or earlier) on the date the package arrives at the destination Express Mail Post Office.
5. If for some reason the package does not arrive at the destination Express Mail Post Office by 10 a.m. the next business day, the sender can receive a 100 percent refund of the Express Mail postage by completing an application for a refund at the post office where the package was originally mailed.

Express mail service was designed for **high-priority** packages. In some ways the cost of mailing a package by Express Mail Next Day Service is rather high. However, it is certainly worth the cost to get an **important** package to its destination by 10 a.m. the next business day!

Express Mail Same Day Airport Service

With this service, a mailable item can be taken to a major **airport mail office** (not an **airline** office) where it will be loaded on a scheduled air flight. The addressee may pick up the item at the **destination airport mail office** on the same day. (Therefore, the addressee must be notified in advance that the item is being sent.) This service can be used only if air flights are already scheduled between the cities involved.

Express Mail Custom Designed Service

This service is used by companies that send important mail to the same locations regularly (payroll checks to branch offices, for example). The mail is shipped in a bright blue and orange pouch, and delivery is guaranteed within 24 hours. The mail may be taken to the post office or the airport mail office for dispatching, or it can be picked up at the sender's office by the U.S. Postal Service. The mail can be delivered to the destination post office, the airport mail office, or directly to the addressee. Terms for payment for custom designed service can also be arranged. Once a company and the U.S. Postal Service have agreed on a plan for using Express Mail Custom Designed Service, the details of the plan agreed upon will be put in writing by the U.S. Postal Service.

Express Mail International Service

Express mail service is also available between cities in the United States and several major foreign countries. You will need to contact your local post office for details about this service.

Precanceled Stamps and Envelopes

Precanceled stamps and envelopes may be used only by those persons or companies who have been issued a permit to use them. They must also be presented for dispatching at the post office where the precanceled stamps and envelopes were purchased. The advantage of this service is that it saves canceling time at the post office.

Stamped Envelopes and Cards

Stamped envelopes and cards may be purchased at the post office in various sizes and kinds and in various denominations either in quantity or individually. When envelopes are purchased in quantity, the post office will (for an additional fee) have the sender's return address and return request imprinted. First-class postal cards in single or double form are also available individually or in quantity. Soiled or unserviceable stamped envelopes and cards may be exchanged at the post office—envelopes at postage value and postal cards at a percentage of their value. Exchanges are made in stamps, stamped envelopes, or postal cards, but not in cash.

Metered Postage

The postage meter machine prints the postmark and the proper amount of postage on each piece of mail. Because of this, metered postage need not be canceled or postmarked when it reaches the post office, making it possible for this mail to be dispatched sooner. When metered mail is presented at the post office for dispatching, it **must be bundled** according to local and out-of-town delivery.

A postage meter machine is purchased outright, but the meter section of the machine is leased. To use the postage meter, a company must obtain a meter license by filing an application with the post office where its mail is handled. The application form must indicate the make and model of the meter. A record of meter transactions must be maintained in a **Meter Record Book** supplied by the post office.

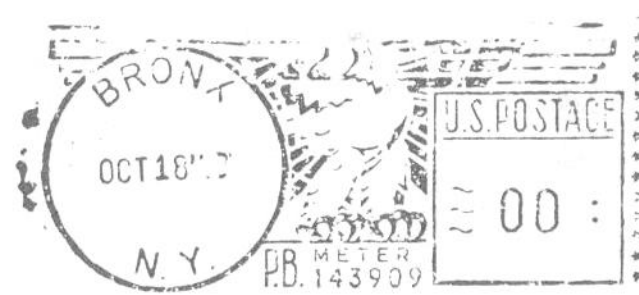

Fig. 47. Metered Postage

When postage is purchased, the meter is taken from the machine to the post office. The meter is set for the amount of postage purchased and sealed. When the amount of postage purchased is consumed, the meter locks. It must then be taken to the post office, and additional postage must be purchased.

Forwarding Mail

First-Class Mail—No additional postage is required on first-class mail up to 12 ounces. Change the address, and deposit in the mail.

Second-Class Publications—Full postage must be paid at the transient rate. To forward second-class mail: change the address, endorse the item as SECOND-CLASS MAIL, affix the postage required, and redeposit the mail.

Third-Class Mail—Full postage must be paid at the single-piece rate. To forward third-class mail: change the address, affix postage, and deposit in the mail.

Fourth-Class Mail—Additional postage at the applicable rate is required to forward fourth class mail. In addition, the address must be changed before it can be remailed.

Priority Mail—Additional postage must be paid at the rate applicable between the forwarding post office and the delivering post office.

Registered, Insured, COD, and Special Handling Mail—The forwarding procedure for mail bearing these special services depends upon the class of mail used.

Undeliverable Mail

First-Class Mail up to 12 ounces—will be returned to the sender without additional charge by ordinary mail. (Postcards and postal cards are excepted.)

Priority Mail—Priority Mail will be returned by the same transportation as first-class mail at no additional charge.

Third- and Fourth-Class Mail—will be returned to the sender with postage due if the parcel is of obvious value. (If the sender wants to guarantee return of undelivered third- and fourth-class mail and postal and postcards, he/she should write, type or print ADDRESS CORRECTION REQUESTED below return address. On postal cards, use the notation RETURN POSTAGE GUARANTEED.)

When letters and packages that are undeliverable do not contain a return address, they are sent to the dead letter office, where they are opened to find a return address. If a return address is found, the mail is sent to that address for a fee. Undeliverable dead mail is either sold or destroyed.

Remailing Returned Mail

Any mail returned with the RETURN TO SENDER stamp must be put in a fresh, correctly addressed envelope and additional postage must be paid if it is remailed.

Fig. 48. Return to Sender Stamp

Change Of Address

When they change their addresses, post office patrons should notify the post office serving them by a letter or by completing the appropriate post-office form. Both the old and the new address should be given. In addition, correspondents should be notified promptly of the change of address either by letter or on forms provided by the post office.

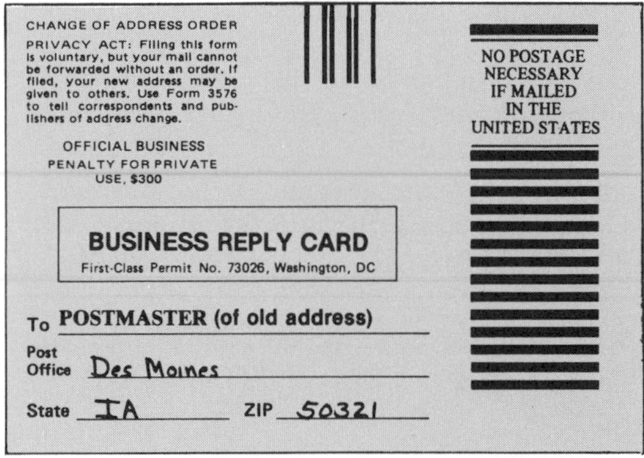

CHANGE OF ADDRESS ORDER

PRIVACY ACT: Filing this form is voluntary, but your mail cannot be forwarded without an order. If filed, your new address may be given to others. Use Form 3576 to tell correspondents and publishers of address change.

OFFICIAL BUSINESS
PENALTY FOR PRIVATE USE, $300

NO POSTAGE NECESSARY IF MAILED IN THE UNITED STATES

BUSINESS REPLY CARD
First-Class Permit No. 73026, Washington, DC

To **POSTMASTER (of old address)**
Post Office Des Moines
State IA ZIP 50321

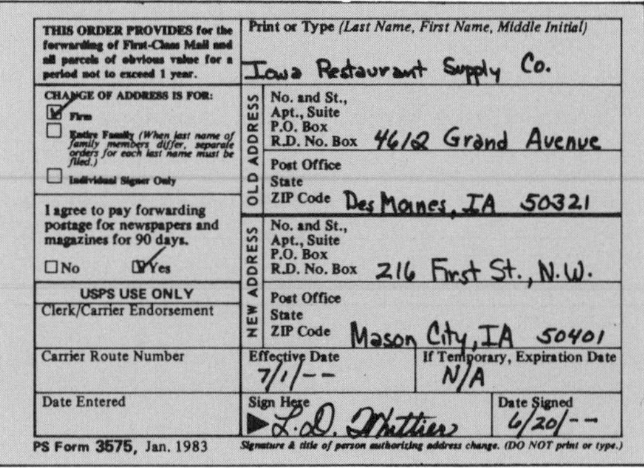

THIS ORDER PROVIDES for the forwarding of First-Class Mail and all parcels of obvious value for a period not to exceed 1 year.

Print or Type *(Last Name, First Name, Middle Initial)* Iowa Restaurant Supply Co.

CHANGE OF ADDRESS IS FOR:
☑ Firm
☐ Entire Family *(When last name of family members differ, separate orders for each last name must be filed.)*
☐ Individual Signer Only

OLD ADDRESS
No. and St., Apt., Suite P.O. Box R.D. No. Box 4612 Grand Avenue
Post Office State ZIP Code Des Moines, IA 50321

I agree to pay forwarding postage for newspapers and magazines for 90 days.
☐ No ☑ Yes

NEW ADDRESS
No. and St., Apt., Suite P.O. Box R.D. No. Box 216 First St., N.W.
Post Office State ZIP Code Mason City, IA 50401

USPS USE ONLY
Clerk/Carrier Endorsement
Carrier Route Number
Date Entered

Effective Date 7/1/--
If Temporary, Expiration Date N/A
Sign Here ▶ L.D. Mittiers
Date Signed 6/20/--

PS Form 3575, Jan. 1983
Signature & title of person authorizing address change. (DO NOT print or type.)

Fig. 49. An official Change of Address Order

General Delivery

Mail may be addressed in care of General Delivery (for example, to a person who is traveling). Mail is held for a certain number of days. If the person to whom it is addressed does not call for it within that time, it is returned to the sender. Figure 50 shows the way an envelope addressed to General Delivery should look. The words **Transient** or **To Be Called For** may also be added to the address.

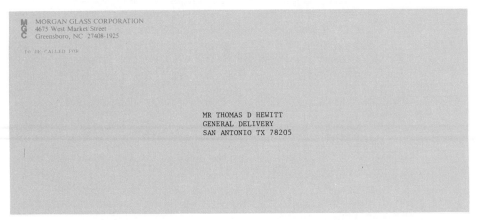

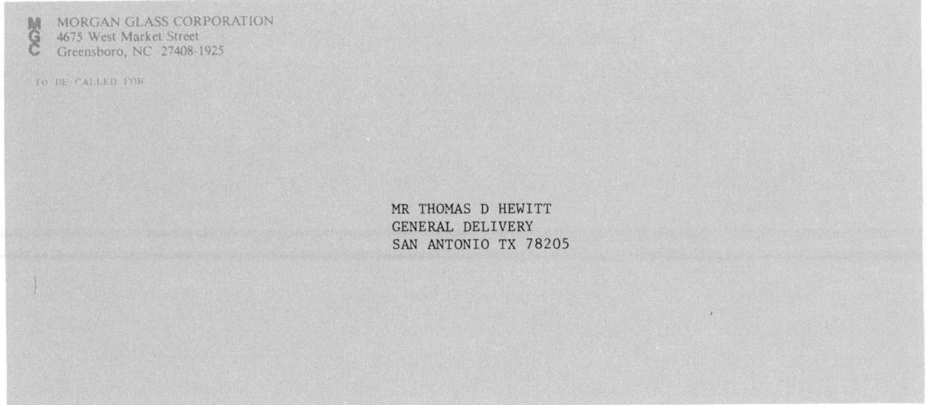

MGC
MORGAN GLASS CORPORATION
4675 West Market Street
Greensboro, NC 27408-1925
TO BE CALLED FOR
MR THOMAS D HEWITT
GENERAL DELIVERY
SAN ANTONIO TX 78205

Fig. 50. An envelope correctly addressed for General Delivery

Postal Money Orders

1. **Domestic**
   Postal money orders up to $400 in value (each) may be purchased at post offices, branches, and postal stations. Any number of money orders may be purchased at one time.
2. **International**
   An International Money Order is a method of sending money to a person in a foreign country, and it may be purchased at almost all post offices. The purchaser receives a receipt for the money from the postal clerk, who then arranges to send the money. Exact information is required about the payee, his/her address, and—in the case of a woman—her marital status. The purpose of the payment must also be stated. (Note: Money orders to Canada are the same as U.S. domestic money orders.)

International Mail

Because many companies today do business in both the United States and in foreign countries, it is important to have a general understanding of international mail services as well as domestic mail services.

International mail service provides for both Postal Union Mail and Parcel Post Service.

Postal Union Mail

Postal Union Mail is divided into two groups, LC Mail and AO Mail. **LC Mail** (letters and cards) consists of letters, letter packages, aerograms, and postal cards. **AO Mail** (other articles) includes printed matter, matter for the blind, samples of merchandise, and small packets. Postage on letters and postal cards mailed to Mexico and Canada is the same as postage for the United States. Postage to all other countries is at a higher rate, and weights are limited. Insurance is not available on Postal Union Mail, and certified mail service is not available to any foreign countries.

Parcel Post

When a parcel is to be mailed overseas, it must be packed with greater care than parcels mailed to destinations within the United States and Canada. Parcels sent by international parcel post may be registered or insured, and special-delivery and special-handling service is also available. However, there is no COD service on international parcel post. A customs declaration must be attached to every package sent by international parcel post, containing a complete description of the contents.

Weight, size limitations, and other regulations on international mail differ from country to country. For that reason, it is a good plan to consult your local post office when you are planning a mailing by international mail.

DIRECT MAIL

Direct mail is an extremely helpful sales technique when:

1. It is used in combination with other sales procedures.
2. Each direct-mail program is sent to a carefully selected mailing list.

Developing A Mailing List

Once it has been decided what product or service will be promoted by a direct-mail advertising campaign, the all-important task begins of developing a mailing list that will reach the people who have the greatest need for the product or service. Here is a helpful procedure to follow:

1. Identify broad markets that could use the product or service that can also be reached effectively by direct mail.
2. From the various fields identified, select people or companies that are potential buyers of the product or service. The following are excellent sources of names for a mailing list:
   - Sales Records
   - General Correspondence
   - Directories (A directory of directories—Principal Business Directories for Building Mailing Lists—is available from the Dartnell Corporation of Chicago.)
   - List Brokers
3. Ask the marketing people in the company for which you work who should receive the mailing in the companies you choose (executive officers, sales personnel, and purchasing department).

When you have accomplished these three steps, you will have taken a major step toward developing a realistic mailing list that will reach the people who have a need for the products or services that will be the subject of your mailing. Once a mailing list has been created, it is very important to keep it up to date. Carrying "dead wood" on a mailing is costly, and it will not produce the desired results. Here are some ways a mailing list can be kept up to date:

1. Using a double postal card, send a mailing to everyone on your mailing list asking him/her to indicate on the return portion of the card whether or not he/she wants to continue to receive your direct mail. At the same time, ask the people on your mailing list if they know of other firms or individuals who would like to receive your mailings.
2. Check names in new directories.
3. Submit the names and addresses on your mailing list on typed cards to the post office serving the addressee. The post office will check the address (for a fee) and return the card to you with an address correction if one is required.
4. Remove the names of companies that have never responded to any of your mailings.

Scheduling A Direct-Mail Campaign

When you are planning a direct-mail campaign, timing is extremely important. If the mailing is to get maximum attention from the people on your list, it must arrive at the time when they will be most receptive to the message it bears. Careful advance planning is essential to determine when the mailing should arrive at its destination for best results. Once the target date has been determined, work backwards to determine the time that preparations must begin in order to have the mailing ready to go on that date. Allow yourself plenty of time and check frequently to be sure preparations are progressing according to schedule.

Postage For Direct-Mail Campaigns

There seems to be little question that mail sent first class gets a more interested reception than mail sent third class. When you are preparing a direct-mail campaign, check post office regulations to determine the best way to send the mailing consistent with the budget provided.

By following the procedures outlined here, you can help assure your company of more successful direct-mail campaigns.

BUSINESS-REPLY MAIL

Frequently the sender of direct mail encloses a business reply-card or envelope with the mail to make it easier for the recipient of the mailing to reply. The postage on business-reply mail is guaranteed by the addressee, and it is paid when the envelope or card is returned. If the business-reply envelope or card is not returned, no postage is paid. To use business-reply mail (a first-class mail service), the sender must register at the post office and get a permit number that must be printed on the business-reply card or envelope in the place of the stamp.

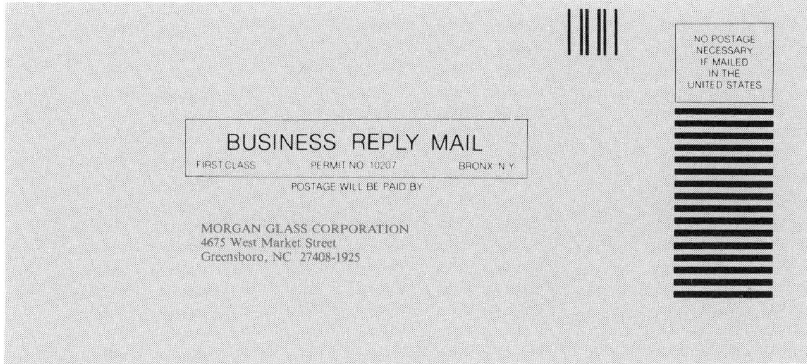

NO POSTAGE
NECESSARY
IF MAILED
IN THE
UNITED STATES
BUSINESS REPLY MAIL
FIRST CLASS PERMIT NO 10207 BRONX N Y
POSTAGE WILL BE PAID BY
MORGAN GLASS CORPORATION
4675 West Market Street
Greensboro, NC 27408-1925

Fig. 51. A business-reply card

PROCESSING OUTGOING MAIL

Even though outgoing mail is written and prepared with great care, chances are it will not be sent as rapidly as it should be if it isn't processed according to a set, prescribed method. Actually, the way the outgoing mail is processed usually depends on whether the office is large or small.

Large Offices

In large offices, outgoing mail is usually placed in an outgoing mail basket within each department. Only mail marked "personal" or "confidential" is sealed. (The other mail will be sealed as it is posted in the mail room.) At certain preset times during the day, someone from the mail room will go to each department to pick up the contents of the outgoing mail basket. When the mail reaches the mail room, it is stamped or metered, sealed, and sorted according to in-town and out-of-town delivery. In large companies, mail is usually taken to the post office two or three times during each business day—in time for major sorting and dispatching periods at the post office. From this point of view, the people in each department who prepare outgoing mail—letters, invoices, checks—should carefully plan their work in order to have as much outgoing mail as possible ready to go at each departmental pickup time and to have **all** the outgoing mail for the day ready to go by the last departmental pickup of the day.

Small Offices

In small offices, where there is no mail room, there is usually a specific place within the office where outgoing mail is deposited. Each person preparing a piece of outgoing mail seals the envelope and puts the correct amount of postage on it before depositing it in the outgoing mail basket. (Here is a time when it is essential to understand mail regulations, procedures, and rates!) At certain preset times during each workday—usually at noon time and again at closing time—someone from the office takes the mail to the mail collection box closest to the office or to the post office. If the mail is taken to a mail collection box in the neighborhood near the office, it is important to have it there before the last pickup of the day; or the mail could stay in the collection box for 10 or 12 hours without being collected. (Collection hours are posted on the outside of each mail collection box by the United States Postal Service.) Outgoing mail taken to the post office will be sorted and dispatched more quickly.

Whether you work in a large office or a small office, it is important to have an established procedure that will enable the outgoing mail to move from your office to the post office for sorting and dispatching in the shortest time possible. If there is not an established procedure in the office where you work, perhaps you can help to establish one!

SHIPPING SERVICES

Every office worker who has responsibility for seeing that company products are sent to buyers should be aware of shipping services—other than postal services—that are available. Even though a wide variety of shipping services is possible, we will confine our study to the most commonly used shipping services—express and freight.

Express

Parcels can be shipped by air express or bus express. The service that is chosen depends upon the material to be shipped and the distance it is to travel.

Air Express

Air Express (not to be confused with Air Freight that is to be described later in this chapter) is a service of private companies that specialize in Air Express shipments throughout the United States. A unique feature of **Federal Air Express** (the largest Air Express company in the United States) is that items to be shipped are picked up and they are delivered at the destination **without an additional charge.** Therefore, shipments to small towns that may be some distance from an airport are entirely practical. Since overnight delivery to any airport in the United States handling Air Express shipments is almost a certainty, next-day delivery to almost any point in the United States is also certain.

The charges for an Air Express shipment are figured by the **weight** of the parcel being shipped and the **distance** it will travel. Air Express is primarily designed for small package shipments.

A company that does a limited amount of shipping by Air Express can obtain information about rates by calling a local Air Express office. A company that does considerable shipping by **Federal Air Express** would want to have a copy of SYSTEM ROUTES AND TARIFFS, which can be obtained without charge from any Federal Air Express office.

There is a **weight limit of 70 pounds** for each package and a **total weight limit of 300 pounds** for an entire shipment **to one destination each day.** The **size limit** for each package is a total of 108 inches (combined length and girth). Insurance up to a value of $100 is included in the cost of shipment. Additional insurance, up to a maximum value of $2,000, may be purchased for a nominal fee.

Bus Express

When smaller packages must be shipped to small towns within the same state or in a nearby neighboring state where there are no airports, Bus Express service should be considered. Although most bus companies offer shipping services, Greyhound Package Express is probably the best-known service of this type. Items traveling by Bus Express are limited in weight to 100 pounds per package with a size limit of 24 by 24 by 45 inches. All parcels receive insurance up to a $50 limit as a part of the shipping charges. Additional insurance may be purchased for parcels valued at more than $50. Pickup service is also available at an additional charge. Information about rates and other details can be obtained from the bus companies in your locality offering Bus Express service.

Freight

Freight is the most complicated of the shipping services; but it is also the most economical way to ship bulky, heavy goods in large quantities. Usually companies who have need for this type of shipping have a separate shipping department manned by employees who have expertise in routing. However, as an office worker you should have at least a basic understanding of the following freight services:

Air Freight

Air Freight is a shipping service that is operated entirely by the airlines, and it is not to be confused with **Air Express** that was explained previously.

All of the major passenger-carrying airlines have cargo departments that compete with other airlines and with other cargo carriers for business. In addition, some airlines are strictly cargo carriers and do not carry passengers. In recent years, Air Freight services have expanded extremely fast. Now, almost every type of item is carried by Air Freight. Originally, however, Air Freight was used only for rush shipments of perishable items such as flowers and foods.

Pickup service for Air Freight shipments is available at an additional charge; but delivery service is included, without additional charge, in the cost of the shipment. The higher cost of Air Freight shipments is offset by the reduced cost of inventory and warehouse space and by the reduced cost of heavy crating usually required for surface shipments.

Information about rates and requirements of particular Air Freight shipments may be obtained by calling the freight department of any airline or by calling one of the air cargo carriers.

Motor Freight

Motor (truck) Freight is used for hauling materials both locally and over long distances. Some truck companies operate from coast to coast. Other companies have arrangements for connecting services with other trucking companies in various parts of the country and, by that means, provide coast-to-coast service.

Specialized contract carriers often carry only one item, such as beer, milk, or gasoline, by truck.

Trucking companies often work in conjunction with railroads on what is called **piggyback** service. In this type of service, loaded truck trailers are driven to the railroad freight yards and left. The trailers are then loaded aboard flatcars and moved by train to their destination cities, where they are unloaded from the flatcar and driven to their final destinations. The combination use of truck and railroad makes it possible to use this service in areas not served by regular railroad service.

One disadvantage of shipping less than a full truckload by Motor Freight is that shipments are sometimes held by the trucking company until they have a paying (full) load to a particular destination.

Information about rates and requirements of particular Motor Freight shipments can be obtained by calling any trucking company.

Railroad Freight

In the past, when goods were shipped by Railroad Freight, the shipper had to take the goods to the freight office of the railroad. When the goods arrived at their destination city, the person or company to whom the shipment was addressed had to call for the shipment at the freight office or arrange to have it delivered at his/her own expense. Today, in order to encourage more companies to ship by Railroad Freight, many railroads have started "door-to-door" service. They pick up and deliver Railroad Freight shipments with trucks owned and operated by the railroad. Another innovation in Railroad Freight is the **piggyback** service described under the preceding heading—Motor Freight.

Freight forwarding companies gather smaller Railroad Freight shipments going to a given destination from several shippers. By doing this, the freight forwarding companies are able to gain a carload (less expensive) rate from the railroads.

Information about rates and the requirements for particular shipments by Railroad Freight can be obtained by calling the freight department of any railroad.

Water Freight

Water Freight, as used here, refers to materials carried by river barges and ships on inland waterways in the United States. Water freight is usually cheaper than any other method of freight transportation. Such items as lumber, ore, coal, and chemicals are carried by Water Freight. Information about rates and shipping requirements can be obtained by contacting any shipping company handling Water Freight.

Bills Of Lading

Either a Straight Bill of Lading or an Order Bill of Lading must accompany every freight shipment no matter what type of freight carrier is used. A bill of lading lists the goods being shipped and explains the circumstances of the shipment (such as how the goods will be shipped and who will pay for the shipping).

Straight Bill Of Lading

When a shipment is made on open account or when the freight carrier is to collect the amount of the shipment on a COD shipment, a Straight Bill of Lading is used. In the latter case, the letters COD and the amount to be collected must be written on the face of the bill of lading.

Order Bill Of Lading

When a bank at the destination city is to collect the amount due for the shipper, an Order Bill of Lading and a sight draft are used. The consignee (recipient of the shipment) pays the bank the amount of the sight draft (due and payable on "sight") and the bill of lading is transferred to him/her. The consignee then presents the bill of lading to the carrier and takes delivery of the shipment.

International Shipments

If you work for a company that does extensive shipment of freight to foreign ports, it will probably have its own export department with employees who have expertise in international shipments. If it does not, you can obtain information about international shipments from **Foreign Freight Forwarders, Cargo Agents,** or from Combination Export Management firms whom you will find listed in the yellow pages of large city telephone directories.

STRAIGHT BILL OF LADING — SHORT FORM — ORIGINAL — NOT NEGOTIABLE

RECEIVED, subject to the classifications and tariffs in effect on the date of issue of this Original Bill of Lading,

the property described below, in apparent good order, except as noted (contents and condition of contents of packages unknown), marked, consigned, and destined as indicated below, which said carrier (the word carrier being understood throughout this contract as meaning any person or corporation in possession of the property under the contract) agrees to carry to its usual place of delivery at said destination, if on its route, otherwise to deliver to another carrier on the route to said destination. It is mutually agreed, as to each carrier of all or any of said property over all or any portion of said route to destination, and as to each party at any time interested in all or any of said property, that every service to be performed hereunder shall be subject to all the terms and conditions of the Uniform Domestic Straight Bill of Lading set forth (1) in Uniform Freight Classification in effect on the date hereof, if this is a rail or a rail-water shipment, or (2) in the applicable motor carrier classification or tariff if this is a motor carrier shipment. Shipper hereby certifies that he is familiar with all the terms and conditions of the said bill of lading, set forth in the classification or tariff which governs the transportation of this shipment, and the said terms and conditions are hereby agreed to by the shipper and accepted for himself and his assigns.

From Morgan Glass Corp.

At Greensboro, NC 10/15 19-- BY DESIGNATE WITH AN (X) TRUCK [✓] FREIGHT [ ] Shipper's No.

Carrier Roadway Agent's No.

(Mail or street address of consignee—For purposes of notification only.)

Consigned to Restaurant Supply Co., 1839 Peachtree Road, Northeast, Atlanta, GA 30308

Destination Atlanta State of GA County of

Route Roadway

Delivering Carrier Roadway Vehicle or Car Initial No.

NO. PACKAGES	HM	KIND OF PACKAGE, DESCRIPTION OF ARTICLES, SPECIAL MARKS AND EXCEPTIONS	*WEIGHT (SUBJECT TO CORR.)	CLASS OR RATE	CHECK COLUMN
27		Hansford Wine Glasses	100		
10		Glass Dessert Plates	20		
25		Hansford Goblets	110		
TOTAL PIECES		1			

Subject to Section 7 of conditions of applicable bill of lading, if this shipment is to be delivered to the consignee without recourse on the consignor, the consignor shall sign the following statement:
The carrier shall not make delivery of this shipment without payment of freight and all other lawful charges.

Per ______ (Signature of Consignor.)

If charges are to be prepaid, write or stamp here, "To be Prepaid."
To be prepaid

Received $______ to apply in prepayment of the charges on the property described hereon.

Agent or Cashier.

Per ______

(The signature here acknowledges only the amount prepaid.)

Charges Advanced:
$______

†The fibre boxes used for this shipment conform to the specifications set forth in the box maker's certificate thereon, and all other requirements of Rule 41, of the Consolidated Freight Classification.

†This is to certify that the above named articles are properly classified, described, packaged, marked and labeled, and are in proper condition for transportation, according to the applicable regulations of the Department of Transportation.

*If the shipment moves between two ports by a carrier by water, the law requires that the bill of lading shall state whether it is "carrier's or shipper's weight."

†Shipper's imprint in lieu of stamp; not a part of Bill of Lading approved by the Department of Transportation.

NOTE—Where the rate is dependent on value, shippers are required to state specifically in writing the agreed or declared value of the property.

The agreed or declared value of the property is hereby specifically stated by the shipper to be not exceeding ______

C. O. D. SHIPMENT
C.O.D. Amt. ______
Collect on Fee ______
Total Charges ______

THIS SHIPMENT IS CORRECTLY DESCRIBED
CORRECT WEIGHT IS ______ LBS.

This is to certify that the above named materials are properly classified, described, packaged, marked and labeled and are in proper condition for transportation according to the applicable regulations of the Department of Transportation.
NOTE: Preprinted certificates complying with 49 CFR 173.430 (a) in effect on June 30, 1976 may be used through June 30, 1979.

Shipper
Per ______

4675 West Market Street
Greensboro, NC 27408
Permanent post office address of shipper

Shipper, Per ______ Agent, Per ______

Fig. 52. A Straight Bill of Lading

Printed in U.S.A.

UNIFORM ORDER BILL OF LADING

ORIGINAL

Shipper's No. ______

Agent's No. ______

NEW YORK CENTRAL SYSTEM

THE NEW YORK CENTRAL RAILROAD COMPANY

RECEIVED, subject to the classifications and tariffs in effect on the date of the issue of this Bill of Lading,

at Greensboro, NC March 10, 19--

from Morgan Glass Corporation, 4675 West Market St., Greensboro, NC

Consigned to ORDER OF Reno Wholesale Distributors

Destination Reno State of NV County of

Notify Reno Wholesale Distributors

At Reno State of NV County of

Route Roadway System

Delivering Carrier Roadway Car Initial Car No.

No. Packages	Description of Articles, Special Marks and Exceptions	Weight	Class or Rate	Check Column
20	Hansford Wine Glass	60		
150	Hansford Goblets	750		

$8820.00

At Sight------------------------ March 10, 19--

Pay to the order of First National Bank, Reno, NV

Eight Thousand Eight Hundred and Twenty Dollars

Value received and charge the same to account of

To Reno Wholesale Distributors

No. 62 Concord Road, Reno, NV

Morgan Glass Corporation Shipper

Per R. L. D. Per

Permanent post-office address of shipper 4675 West Market Street, Greensboro, NC 27408

Fig. 53. An Order Bill of Lading

For Review And Discussion

1. What is the final authority on all postal regulations?
2. Name and explain briefly the classes of domestic mail.
3. Name and explain briefly the special mail services.
4. Describe the mail forwarding procedures for the various classes of mail.
5. Explain what happens to undeliverable mail (by classifications).
6. What is the proper way for a post office patron to notify both the post office and his/her correspondents of a change of address?
7. Explain what is meant by the term "General Delivery Mail."
8. Explain the term "Direct Mail."
9. Explain a typical procedure for processing outgoing mail in a large office and in a small office.
10. Name and explain briefly the three express services described in this chapter.
11. Name and explain briefly the four freight services described in this chapter.
12. Explain the Straight Bill of Lading and the Order Bill of Lading.

Turn to your workbook and complete Student Projects 14 and 15.

CHAPTER 8

The Telephone

OBJECTIVE

After studying Chapter Eight you will understand the following telephone procedures:

- Using telephone equipment correctly
- Answering incoming calls correctly
- Placing outgoing calls correctly
- Using the alphabetical and classified directories
- Using special telephone equipment and telephone services available to business
- Placing telephone calls to other time zones
- Keeping track of long-distance calls

JOB-RELATED VOCABULARY

Transmitter—The part of a telephone into which one speaks and which contains a mechanism to convert sound waves into radio waves.

Modulated—Using stress or pitch in the voice to convey meaning.

Consolidates—Brings together in one place for the purpose of strengthening.

No other business instrument is used (in many instances misused!) as much as the telephone. For many businesses, the telephone is a major means of getting orders and adjusting business situations. From that point of view, it is crucial that every employee of a business has a clear understanding of the proper use of the telephone. Otherwise, valuable business might be lost!

USING THE TELEPHONE CORRECTLY

Certain basic telephone techniques make telephone conversations more pleasant, and they present you and your company in a strong, positive manner to other people. To be **phonogenic,** follow these suggestions:

1. Place the telephone transmitter directly in line with your lips at a distance of about the width of two fingers from the mouthpiece.
2. Speak in a clear, well-modulated voice. Do not yell.
3. Be polite and considerate of other people.
4. Terminate the call when the reason for the call has been accomplished.

Incoming Calls

The way you answer the telephone will "set the stage" for the conversation that follows. Here are some suggestions for a good beginning:

1. Answer the telephone promptly—on the first ring whenever possible.
2. If calls come directly to your desk from the outside, identify your company and yourself.
3. If calls come to your desk through the company switchboard, identify your department (or office) and yourself.
4. Listen carefully to what the caller is saying. Try to help him/her.
5. If a delay is necessary to gather information, offer to call back.
6. If you must leave the telephone for any reason, excuse yourself; and tell the person on the other end of the telephone that you are putting the line on "hold."
7. If it is necessary to take a message for someone, be sure to record **the date** and the **exact time** of the incoming call. Also be sure to repeat the essentials of the message to the caller so he/she will be sure you understand. If it is necessary to repeat a telephone number, do it in the following manner: "area code 314 (pause) 864 (pause) 47 (pause 21." A properly completed telephone message form is shown in Fig. 54.

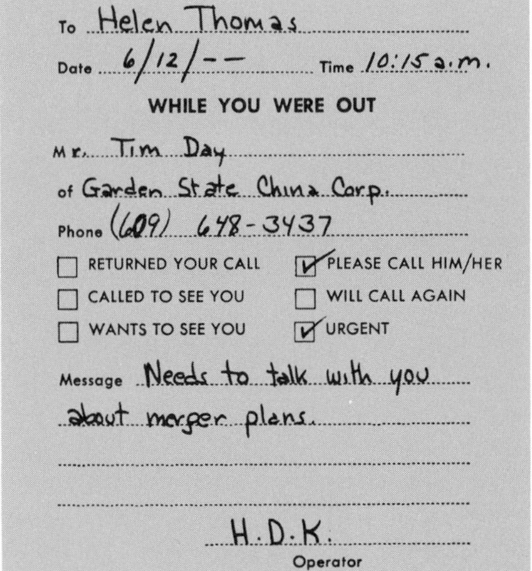

To Helen Thomas

Date 6/12/-- Time 10:15 a.m.

WHILE YOU WERE OUT

Mr. Tim Day

of Garden State China Corp.

Phone (609) 648-3437

☐ RETURNED YOUR CALL ☑ PLEASE CALL HIM/HER

☐ CALLED TO SEE YOU ☐ WILL CALL AGAIN

☐ WANTS TO SEE YOU ☑ URGENT

Message Needs to talk with you about merger plans.

H.D.K.
Operator

Fig. 54. Message form

Outgoing Calls

When you place outgoing calls, follow these techniques:

1. Observe the indicator lights on the telephone you are using. Be sure the line is free **before** you pick up the receiver.
2. When you pick up the receiver, be sure you hear a dial tone before you start to dial.
3. When the person you are calling answers the telephone, identify yourself and your company. For example—"Good afternoon, Mr. Parker, this is **Helen Lewis** of **Morgan Glass Corporation.**"

4. Make the call easier for everyone; begin immediately to discuss your business in clear, concise terms.
5. Be considerate of other people's time. When you have completed your business, end the call in a courteous manner.

Screening Telephone Calls

Sometimes a busy executive must protect his/her time in order to get his/her work done. In order to use his/her time to best advantage, the executive may ask someone in the office to find out who is calling and to relay only the most important calls.

If you answer a call and the caller does not identify himself/herself, say: "May I tell Ms (or Mr.) .... who is calling please." If the name of the caller does not identify the nature of his/her business, it is perfectly proper to say: "May I tell Ms (or Mr.) .... what the call is about, please."

If you answer a call you know your employer does not want to take, always be sure to offer to take a message. Remember, too, that the tone of your voice and your attitude, expressed by your "manner," will do much to keep callers from getting annoyed.

Personal Calls

Rules governing personal telephone calls vary greatly from company to company. Some companies permit a **limited number** of personal calls; other companies discourage such calls. As a general rule, brief important personal calls and emergency calls are permitted.

TELEPHONE DIRECTORIES

Before placing a call, it is often necessary to refer to the telephone directory published by the local telephone company. The telephone directory has two parts: the Alphabetical Directory (white pages), in which subscribers' names, addresses, and telephone numbers are listed; and the Classified Directory (yellow pages), in which major headings are products or services with the names, addresses, and telephone numbers of companies or individuals offering those products or services listed alphabetically under each major heading. In order to help subscribers to locate the correct page, the first and last name on the page (white pages) or headings (yellow pages) are printed on the upper outside corner of each page.

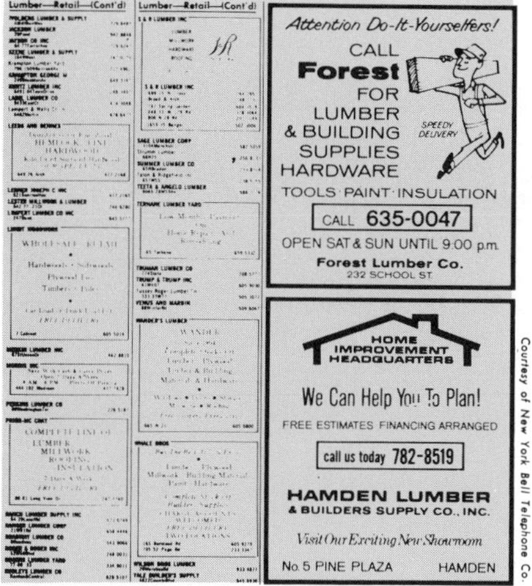

Fig. 55. An excerpt from the yellow pages

Alphabetical Directory

Although numbers are usually fairly easy to find in the Alphabetical Directory, some numbers become more difficult to find because of the long lists of names with one surname. For example—In the New York City Telephone Directory for the Borough of Manhattan, there are 31 columns of the surname Smith. In addition, the heading to the Smith listings refers users to the alternate spellings of Smyth and Smythe. For that reason, users of telephone directories must pay close attention to the given (first) names or initials for those surnames having long lists of names so they can find quickly the name for which they are looking.

When you are looking for telephone numbers of public services and governmental offices, you will need to be aware of the following:

NY STATE OF—
ATHLETIC COMM 496 W84 - - - - 762-9100
ATOMIC & SPACE DEVELOPMENT AUTHORITY 54 Porter - - - - - 461-8346
AUDIT & CONTROL DEPT OF—
COMPTROLLER 2701 ParkAv - - 676-4793

1. State offices are usually listed under the name of the state first, then alphabetically by the name of the office.

NY COUNTY—See Also NY City Of
NY County Master Plumbers Assn 46 W89 471-4901
NY County Medical Soc 21 Chambers 537-9604
NY County Merchants Assn 461 West 741-8907

2. County offices are usually listed under the name of the county first, then alphabetically by the name of the office.

NY CITY OF—
C
CHELSEA TASK FORCE 218 W96 - 741-0468
CITY ADMNSTRTR 290 Lex - - - - 517-9048
CITY CLERK'S OFFICE Municipal Bldg 714-0826
CITY COUNCIL THE CityHall - - - 362-2901

3. City offices are usually listed under the name of the city first, then alphabetically by the name of the office.

UNITED STATES GOVERNMENT—
A
AGRICULTURE DEPT OF—
ANIMAL & PLANT HEALTH INSPEC
SVCE 96 FedrlPlz - - - - - - - - - 496-0108
Export Certification - - - - - - - 478-9104
Port Inspection - - - - - - - - - 676-4104

4. Federal offices are listed first under the heading, United States Government, then alphabetically by the name of the office.

NY CITY OF—
EDUCATION—
CITY BOARD OF—
High Schools—
George Washington High School YorkAve&112 471-0716
HC 20 Classes PS199 241 W96 - 541-0671
Haaren Hgh School 9Av&79 - - 374-0177
Harlem Hgh School 207 W138 - 748-0214

5. Public schools are usually listed first under the name of the municipality or county, then under the Board of Education, then alphabetically by school name.

Saint Bernard School 471 W95 - - - 376-0492
St Bernard's Rectory 478 E79 - - - 710-4111
St Bernard's School 371 E71 - - - - 471-0752
St Bridgid's Guild 4918 Hall Bx - - 947-0146

Format Courtesy of New York Bell Telephone Co.

6. Parochial schools are usually listed alphabetically by the name of the school.

Figs. 56-61. Selections from the Alphabetical Directory

When there are identical listings, look at the street names (in **alphabetical** order). If the street names are also identical, look at the street number (in **numerical** order).

Classified Directory

Frequently someone in a business office (or at home) will want to telephone "that printing company on Maplewood Road," but he/she does not know the name of the company; and for that reason, he/she cannot use the Alphabetical Directory. By looking in the Classified Directory (yellow pages) under the heading, PRINTERS, then following the listings down the columns under that heading until he/she comes to a listing for a printing company on Maplewood Road, the person can find both the name of the company and the telephone number.

It is a good practice to circle the listings of frequently called numbers in both the Alphabetical Directory and the Classified Directory. This practice makes the number easier to find the next time it is needed.

Many companies keep in their offices a collection of Alphabetical and Classified Directories from cities where they do a great deal of business. In this way, the company has a ready reference for numbers it needs to check in the cities where it does a large volume of business.

Some telephone directories are now divided into **three** parts: alphabetic listings for home telephones, alphabetic listings for business telephones, and the Classified (or yellow pages) Directory.

Personal Telephone Directory

It is far more efficient to keep a listing of the frequently called numbers of companies and individuals in a Personal Telephone Directory than it is to take the time to locate the number in the Alphabetical or Classified Directories each time. In addition, unlisted numbers must be kept in a Personal Telephone Directory, because they cannot be obtained by calling the Directory Assistance Operator.

Numbers in the Personal Telephone Directory are entered alphabetically by the name of the subscriber. In some areas, you can obtain a Personal Telephone Directory from your local telephone company business office.

If you work as a secretary, it is a good plan to prepare two Personal Telephone Directories, one for your desk and one for your employer's desk. (Remember to make additions and corrections in **both** of them.)

TELEPHONE EQUIPMENT AND SERVICES

It is important for an office worker to be aware of the various types of telephone equipment the telephone company makes available to businesses. Very often the general office workers, not the executive staff, first become aware of the need for additional telephone equipment and services. By being aware of what is available in both equipment and service, you might be able to bring the need for that equipment or service to the attention of the executives in the company for which you work.

A. PBX Console
This equipment consolidates all of the features normally associated with a switchboard in a modern, compact desktop unit. Ordinarily this type of equipment is placed on the receptionist's desk.

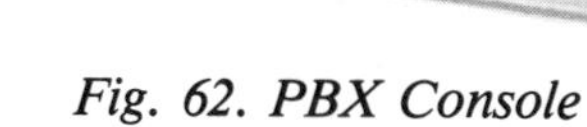

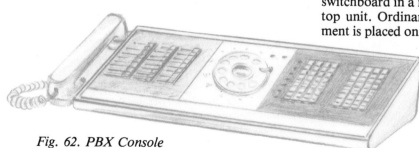

Fig. 62. PBX Console

Telephone Equipment

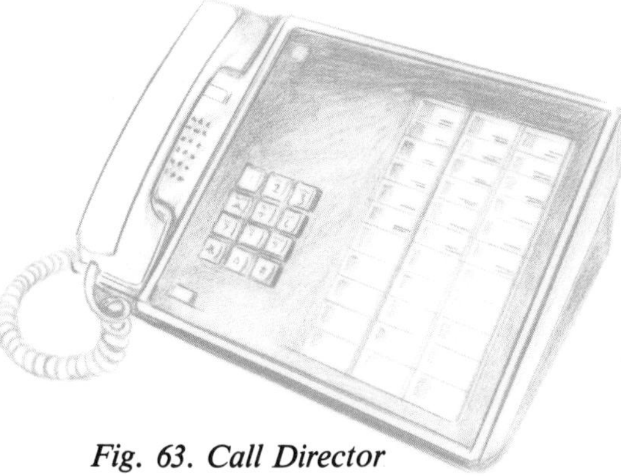

Fig. 63. *Call Director*

B. Call Director
The Call Director enables a secretary to answer many lines at one location. A Call Director may be arranged to provide interoffice telephone service, conference call service, and the "add on" feature. The Call Director is available in two sizes: 12-button and 30-button. Call Directors are available with either rotary dials or TOUCH-TONE.®

C. Six-Button Desk Telephone
This type of equipment is frequently found in business offices. Available with either a rotary dial or TOUCH-TONE®, it usually provides four trunk lines, a hold button, and an intercom button for interoffice communications.

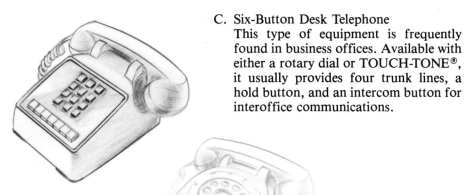

Fig. 64. *Six-Button Desk Telephones*

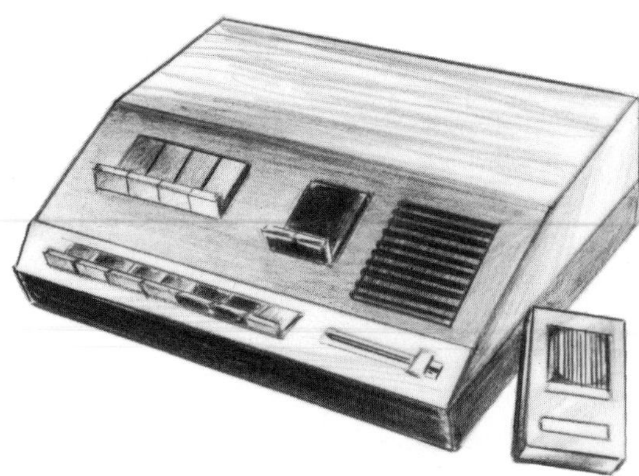

Fig. 65. *Telephone Answering Device*

D. Telephone Answering Device
Automatic telephone answering equipment can deliver any message that the subscriber records. Before leaving the office, the business executive or his/her secretary turns on the equipment and records a message including instructions for the caller to leave a message. The caller listens to the announcement and then records his/her own message. An innovation permits the business person to call from an outside telephone and revise his/her own message as necessary.

Fig. 66. DATA-PHONE®

E. DATA-PHONE® Service
The "DATA-PHONE®" data set permits business data, converted into tones, to be transmitted between one business machine and another over telephone lines. By using this equipment, businesses can transmit large amounts of data between branch offices and home office in a relatively short period of time.

Fig. 67. Speakerphone®

F. Speakerphone®
The Speakerphone® has a built-in transmitter and volume control. It permits "hands-free" operation of the telephone—the voice of each person in the room is picked up by a microphone and the calling party's voice is heard over a loudspeaker with volume adjustable to the listener's preference. The Speakerphone® is especially valuable for conference calls.

Fig. 68. Picturephone®

G. Picturephone®
The Picturephone® has been developed to permit people to have face-to-face discussion, demonstrations, and presentations via the telephone. This particular type of telephone is now in the developmental stage, but it is expected to be widely used in the future. Usually a secretary must call and arrange an appointment for Picturephone® service.

Fig. 69. Bellboy® Unit

H. Bellboy®
Bellboy® service is a personal signalling service. A doctor, salesman, or any other person who must be close to the telephone at all times, carries a lightweight unit in his/her pocket. When his/her office wishes to contact him/her, someone merely dials his/her BELLBOY® number; and the unit he/she is carrying begins to buzz. The subscriber then goes to a nearby telephone and calls his/her office or answering service for a message.

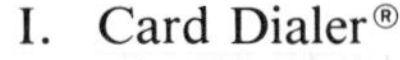

Fig. 70. Card Dialers®

I. Card Dialer®
The Card Dialer® telephone is particularly valuable when repeated calls are to be made to the same number or when a number of calls are to be made in sequence. The subscriber places a punched-hole plastic card into a slot in the telephone and pushes the start bar. The punched-hole card dials the correct number. Notice that the cards are stored in the special compartment at the top of the telephone instrument.

Fig. 71. Touch-A-Matic®

J. Touch-A-Matic®
The Touch-A-Matic® is a Touch-Tone **automatic dialer** that is a combination of the six-key Touch-Tone telephone and an automatic dialer with storage capacity for up to 31 telephone numbers.

Fig. 72. Com Key®

K. Com Key®
The Com Key® telephone system can set up conference calls instantly, reach co-workers by buttons with names instead of extension numbers, and permit employees to update themselves without leaving their offices. Optional features permit users to keep a separate line for special callers and talk on the telephone without holding a handset.

Fig. 73. Princess® Phone

L. Individualized Equipment

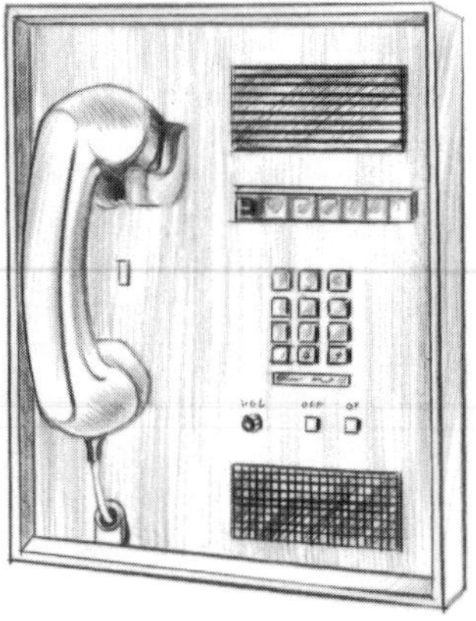

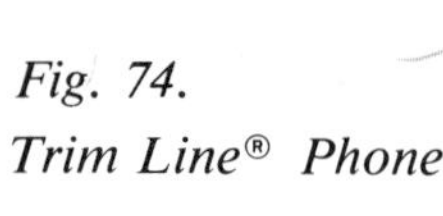

Fig. 74.
Trim Line® Phone

Telephone Services

A. Telephone Answering Service
An outside operator (not a telephone company operator) actually answers the company (or personal) telephone when the subscriber is away. The operator is able to deal with callers in a personal way that a recorded message cannot. It is the subscriber's responsibility to let the answering service know when it will be responsible for answering the telephone. In addition, the subscriber should check with the answering service for messages immediately upon returning to the office.

B. Taped Announcements
Taped announcements such as the time of day, the weather, flight information, stock-market information, movie schedules, and prayers play automatically when certain telephone numbers are dialed.

C. Special Reverse-Charge Toll Service
If a business wants to make its services available to telephone subscribers in another city, the business may have a special **local** telephone number listed in the directory for that city. When a caller dials the number, the long-distance charge will be billed to the listed number, permitting the caller to make the call as a local call.

D. Station-to-Station Call
When you place a station-to-station call, you dial a telephone number with the understanding that you will speak with whoever answers. This type of call should be made when you are reasonably sure that the person you want will be within easy reach of the telephone. Charges begin at the time someone at the called number answers.

E. Person-to-Person Call
A person-to-person call is made when you must talk to a particular person. Charges (which are more than for a station-to-station call) begin when the designated person answers. In most areas, if the operator is asked to do so he/she will try repeatedly to complete a person-to-person call until he/she is successful in reaching the party requested.

F. Direct Distance Dialing (DDD)
DDD is the process of dialing the entire long-distance call yourself. First, dial the 3-digit area code; then dial the 7-digit telephone number. (Note: In some areas, you must dial the access code 1 to get a long-distance line before dialing a toll call.) This process will complete a station-to-station call. In some areas, it is possible to use DDD to place person-to-person, credit card, and collect calls too. If it is possible in your area, follow these steps:
1. Dial O.
2. Dial the 3-digit area code.
3. Dial the 7-digit telephone number.
4. You will hear a "beep" tone, and the operator will come on the line. Give him/her the name of the person you are calling. When someone at the number you are calling answers, the operator will help you to obtain your party. In the case of a person-to-person call, you will not have to pay for the call if you are not able to reach the person you are calling.

G. Collect Calls
On collect calls, toll charges are billed to the telephone number being called, not the one from which the call is placed. The request to reverse the charges must be made to the operator at the time the call is placed. In addition, the receiving number must accept the charges before the conversation can begin.

H. Telephone Credit Cards
Business people frequently have occasion to make long-distance calls when they are traveling for business. Upon application, the telephone company will issue credit cards that will enable business people to charge calls to their home or business telephone. The credit card shows the subscriber's code number, name, and business affiliation. When making a credit-card call, the subscriber tells the long-distance operator that he/she is placing a credit-card call and gives the operator the code number and the number of the party he/she is calling. Credit-card calls are identified by a special code letter on the monthly statement of charges. In some instances, special telephones are available in public buildings on which an entire credit-card call can be placed without the assistance of an operator.

I. Wide Area Telephone Service (WATS)
WATS enables the subscriber to place an unlimited number of calls within a specific radius of his/her place of business for a flat rate monthly. The number of calls and the length of the calls are unlimited. A measured-time service is also available that provides ten hours of unlimited calls. For WATS, the country is broken into six regions. The area of coverage for WATS will be determined by the needs of each individual business.

J. Extended Area Service (EAS)
A business located in a metropolitan area may need to place many calls to the nearby suburban area. Such calls can be placed as "local" calls with EAS. Here is an example: A business in New York City may have need for "local" service to Mount Vernon, New York, Newark, New Jersey, and Hyde Park, New York. Such a company could purchase reduced-rate EAS at a flat monthly fee. The savings over individual, full-rate, long-distance calls to these areas would be considerable.

K. Leased Lines (Private Lines)
Companies can lease telephone lines betweeen one location and another for their exclusive use.

L. Tie-Line Service
Tie lines are used for direct connection of different PBX locations. The locations may be in the same city or in another city. The lines can be used to transmit the voice or data (DATA-PHONE® Service).

M. Foreign-Exchange Service (FX)
When a company does much business in a distant city, the company's telephone number can be listed in the local directory so that the call goes through as a local call. For example, the New York City directory might list the number of a firm in Camden, New Jersey as NYC 968-4617. By using that number, a caller in New York City can call the Camden, New Jersey, firm without paying a toll charge. The subscriber could also place calls to New York City on a local basis rather than incur toll charges.

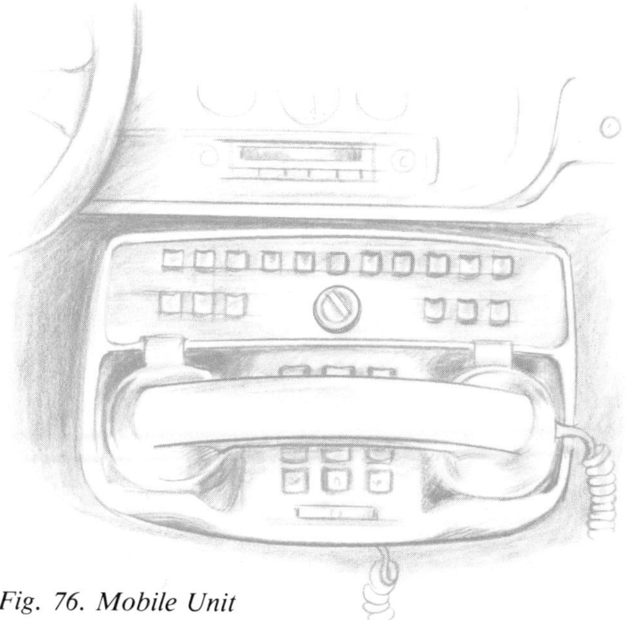

Fig. 76. Mobile Unit

N. Mobile Service
Trucks, news services, private automobiles, buses, trains, and planes all may have mobile service. Anyone can make a call to a mobile unit from any telephone, and any telephone can receive a call from a mobile unit. Calls are placed through the mobile service operator. The conversation travels part way by radio and part way by conventional telephone circuits.

O. Third Number Billing
Third number billing is placing a long-distance call from one telephone number to another and having the charges billed to a third telephone number. For example: A salesperson who is traveling for his/her company might place a call from a coin-operated telephone to one of his/her clients and have the charges billed to his/her company (the third number).

P. Conference Call
A conference call is placed when the caller wants to talk with several persons at from 3 to 14 different locations at the same time. To place such a call, the person arranging a conference call asks for the conference call operator. The caller gives the conference operator the names and telephone numbers of the persons to be included in the call. It is always necessary to specify the time the call is to be made. With special equipment such as the Speakerphone®, several people can hear and participate in the conference call at each location. On a one-way conference call—one in which the voice of only one caller is transmitted—up to 49 locations can be connected.

Q. Sequence Calls
Sequence calls are used when a business has a special group of offices, salespeople, and clients who must be called week after week. The secretary prepares a list of numbers and names to be called in sequence and files it on the required telephone company form with the Sequence Call Service. When he/she is ready to place the calls, the secretary asks for the sequence operator and tells the operator which list is to be called. The operator does the work of dialing the

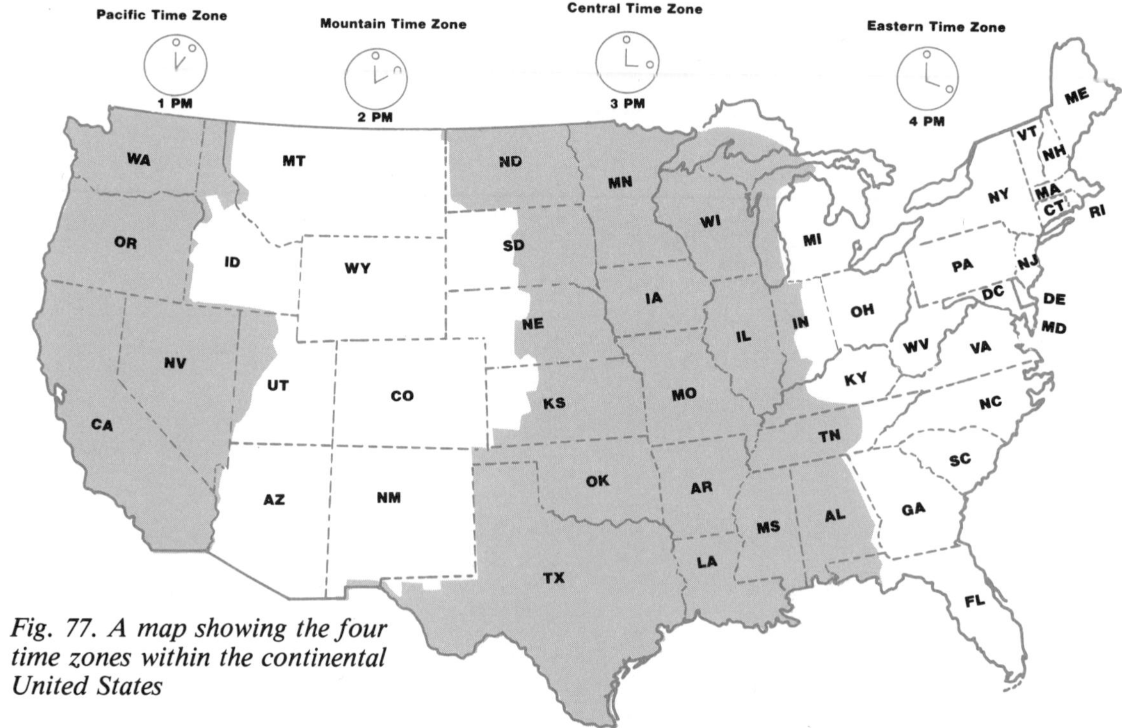

Fig. 77. A map showing the four time zones within the continental United States

calls in sequence, one after the other, until the entire list has been completed. The telephone company provides this service without extra charge.

Time Zones And Using The Telephone

When you place telephone calls to different parts of the continental United States, it is important to keep in mind the four time zones—Eastern (EST), Central (CST), Mountain (MST), Pacific (PST). As you move from **East to West,** the time is **one hour earlier** as you move from one time zone to another. Here are some time comparisons for you to study:

Boston (EST) 2 p.m.—	Chicago (CST) 1 p.m.
San Diego (PST) 5 p.m.—	New York (EST) 8 p.m.
Denver (MST) 9 a.m.—	Raleigh (EST) 11 a.m.
Dallas (CST) 6 p.m.—	Reno (PST) 4 p.m.
Philadelphia (EST) 4 p.m.—	Salt Lake City (MST) 2 p.m.

If you work in an office in Philadelphia (EST) that has a branch in San Diego (PST), you would not call San Diego before 12 noon (EST), because that would be 9 a.m. (PST) San Diego time. By the same token, the San Diego branch would not call Philadelphia after 2 p.m. (PST) because that would be 5 p.m. (EST) Philadelphia time.

Telephone calls should be placed to coincide with the business day of the place called. The time at the place where the call originates determines whether day, evening or night rates prevail.

Paying For Long-Distance (Toll) Calls

It is important for each person in a company who makes a long-distance call to keep a record of the call including: the name of the person or company called, the telephone number, and the date of the call. The person who accepts a collect call should keep a record of the name of the person calling, the city from which the call originated, and the date of the call.

When the telephone bill comes each month, it contains a Statement of Long-Distance Service (see Fig. 78). Each long-distance or collect call for that month is checked against the statement. The initials of the person or department responsible for the call are placed beside each call. This procedure serves two purposes:

1. It enables the Accounting Department to charge the cost of long-distance calls to the proper department.
2. It enables the company to exercise control over the use of the telephone for long-distance purposes.

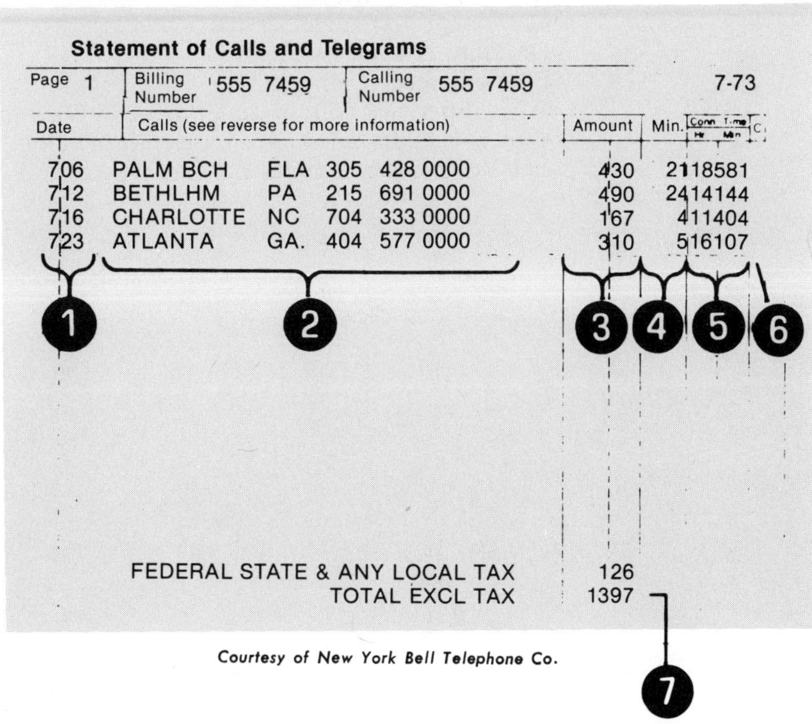

Statement of Calls and Telegrams

Page 1 | Billing Number 555 7459 | Calling Number 555 7459 | 7-73

Date	Calls (see reverse for more information)	Amount	Min. Conn Time Hr Min C
706	PALM BCH FLA 305 428 0000	430	2118581
712	BETHLHM PA 215 691 0000	490	2414144
716	CHARLOTTE NC 704 333 0000	167	411404
723	ATLANTA GA. 404 577 0000	310	516107
	FEDERAL STATE & ANY LOCAL TAX	126	
	TOTAL EXCL TAX	1397	

Courtesy of New York Bell Telephone Co.

Fig. 78. A Statement of Long-Distance Telephone Service

Here is an explanation of the Statement of Long-Distance Telephone Service in Fig. 78:

1. The date each long-distance call was made.
2. The city, state, and telephone number called.
3. The cost of each telephone call or telegram before taxes.
4. The length (in minutes) of each long-distance telephone call.
5. The time of day each telephone call was made using the 24-hour clock. (21:18 on the 24-hour clock would be 9:18 p.m. on the 12-hour clock.)
6. The rate classification code of the call or the way the call was placed. (The code is explained on the back of the bill.)
7. Total charges for long-distance calls and telegrams **excluding** federal, state, and local (if applicable) taxes.

FOR REVIEW AND DISCUSSION

1. Explain the four basic techniques for using the telephone.
2. Explain the seven procedures for handling incoming telephone calls.
3. Explain the five procedures for placing outgoing telephone calls.
4. Explain the contents and the listings in the Alphabetical Directory and the Classified Directory.
5. What is a Personal Telephone Directory? For what is it used?
6. Explain briefly the purposes of the following telephone equipment:
   A. Call Director
   B. Telephone Answering Device
   C. DATA-PHONE®
   D. Speakerphone®
   E. Bellboy®
7. Explain briefly the use of the following telephone company services:
   A. Wide Area Telephone Service (WATS)
   B. Extended Area Service (EAS)
   C. Foreign-Exchange Service (FX)
   D. Third Number Billing
   E. Conference Call
8. What difference do time zones make in using the telephone?
9. Why is it important to keep a record of toll calls made and collect calls accepted each month?

Turn to your workbook and complete Student Project 16.

CHAPTER 9

Telegraph Services

OBJECTIVE

After studying Chapter Nine you will understand the types of domestic and international telegraph services available and the procedures to be followed for using those services.

JOB-RELATED VOCABULARY

Transmitted—(A signal) sent by radio waves or by wire.

Sophisticated—Highly complicated or complex.

Capability—Potentiality or capacity.

Telegraph services are a means of rapid written communication for thousands of businesses. A telegram can be the solution to a communication problem when an urgent message must be delivered extremely fast. In addition to high-speed delivery, a telegram commands immediate attention. It is usually read and acted upon immediately. Finally, a telegram provides a lasting, written record for future reference.

In addition to rapid message service, telegrams can be used to send and receive money rapidly, to send flowers or gifts to another city, to find an available hotel or motel room rapidly, and to receive instant quotations from stock and commodity exchanges.

The telegraph services provide one more way for people to conduct business rapidly and efficiently. Because of this fact, every prospective business person should understand the basic telegraph services described here.

DOMESTIC TELEGRAPH SERVICES

Full-Rate Telegrams

Full-rate telegrams (sometimes referred to as Fast Telegrams) are sent as soon as they are received at the Western Union office at any time of the day or night. The rate for this service is based on a minimum of 15 words with an additional charge for each additional word.

Overnight Telegrams

An attempt to deliver overnight telegrams is made before 2 p.m. on the day following the date the overnight telegram is filed. The message can be sent at any time up to midnight. The rate is based on a minimum of 100 words with an additional charge for each additional word.

Teletypewritten messages are one type of **electronic mail** media. (Note: Electronic mail will be discussed in detail in Chapter Ten.)

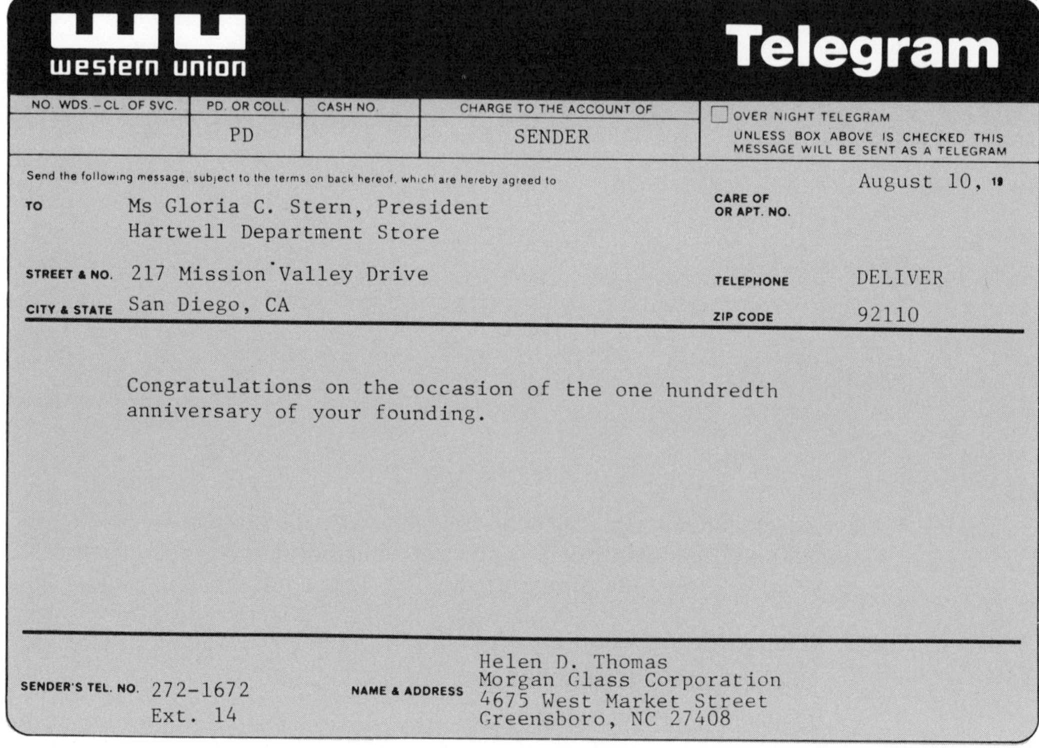

western union Telegram

NO. WDS.-CL. OF SVC.	PD. OR COLL.	CASH NO.	CHARGE TO THE ACCOUNT OF	☐ OVER NIGHT TELEGRAM
	PD		SENDER	UNLESS BOX ABOVE IS CHECKED THIS MESSAGE WILL BE SENT AS A TELEGRAM

Send the following message, subject to the terms on back hereof, which are hereby agreed to

August 10, 19

TO Ms Gloria C. Stern, President
Hartwell Department Store

CARE OF OR APT. NO.

STREET & NO. 217 Mission Valley Drive

TELEPHONE DELIVER

CITY & STATE San Diego, CA

ZIP CODE 92110

Congratulations on the occasion of the one hundredth anniversary of your founding.

SENDER'S TEL. NO. 272-1672
Ext. 14

NAME & ADDRESS Helen D. Thomas
Morgan Glass Corporation
4675 West Market Street
Greensboro, NC 27408

Form Courtesy of Western Union

Fig. 79. A properly typed telegram

MAILGRAM®

MAILGRAM® —another medium of **electronic mail**—is a distinctive, low-cost message service combining the fastest electronic transmission facilities of Western Union with the economical delivery system of the U.S. Postal Service. MAILGRAMS® are transmitted by Western Union's high speed switching computer to a post office serving the zip code area of the addressee. MAILGRAMS® filed during business hours will be delivered at almost all locations in the next day's mail. There is a base rate for the first 100 words or less, and an additional charge is made for each additional group of 100 words or less.

Send This Message By Mailgram
.... Electronic Mail Via western union

Send To:
NAME
Mrs. H. C. Loomis
COMPANY
D. L. Stevens Supply House
STREET ADDRESS
2981 Carter Highway
CITY AND STATE
Seattle, WA
ZIP
98101

OR SEND TO: ADDRESS LISTS

From:
NAME AND TITLE
Helen D. Thomas
COMPANY
Morgan Glass Corporation
STREET ADDRESS
4675 West Market Street
PHONE
272-1672
CITY AND STATE
Greensboro, NC
ZIP
27408

Message:

I have just learned of the untimely death of your husband
Mr. Tom Loomis. I take this opportunity to express to you
the sympathy of the officers and staff of Morgan Glass
Corporation. Mr. Loomis had been a distributor of ours
for more than 25 years. In all those years, we enjoyed
the best possible business and personal relationships.
We shall miss Mr. Loomis greatly.

(continue on reverse side or separate sheet if necessary)

Signed: Helen D. Thomas

To send this MAILGRAM
From Telex, dial 6161
From TWX, dial 910-420-1212
From Phone, dial

Fig. 80. A properly typed MAILGRAM®

The Type Of Telegraph Service To Be Used

When a telegraph service is needed, three factors determine the type of service to be used:

Cost
Time of Day
Urgency of the Message

Telegram Copies

Ordinarily, in business offices, three copies of an outgoing telegram are prepared. The original, referred to by Western Union as the "File" copy, is the one from which the message is transmitted. The first carbon copy is usually sent to the Accounting Department of the sender's company, where it will be used to verify the billing of the telegram. The sender usually keeps the third copy for his/her files. (However, many telegrams are now sent to Western Union by telephone. When telegrams are transmitted to Western Union by telephone, only two copies of the telegram are required for use in the business office.)

Delivery Of Telegrams

Messages to business offices ordinarily are delivered by Western Union machines. Other telegrams are usually delivered by telephone. If the sender wants the telegram delivered "in person," he/she should type the word DELIVER on the telegram blank in place of the telephone number of the addressee.

Methods Of Filing A Telegram Or MAILGRAM®

1. Over the counter at the Western Union office
2. Over the telephone (most popular method of filing)
3. At the teleprinter area in the company for which you work
4. By Desk-Fax (at firms that have this equipment)

Canceling A Telegram Already Filed

To cancel a telegram that has already been filed, a person calls the telegraph office where the telegram was filed. If the telegram has not left the office, no charge is made for cancellation. If the message has already been transmitted to the receiving telegraph office, the charge for the original transmission stands; and the sender must also pay for a message to the receiving office to cancel the original transmission. Frequently, however, Western Union's electronic transmission and computer switching system make a follow-up cancellation impractical.

Repeat-Back Service/ Valued Message Service

Repeat-back service is available when the monetary **value** of a telegram is $5,000 or less. Repeat-back service involves repetition of the message to the sending office by the receiving office at each stage (or relay) in its transmission, to insure accurate reception. The charge for this service is 1½ times the regular message toll. If the declared value of a telegram exceeds $5,000, Valued Message Service is available (which is similar to repeat-back service). For this service the sender pays an additional cost of $\frac{1}{10}$ of one percent of the declared value.

Report-Delivery Service

In Report-Delivery Service a **collect** message will be furnished to the sender of a telegram or MAILGRAM® indicating that the message he/she filed has been delivered to the addressee. The charge for this service is the amount of the collect telegram (not to exceed a 15-word minimum charge) and the amount for the addition of the two words REPORT DELIVERY to the original message.

Methods Of Paying For A Telegram

1. Cash—This method of payment is usually chosen by persons who use telegraph services infrequently.
2. Monthly Billing by Western Union—This service can be used by persons who have established an account with Western Union, or any sender can request to have telegram charges billed directly to him/her at his/her home address.
3. Telegrams filed by telephone can be charged to the sender's telephone (either personal account or business account). Charges will appear on the monthly toll statement that accompanies the sender's telephone bill. In addition, telegrams filed by telephone may be charged to any of the other charge methods acceptable to Western Union.
4. Collect (the recipient of the message pays the fee)—To use this service, the sender must give his/her own address and telephone (either personal or business) in case the recipient of the telegram refuses to pay the charges.
5. Credit Cards—Telegraph services may be charged to Visa or to Master Card credit cards.

Ways Of Receiving A Telegram

1. By telephone
2. At your company teleprinter station
3. By Western Union messenger

TELEPRINTER SERVICE (WESTERN UNION TIE-LINE)

Western Union tie-line machines are usually called **teleprinters.** Various types of teleprinters are available. With each machine, the office clerk or secretary types the message directly on the machine, using a keyboard similar to a typewriter. The message is transmitted to the local Western Union office, to the Western Union switching computer, or to a receiving teleprinter machine at a different location. The following is a description of three types of tie-line machines:

A. **Teleprinter Tie-Line**
With this machine, messages can be sent to the local Western Union office for onward relay. A more sophisticated version of this same tie-line service is the **Private Wire System,** whereby messages can be sent to other office locations of the sending company or to Western Union.

B. **Telex (TLX)**
By use of a dialing arrangement, Telex subscribers can send messages directly to other Telex subscribers anywhere in the world. There are Telex subscribers in all 50 of the United States, in Canada, Mexico, and in almost all other countries. Messages may be sent on this same machine to the local Western Union office for delivery to nonsubscribers of Telex or to international message carriers for delivery to nonsubscribers at overseas points. Incoming messages are also received on the Telex machine; and they may be transmitted directly to it from the Telex machines of other subscribers, even from international locations. The Telex machine may also be used to input messages and MAILGRAMS® to Western Union's switching computer. By use of the computer's capabilities, messages may be directed to the receiving machine of a Western Union customer who uses a different type of tie-line terminal (such as TWX).

C. **Teletypewriter Exchange** (TWX—A trademark of the Western Union Telegraph Company)
This machine is similar to Telex with the same general characteristics and capabilities, but service is not extended to international or overseas locations.

Western Union supplies each Telex and Teletypewriter Exchange subscriber with a directory containing dial numbers for other subscribers and detailed instructions for reaching them.

INTERNATIONAL TELEGRAM SERVICE

Messages to overseas (international) points can be filed by any of the methods described for domestic services. Billing procedures are the same. In addition, Telex subscribers can file messages by use of their machines directly with Telex subscribers at overseas points. Telex subscribers can also file messages with the international message centers to be delivered to non-Telex subscribers overseas.

Fig. 81. A satellite receiving and sending communications from one part of the world to another

FOR REVIEW AND DISCUSSION

1. Discuss the rules governing full-rate telegrams, overnight telegrams, and MAILGRAMS®.
2. What factors determine the type of telegraph service to be used?
3. Discuss the delivery of telegrams once they have been transmitted to the destination office.
4. Discuss the methods of filing a telegram or MAILGRAM®.
5. Discuss the method of canceling a telegram that has already been filed. What are the disadvantages?
6. Explain the terms "repeat-back service/valued message service" and "report-delivery service."
7. Discuss the various methods of paying for a telegram.
8. Discuss the teleprinter service available through Western Union.
9. Which of the Western Union services are media of electronic mail?

Turn to your workbook and complete Student Project 17.

CHAPTER 10

Data Processing, Word Processing, Electronic Mail, And The Office Worker

OBJECTIVE

After studying this chapter you will understand:

- The basic functions of computers
- That automation should have a positive rather than a negative effect on the office worker
- The concept of word processing
- The concept of electronic mail
- Basic automation terminology

JOB-RELATED VOCABULARY

Note: A glossary of basic data processing terms appears at the end of this chapter.

A study of office work today will quickly indicate that the nature of office work has changed greatly as the use of data processing, word processing, and electronic mail has increased. Many of the routine duties, such as copying, calculating, sorting, recording, and sending, that were once the primary concern of office workers are being handled by machines. This fact leaves the office worker time to perform the more challenging and more stimulating supervisory and administrative functions that should help the company to grow and prosper in its field.

AUTOMATION IN THE OFFICE

Automation in the office includes the coding, sorting, computing, summarizing, recording, and communicating of business data by automatic means. The need for increased automation in business offices today has resulted from the rapid growth of business, expanding markets, the need for efficiency and productivity, and the need for better control of business through more immediate access to reports and projections.

The office worker has always been aware of the value of such machines as the typewriter, calculator, adding machine, duplicator, and copier for processing data—sometimes automatically. Now it is important for him/her to understand the functions of computers, word processors, and electronic mail, because these processes affect the daily routine of the office staff.

Data Processing

Data processing is the converting of data into machine-readable form and the subsequent processing (storing, manipulating, and retrieving) by a computer. A **computer** is an electronic machine that can work with numbers, words, or a combination of numbers and words to produce output data.

Computers have touched almost every job in business. Secretaries frequently work with computers in word processing applications. Clerks and secretaries are sometimes responsible for entering data into a computer—such as customers' orders—and for retrieving data from a computer—such as customer accounts. Accountants and bookkeepers use computers when they enter financial data and when they make extensive calculations. They also use computers to produce financial reports and the usual financial statements, such as income statements, balance sheets, and various types of data reports. Managers at all levels use computer reports to help them to make intelligent, informed business decisions.

Data

Data for the computer to process are from a variety of sources, such as a sales slip, a time card, or a check. Data may be the price of a single product or the gross sales of a company for a day. Data are handled by the computer in three steps: **Input, Process,** and **Output.**

Data are **recorded** in the computer in a process called **input.**

Data are **acted upon** (or manipulated) in some manner by the computer during the **process** phase.

Data are **displayed in a usable form** (such as a printed report) during the **output** phase.

Input Function. The **input function** of the computer is performed by four **input peripherals:**

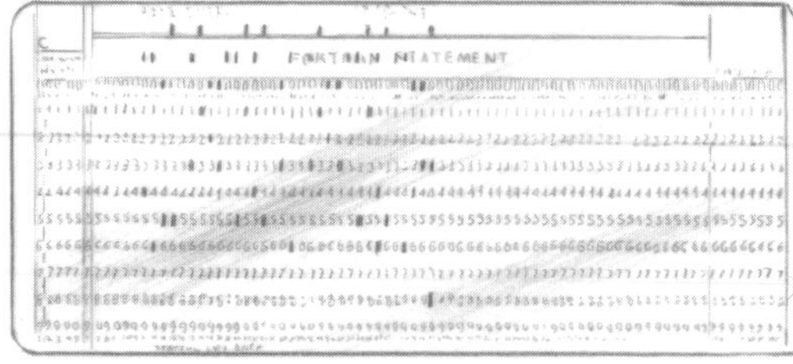

Fig. 82. Punched Computer Card

The **punched computer card** is the oldest method of input, and it is used by **some** businesses where there is a large amount of data to be processed. The card is put on a machine called a card punch (or key punch) machine which punches holes in the card to represent information. The cards are then processed through a card reader which sends the information on the cards to the central processing unit of the computer.

A **keyboard terminal** is very similar to a typewriter. The keyboard is one of the most commonly used input peripherals.

Fig. 83. Keyboard Terminal

Optical scanners are used in retail stores to "read" and record the selling price and the stock number of a product. Optical scanners help store clerks since they do not have to enter the price of each item, the total amount of each item, and the total amount of each sale. Optical scanners are also used by the United States Postal Service to sort mail rapidly and efficiently. (See related information in Chapter Five, pages 27 to 30.)

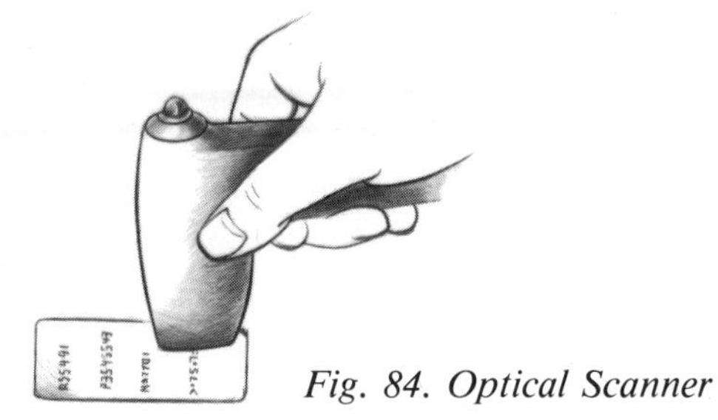

Fig. 84. Optical Scanner

Fig. 85. Product Code

Optical scanners also use **light patterns** to read the **code** stamped on a product and then record the type of product being sold and the price. A scanner can "see" any type of dark ink on a light background. Many supermarkets now use this type of equipment at checkout stations.

Fig. 86. Magnetic Ink Characters on a Bank Check

Magnetic ink characters similar to these can be found on the bottom of almost all checks. ⑆021900325⑆

Fig. 87. Magnetic Ink Character Reader (MICR)

This **Magnetic Ink Character Reader** (or MICR) "reads" **magnetic ink characters** and records the data. Banks use the MICR to process checks.

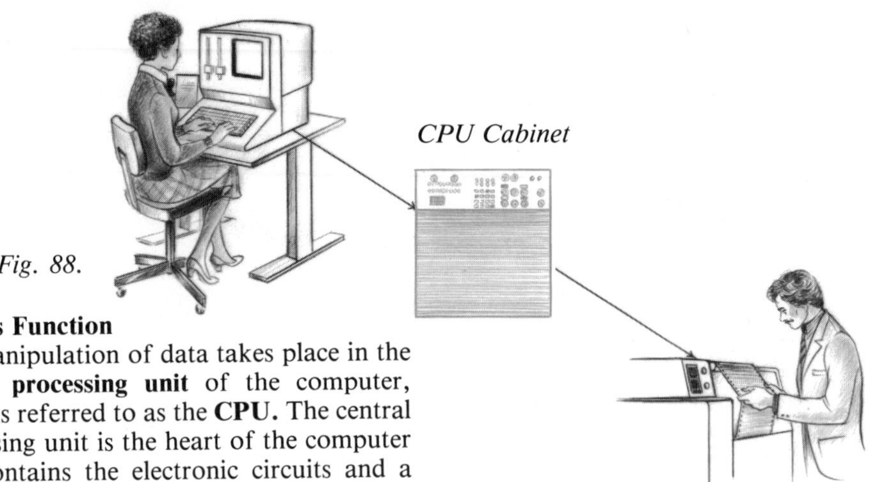

Fig. 88.

Process Function
The manipulation of data takes place in the **central processing unit** of the computer, which is referred to as the **CPU.** The central processing unit is the heart of the computer that contains the electronic circuits and a silicon chip. A **computer program** "instructs" the computer to process data.

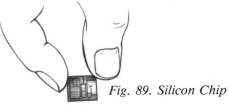

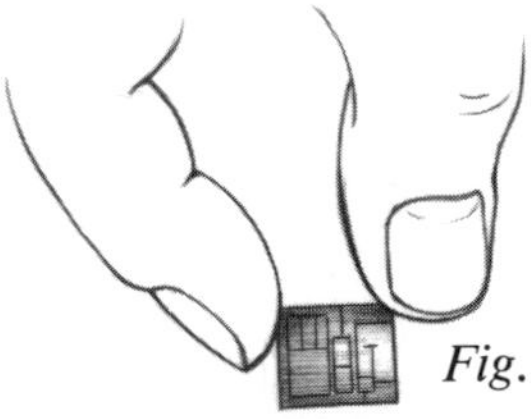

Fig. 89. Silicon Chip

A **silicon chip** is a piece of silicon about the size of the nail on your little finger. A single silicon chip has the capability to process the same amount of data as a large mainframe computer.

Fig. 90. Printer Device

Output Function
The **output function** is performed by the following four **output peripherals:**

A **printed report** is the most common form of business output. Any type of business report can be printed on a printer device such as the one shown in Fig. 90.

Fig. 91. Cathode Ray Tube (CRT)

The second most common form of output is a **display** of data on a device that is similar to a television screen. The device is called a **cathode ray tube** or a CRT.

Whenever the extensive use of graphs or charts is required, a **plotter** is used. The plotter, which is controlled by the computer, produces detailed charts, graphs, and maps.

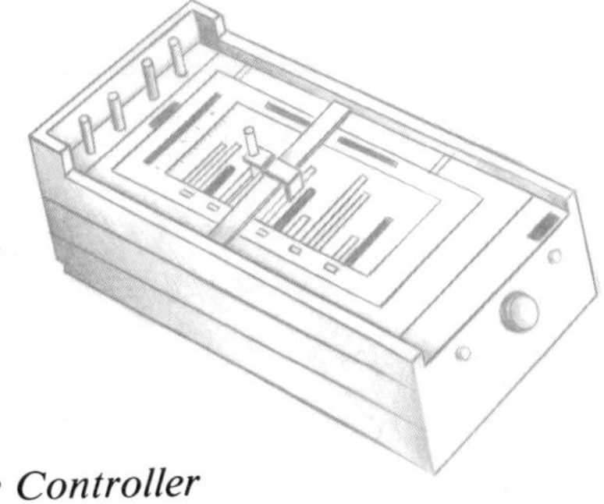

Fig. 92. Plotter

Fig. 93. Audio Response Controller (Voice Synthesizer) A **voice synthesizer** or audio response controller, which can produce music, background noises, or audio similar to the human voice, is also used as output.

Disks

Fig. 94
15-Inch Disk

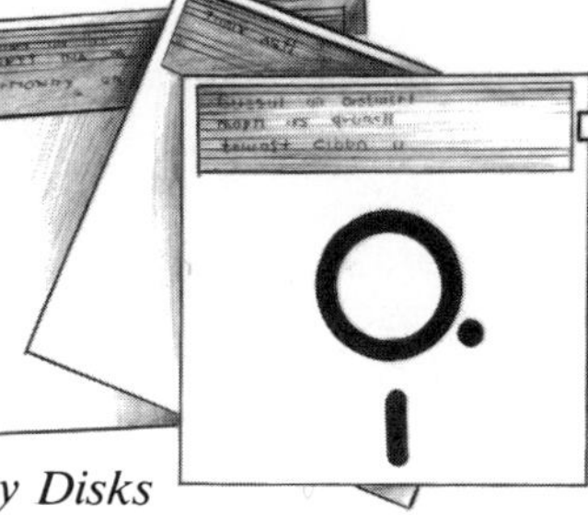

Fig. 95
8-Inch Floppy Disks

A disk is a round piece of plastic that is very much like a record. Disks are stored in disk cases that prevent damage to the disk. Three types of disks, like those shown in Figs. 94 to 96, are commonly used. When it is necessary to store large amounts of data, a standard 15-inch disk is used. A floppy disk, which is 8 inches in diameter, stores less information, but it is more convenient to use. A minifloppy disk measures only 5¼ inches in diameter, and is used on many microcomputer systems.

When a disk is used as an **input device,** information has been electronically recorded on it. When a disk is processed in a disk drive, the information is "read" into the computer. Information on a disk the size of a record can be processed in a matter of seconds.

Fig. 96
5¼-Inch Minifloppy Disks

A disk acts as an **output device** when information is processed by the computer and then read onto it for storage. Storage of data on a disk is in the form of electronic impulses.

The amount of information that a disk can hold varies greatly. A typical disk for a microcomputer (a **minifloppy disk**) can store the equivalent of 100 to 150 typewritten pages. A **disk pack** containing eight 15-inch disks can store the equivalent of about 170,000 typewritten pages.

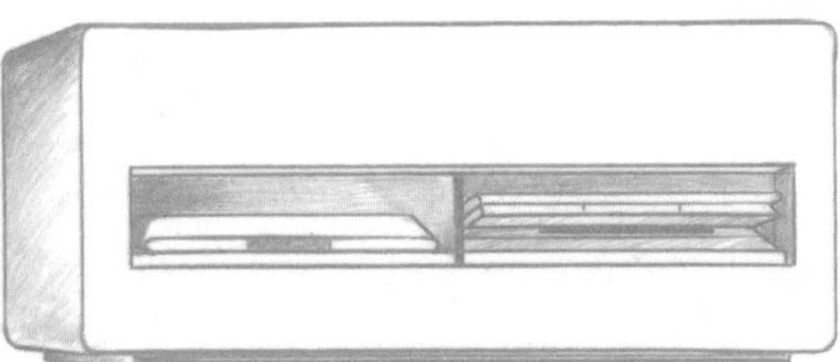

Fig. 97. Disk Drive Unit

The part of a computer which is **both an input device and an output device** is the **disk drive.** A needle-like device called a **read/write head** inside the disk drive **floats** near the surface of a disk and "reads" the information.

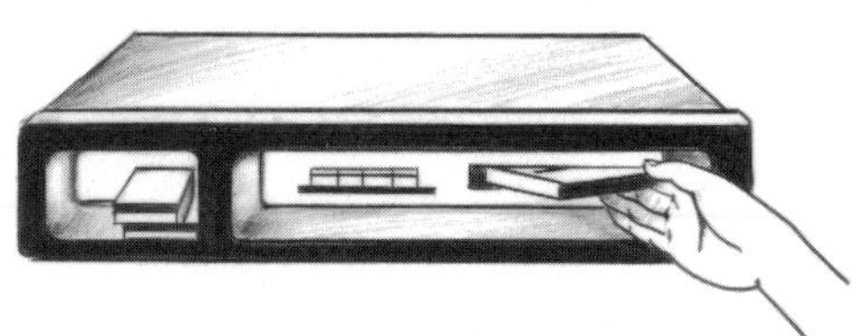

Like disks, reel-to-reel magnetic tapes and 9-inch magnetic cassette tapes are also used for input and output.

Fig. 98. Reel-to-Reel and Cassette Tapes

Computers And Word Processing, Electronic Mail, And Records Management

A computer is at the very "heart" of word processing, electronic mail, and electronic records management systems. The central processing unit of a computer provides electronic circuits and the storage capabilities to carry out the function desired. Therefore, special computer programs have been designed for word processing, data communication (electronic mail), and files storage (records management).

Word processing is a special application of the computer. A word processing program "tells" the computer how to edit a text, how to underline words, how to center columns and headings, how to format copy, and how to perform other word processing applications.

Data transmission (or electronic mailing) is another specialized application of the computer. A computer transmits data to another computer through the use of a **modem.** A modem is a device that translates digital signals into magnetic pulses or audio tones so they can be transmitted to another computer by microwave, by cable, or by telephone lines.

As you have learned, documents are stored in the computer on a variety of media. As documents are filed in a computer, they are assigned a code number or a code word. Documents (or files) are retrieved by inputting the code number or the code word.

(NOTE: Word processing and electronic mail are discussed later in this chapter. Records management will be discussed in Chapter 11.)

Advantages Of Computers

Now that you have a basic understanding of how a computer works, consider the advantages a business gains by using a computer. First, a computer actually saves money for businesses. By using a computer, businesses can do away with many paper files; and they can increase productivity because a computer can process data rapidly and store data efficiently in limited space. Next, the rapid processing possible with a computer increases the timeliness and the accuracy (through reduction of errors in calculation) of business reports. Timely reports that are continuously updated help to improve the decision-making process of business executives. Finally, a computer improves services to customers in the form of timely billing, more accurate billing procedures, and easily updated mailing lists.

Computer-Related Jobs

As the use of computers has increased, a new set of job functions has been developed in order to help businesses to work with computers.

Computer programs are written by **computer programmers** to "instruct" the computer about the function to be performed. Business has a great need for well-trained computer programmers. **Data entry personnel** (or terminal operators) are those people who enter business data into the computer by keyboarding magnetic impulses onto disks and tapes or by punching holes in computer cards. **Systems analysts** are people who help to design computer systems to meet the needs of businesses. To be a systems analyst requires years of experience in data processing and extensive knowledge about various types of computer equipment.

Fig. 99. Word Processing Unit and a Document Production Specialist

WORD PROCESSING

Word processing has many definitions from many different sources. Basically the term word processing means: **a system used to turn rapidly ideas and information into a readable form of communication.** Word processing is accomplished by applying modern technology and systems-management techniques to office routines through the use of trained people, specific procedures, and automatic equipment.

Here is how word processing flows through an office: Someone, probably an executive or a manager, has an idea. The executive writes the idea in longhand or uses a dictating system to transmit the idea to the **word processing specialist** (or operator). The specialist types ("keyboards") material using automatic equipment which is capable of storing information for future use. Word processing makes it easy to record, store, find (recall), and revise information. Once information has been typed and stored in the processing system, it can be used in a variety of ways. For example, a customer's name and address can be recalled from the computer's memory bank when the firm wants to send statements, advertisements, or other types of correspondence. (Keep in mind, though, that word processing does not have to involve a computer.)

If word processing is to be successful, the word processing specialists must work together as a team. Usually there are two types of word processing specialists:

Document Production Specialists—Persons who operate the word processing equipment by keyboarding and preparing documents.

Administrative Services Specialists—Persons who carry out nontyping duties needed by management, such as data gathering, preparing report material, proofreading, dictating, assisting executives with administrative details, and composing communications.

In some companies word processing specialists handle all types of work in a centralized word processing center. In other companies word processing specialists prepare documents for specialized departments such as marketing, public relations, or finance in a series of "satellite" word processing centers.

Language skills, formatting skills, typing skills, proofreading skills, and machine transcription skills are essential for Document Production Specialists. All of these skills plus editing skills, dictating or writing skills, oral communication skills, and general clerical and secretarial skills are essential for Administrative Service Specialists.

Since a wide variety of word processing equipment is available to business, a person who is employed in a word processing center as a Document Production Specialist should expect to have some on-the-job training even though he/she has had "hands-on" training on word processing equipment in school.

Electronic Mail

Today's fast-paced business world requires **instantaneous** transmission of communications. This demand has led to the development of electronic mail. Electronic mail is high-speed information transportation used to transmit communications either within in-house systems or between companies at different locations.

Electronic mail is the integration of four previously separate technologies:

- Word Processing
- Data Processing
- Telecommunications
- Micrographics

Media Of Electronic Mail

Electronic mail is available in four media:

- MAILGRAMS®
- Facsimile Transmissions
- Teletypewritten Messages
- Information Processing

MAILGRAMS® are a cooperative service between the U.S. Postal Service and Western Union. Persons sending MAILGRAM® messages telephone their messages to Western Union. Western Union relays the message to the **MAILGRAM® post office** nearest the recipient's address. The MAILGRAM® message is printed in the receiving post office, placed in a special mailing envelope, and delivered by a letter carrier as a first-class letter.

Teletypewritten Messages, TWX or Telex Services, which are also operated by Western Union, provide electronic mail distribution over an international teletypewriter network. Subscribers to these services must purchase or lease teletypewriter consoles, and they may communicate **only** with persons or organizations that possess similar equipment. Teletypewriter consoles in worldwide locations can receive messages 24 hours a day even when they are unattended.

Facsimile Transmissions—Facsimile is a technology used to transmit an exact copy of graphics (pictures or drawings) and printed materials. While facsimile transmissions account for more transmissions than any other form of electronic mail, this medium is primarily used within companies (branch-to-branch, for example) because directories or facsimile equipment owners and users are not available.

Information Processing

Electronic mail using information processing systems (a combination of word processing and data processing) provides the capability of sending and receiving one's mail over a network, reading the mail on the screen of a terminal, and using the keyboard of the terminal to respond. This system also provides capabilities to distribute messages and data to selected terminal addresses and to maintain copies of messages and data in an **electronic file.** The "mailbox" is the terminal on the recipient's desk.

Information processing systems (computer-based electronic mail) are easy to operate. The user "signs on" and then chooses among several standard features, such as:

- Scanning the mailbox
- Choosing messages to read
- Forwarding messages
- Deleting messages
- Composing messages
- Sending messages (mailing electronically)

Electronic mail systems can be programmed to provide special mailing features similar to those offered by the U.S. Postal Service. These special features include:

- URGENT—An electronic mail message sent as urgent is programmed so it will appear at the **beginning** of the recipient's messages.
- REGISTERED—When a registered message is sent, the sending terminal is **automatically notified** when the recipient has read the message.
- TIMED DELIVERY—Messages can be composed and stored for automatic transmission at a later time. This feature can be particularly valuable to the business person who is frequently out of his/her office.
- VOICE MAIL—Voice mail is a system that will use a computer to convert all incoming (spoken) messages to digital form and then record the messages on a magnetic medium under the intended recipient's telephone number. The recipient receives messages by calling the computer and entering his/her identification code. The computer will then search the storage medium for messages, convert the messages into a synthesized voice, and transmit the messages over the telephone.

Information processing electronic mail systems are expected to expand **rapidly** in the future.

E-COM (Electronic Computer-Originated Mail)

Currently in use and under continuing development is the U.S. Postal Service's electronic mail system known as E-COM, which stands for Electronic Computer-Originated Mail.

Large volume first-class mailers transmit their messages electronically over telephone lines from company computers to a post office having E-COM facilities. At these post offices, an E-COM computer transforms the digital message that has been transmitted into a printed letter. The letter is stuffed into a special E-COM envelope and placed in the first-class mail stream.

The Future Of Electronic Mail

The future holds many new developments in the area of electronic mail. Already the following home and electronic voice mail applications are under development:

- **HOME/OFFICE LINKUPS**—Home television sets incorporating microprocessors will enable employees to communicate with their offices from their homes. This will enable employees to transmit work from home to the office and to have access to company data on the home television screen.

• **HOME/MERCHANT LINKUPS**—On a personal level, consumers will be able to view merchandise catalogues at home on their television sets. Orders for merchandise selected will be keyboarded directly to the merchant's computer. The customer will be billed automatically, and the merchandise will be shipped promptly.

Electronic mail is very much a part of the modern office, and it is expected to be expanded considerably in the future. As you have learned, it is an assortment of message delivery techniques tethered by a common thread—electronic systems used as communications media.

THE EFFECT OF AUTOMATION ON THE OFFICE WORKER

Although it is not necessary for the **general office worker** to be technically trained in the operations of all technical office equipment, it is important for him/her to understand the functions of such equipment because the general office workers usually provide the source documents (sales slips, invoices, time cards) from which the electronic data processing equipment prepares reports and makes calculations. If a general office worker decides that he/she wants to have a "hands-on" job in data processing, word processing, or some other area of office technology, as a machine operator or a programmer, he/she may take additional training specifically for that purpose; or he/she may get training "on the job."

It should be stressed, too, that general office workers need not fear being replaced by office technology. As companies use more and more technology, the general office worker will be freed from the laborious duties of compiling data by hand to the more creative role of contributing to the management function of the business. This shift in the nature of the work done by the general office worker does, however, require new procedures. Office workers must be willing to learn those procedures and to adjust to new methods made necessary by sophisticated technology.

BASIC DATA PROCESSING TERMINOLOGY

Here are 39 basic terms concerning data processing that you should understand. Knowing these terms will enable you to communicate more accurately about electronic data processing with other office workers.

Access Time—The time required by a computer to locate data stored in its memory.

Audio Response Controller—An output device used to produce computer-controlled sounds, music, or human voice reproductions.

Cathode Ray Tube (CRT)—An output device much like a television screen, which presents data, or graphics on a screen.

Card—An **input medium** used when large quantities of data must be processed. Data are coded onto a card by a machine called a card punch (or a key punch) machine for processing by the computer.

Card Reader—An **input device** which reads the data coded onto a card. The data are then transmitted to the Central Processing Unit (CPU) of the computer for processing.

Central Processing Unit (CPU)—The CPU is the heart of the computer. It contains the electronic circuits which process data. The CPU contains neither input nor output devices; it is the **processing** unit.

Data—Any combination of numbers, letters, or symbols such as the unit price of a product, an employee's name, or a dollar sign. Data come from a variety of sources such as a sales slip, a time card, or a check.

Data Entry Operator—The person (or persons) in a business who enter data into a computer.
Device—The machine used to perform an input or output function.
Digital Signal—An electronic signal within a computer that represents data. Digital signals are used so that the computer can send data to other circuits inside the computer and to the peripherals which support the computer.
Disk—A round piece of plastic used to record data electronically. Although disks vary in size, a standard disk is 15 inches in diameter.
Disk Drive—An electronic device used to **read** information off a disk or to **record** information onto a disk. Disk drives vary in size to accommodate various size disks.
Diskette—See Minifloppy Disk.
Disk Pack—One or more 15-inch disks stored together and sealed in their own permanent housing.
Floppy Disk—A semirigid disk, the floppy disk measures 8 inches in diameter, and is permanently sealed in its own protective case.
Hardware—The **machinery** that collectively make the data processing system.
Home Computer—See Microcomputer.
Input Device—Any device used to enter data into the CPU. The input device is the machine which performs that function. An input device is also referred to as an input peripheral.
Input Medium—Any type of physical material such as a punched card that is used to enter data for processing by the CPU.
Input Phase—The first phase in the three-phase process (**input**/process/output) of the computer. In the input phase, data are recorded into the computer for processing.
Input Peripheral—See Input Device.
Keyboard—An input device that is much like a typewriter. The keyboard has regular typewriter keys and special keys to give commands to the computer.
Mainframe—A very large computer used by businesses to process large quantities of data. A mainframe computer may cost up to one million dollars.
Magnetic Ink Character Reader—An input device designed to read characters printed in magnetic ink.
Medium—The physical material (such as a punched card or a printout) used to record data or to display data in some usable form.
Microcomputer—The smallest and usually the cheapest type of computer. The microcomputer functions with the use of a very small silicon chip. The microcomputer is sometimes called a home computer or a personal computer.
Minicomputer—A computer larger than a microcomputer, but smaller than a mainframe computer. A minicomputer overlaps the capabilities of the mainframe computer at the high end of its operation and the capabilities of the microcomputer at the low end of its operation.
Minifloppy Disk—A disk which measures 5¼ inches in diameter and is sealed in its own protective case. The minifloppy disk is used almost exclusively with the microcomputer. It is sometimes referred to as a diskette.
Modem—An electronic device used in data transmission (electronic mail) that converts computer impulses into electronic impulses so they can be transmitted over telephone lines, by cable, or by microwave.
Optical Scanner—An input device which reads marks or lines. This type of scanner is frequently used in grocery stores and department stores. It is also used by the U.S. Postal Service to sort mail.

Output Phase—The final of the three phases of the computer process (input/process/**output**). In this phase, the data are displayed in some usable form after the data have been processed by the CPU.
Peripheral(s)—Any device attached to the CPU which may perform either the input function or the output function.
Personal Computer—See Microcomputer.
Plotter—An output device, which is controlled by the computer, that produces graphs, charts, or drawings.
Printer—The output device used to print data during the output phase. The printer is used to print a wide variety of reports and written messages.
Process—The second phase in the three-phase computer process (input/**process**/output). In the process phase, the data are acted upon in some manner by the CPU.
Program—A set of instructions that "instruct" a computer to process the data in a certain way.
Programmer—The individual responsible for writing or modifying programs (or instructions) for the computer.
Systems Analyst—The individual responsible for designing a computer system. The systems analyst decides upon the size of the CPU required by a company, the type of computer to be used, and the types of peripherals required.

FOR REVIEW AND DISCUSSION

1. Define the term, data processing.
2. Define the term, computer.
3. Explain the three-step procedure by which a computer handles data.
4. Name and describe four **input peripherals.**
5. In what part of the computer does the manipulation of data take place? How does the computer understand how to process data?
6. Name and describe four **output peripherals.**
7. Name and describe three types of disks. How is a disk "read" in a disk drive?
8. Explain three advantages of computers to businesses.
9. Explain the following computer-related jobs:
   Computer Programmer
   Data Entry Personnel
   Systems Analyst
10. Define the term, electronic mail.
11. Electronic mail is an integration of what four **technologies**?
12. Name and explain the four **media** of electronic mail.
13. Name the standard features of a computer-based electronic mail (information processing) system.
14. Name and explain the special features for which electronic mail systems can be programmed.
15. What is E-COM? How does E-COM work?
16. Name and explain the future applications being developed for electronic mail systems.
17. Define the term, word processing.
18. Describe the two types of word processing specialists explained in the chapter.
19. Describe the difference between centralized and satellite word processing.

CHAPTER 11

Records Management

OBJECTIVE

After studying Chapter 11 you will understand the following file information:

- File department setup
- Preparation of paper records to be filed
- Arrangement of file folders
- Requesting paper records that have been filed
- Out cards
- Cross referencing
- Finding lost records
- Transferring paper records that have been filed
- The management of nonpaper records
- Types of filing methods
- ARMA rules for alphabetic filing

JOB-RELATED VOCABULARY

Transactions—Business dealings.

Functional—Designed from the point of view of use.

Obsolete—To grow old or become disused.

Accessible—Easy to get to or easy to reach.

Disassemble—To take apart.

Every reputable firm builds its future upon the anticipation of doing continued business with its customers. From that point of view, records are vital to the success of the business, because they provide a history of a company's transactions with its customers.

Stored records, if they are to be helpful, must provide **instant access** to the details of past transactions; and they must keep records **safe.** If stored records perform their functions effectively, two additional ingredients are necessary:

Simplicity—All records must be so easy to use that every person having access to them will understand how they are set up and will be able to find materials with a minimum of effort.

Consistency—To aid those people who refer to stored records to find materials quickly and easily, materials of the same type must be stored the same way time after time.

OFFICE RECORDS

In most offices, records to be filed include correspondence, orders, invoices, and checks. In smaller offices, paper records are usually kept in a **centralized** area; and every person working for the company has access to those files. In larger companies, each department usually has its own set of **(decentralized)** paper records for the use of the people in the department; and all the departments contribute materials to become a part of the central files for everyone's use. In addition, some executives in both larger and smaller companies have their secretaries maintain a personal file for the executive's exclusive use.

The records storage needs of a company are rarely ever constant. As a business changes—grows and shifts—new files must be established, and sometimes older files for which there is no further need must be disassembled (and destroyed).

Someone in every company, perhaps you, must be constantly watching the types of records storage being requested; and that person must be ready to make the necessary changes so the records storage system will be more efficient and more functional.

File Department Personnel

In larger offices, the centralized paper files are frequently kept by the employees of the filing department. They are responsible for:

1. preparing and filing the materials that come to their department,
2. establishing new files and disassembling obsolete files as business functions call for it,
3. taking materials from the files for company personnel requesting them, keeping a record of who has the materials taken from the files, and following up to see that those materials are returned after a reasonable period of time.

In smaller offices and for department files, these same functions are performed by a general office clerk or by a secretary.

Whoever keeps the files has the additional responsibility for seeing that important records and documents are kept safe in fireproof cabinets or vaults. The responsibility for seeing that confidential files are kept locked and unavailable to the prying eyes of people who have no need to be concerned with them is also an important part of the work of office personnel who are responsible for filing.

A File Index

In order to make the files easier to use, it is a good idea to develop a File Index, which explains the locations of various documents by file section and drawer number. For a file system to function most effectively, file sections and file drawers should be clearly marked with labels.

Figure 100 shows part of the File Index to the central files at the Morgan Glass Corporation.

Preparing Paper Records To Be Filed

In each office, there is ordinarily a "file basket" where records to be filed are placed. When the person responsible for doing the filing removes the records from that basket, he/she must prepare them for filing by following a carefully planned procedure:

1. All documents to be filed (other than carbon copies of outgoing letters) must be released for filing. The release can be a FILE stamp plus someone's initials or the initials of the executive to whom the letter is addressed. These releases usually appear in the upper left-hand corner of the page. Another means of releasing material for filing is drawing a diagonal line (from the upper left-hand corner to the lower right-hand corner) across the page (usually with a red pen).
2. Pins, brads, rubber bands, and paper clips must be removed from papers to be filed. Enclosures that are to remain with letters to be filed are attached to letters with staples.

FILE INDEX		
MORGAN GLASS CORPORATION		
Type of File	Location	
	File Section	Drawer(s)
Correspondence		
Dealers	6	4 and 5
Government	6	6
Suppliers	6	7 and 8
Orders (completed)	3	4 and 5
Personnel Materials		
Applications	1	1 and 2
Medical Forms	1	3 and 4
Security Investigations	1	5
Reports		
Company (annual)	4	3
Departmental (quarterly)	4	4
Subsidiary (monthly)	4	5

Fig. 100. A File Index

3. When a piece of material to be filed is smaller than standard page size, it should be pasted to a regular sheet of paper to make it easier to file and find.
4. Oversized sheets of paper to be filed should be folded to the size of the file folder (unless special file equipment is used).
5. The materials to be filed must be **coded;** that is, a notation must be made on the face of each sheet indicating where that paper will be filed (usually done with a colored pencil).

A. Alphabet Filing
Materials are usually filed according to the most important name appearing on the sheet to be filed. (Incoming letters are usually filed according to the names of the companies in the letterheads or names of individuals who sent them. An outgoing letter is usually filed according to the name of the person or company to whom it is addressed.)

B. Subject Filing
When materials are being prepared for subject filing, the subject has to be determined from the body of the letter.

C. Numeric Filing
The number code for a letter being filed in a numeric system must be determined from a card index.

D. Geographic Filing
The name of the city and state in the letterhead is coded for incoming letters, and the name of the city and state in the inside address is coded on the carbon copy for outgoing letters.

E. Noncorrespondence Filing
Most materials involved in noncorrespondence filing (checks, invoices, purchase orders) have their own numbering systems, and they are filed by those numbers.

6. Once materials to be filed are coded, they must be sorted; that is, the materials must be arranged in order for filing. Materials might be sorted first by methods of filing—alphabetic, numeric, subject, geographic, noncorrespondence. The method of filing determines how materials will be sorted and arranged for filing.
7. As you file materials in the file cabinets, it may be necessary to prepare new file folders for some correspondence. If so, type the caption on a gummed label approximately three lines from the top edge of the label and three spaces from the left edge. When you put the label on the file folder, be sure you press all the edges down firmly. Type file labels in the following manner:

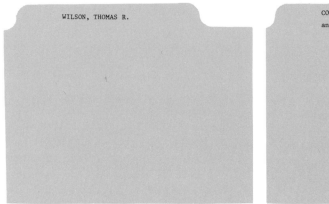

Fig. 101. A one-line file folder caption

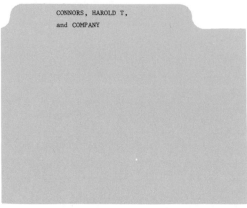

Fig. 102. A two-line file folder caption

8. Arrange materials with the latest date toward the front of the folder.

The Folders In A Drawer File

Ordinarily, an individual folder is used for each correspondent for whom there are five or more records on file. A miscellaneous folder is placed at the end of the individual file folders for each file designation (for example, "A" Miscellaneous, Printers Miscellaneous, Utah Miscellaneous, etc.) for correspondents with fewer than five records each. Sometimes, colored tabs are used on folders to show special situations—high quality buyers, good credit, bad credit, or special shipping needs.

Requesting Materials From The Files

Whether you are requesting materials from the central files or from the files of another department, it is extremely important to ask the person responsible for the files for the materials you want. **Never** simply go into the files yourself and take out what you need **unless** you are responsible for the files yourself.

It is extremely important to keep an accurate record of what materials are out of the files and who has them. It is advisable to have each person requesting materials from the files complete a FILE REQUEST FORM (see Fig. 103), particularly in a large company with centralized files. The File Request Form is then filed by an upcoming date, and it becomes a reminder to the person controlling the files that a file folder has been removed from the files. The file clerk follows up until the folder has been returned.

FILE REQUEST FORM

Folder Requested__________________________

Folder Requested By________________________

Department______________Date Requested_____

Date to be Returned_______________________

Date Returned________________File Clerk_____

Fig. 103. A form for requesting materials from the files

In some companies, a request for materials from the files can be made either in person or over the telephone without completing a File Request Form.

Each person who borrows a file folder has a special responsibility to return it only to the Filing Department as soon as he/she no longer needs it. In that way, the Filing Department maintains complete control over the records at all times.

Many filing departments would rather release the entire folder even though the request is for only one item in the folder, because it is considerably less likely that the entire folder would be misplaced than it is that one document in the folder would be misplaced.

"Out" Cards

When the person responsible for the files removes a folder or a piece of correspondence from the files, he/she should put an "out" card or an "out" folder, which may be used to hold material that accumulates while the regular folder is removed, in the place of the original folder. The "out" card is the size of a file folder with the word "out" printed in boldface type on the tab. A pocket on the card permits inserting an index card containing the caption of the folder that is missing, the name and department of the person who has taken the folder, and the date it was removed. (See Fig. 104.) This procedure tells anyone else who is looking for the folder that it is "on loan" and not lost or stolen. When the folder is returned, the file clerk removes the "out" card and replaces the folder in the file.

Fig. 104. "Out" folders

Cross Referencing

When you file a record, you file it under the caption by which it is most likely to be requested. Occasionally, however, you will have a record that might be requested under a caption different from the one under which it is filed. Consider the following:

> You have a letter from Hancock Glass Corporation that refers to information about work they are doing on a special order of dinnerware for your company with another contractor, Design Associates. Ordinarily, the letter would be requested by the caption Hancock Glass Corp. Occasionally, though, it may be needed with the letters filed under the caption, Design Associates. Therefore, the letter would be filed under the caption, Hancock Glass Corp., and a **cross reference** sheet referring to that letter would appear under the caption, Design Associates.

Here are two cross reference sheets that have been properly prepared.

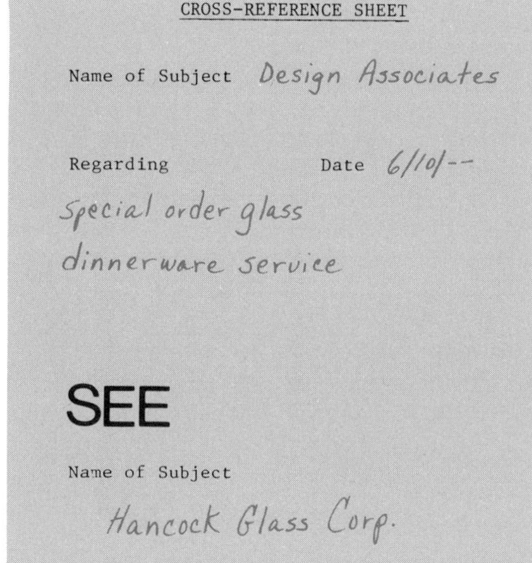

CROSS-REFERENCE SHEET

Name of Subject Design Associates

Regarding Date 6/10/--

Special order glass dinnerware service

SEE

Name of Subject

Hancock Glass Corp.

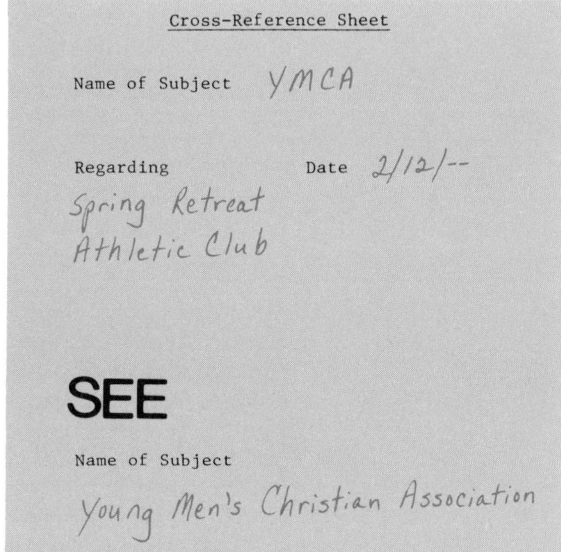

Cross-Reference Sheet

Name of Subject YMCA

Regarding Date 2/12/--

Spring Retreat Athletic Club

SEE

Name of Subject

Young Men's Christian Association

Figs. 105 and 106. Cross reference sheets

Finding Lost Paper Records

When filed records are lost, the best way to look for them is to conduct an organized search in the following way:

1. See if the paper is in the folder where it belongs but out of order.
2. Look in the "file basket."
3. Look in the **folders** in front of and behind the proper folder.
4. Look in the **space** in front of, behind, and under the proper folder.
5. In an alphabetic filing system, look in folders with names that have similar spelling or sound.
6. In alphabetic systems, look in folders containing other indexing units.
   Example: Look for a letter to Carl Thomas in a folder with the caption Karl, Thomas L.
7. Look under names or captions that might be related to the lost record in some way.
8. In numeric systems, try every possible arrangement of the folder number for which you are looking.

Transferring Materials Filed

Files that serve no immediately necessary purpose should be transferred for storage to less accessible locations so they will not get in the way of the active files.

Many records have most value to a company within four to six weeks after they are stored in the files. After that time, they are rarely—if ever—referred to. For that reason, older records should be moved to "transfer files" in an area of the building that is less valuable in terms of high cost space and leave the prime filing areas for active, frequently used files. (Transfer files are frequently cardboard file drawers or older file equipment that has been moved to storage areas because it no longer looks attractive and businesslike.)

In other situations, files that are several months old are still referred to periodically. In those situations, the middle drawers in the file cabinets usually contain the active files and the upper and lower drawers (because they are not as accessible) contain the older files. Periodically, the files are sorted; older materials are transferred to storage areas; and less frequently used files are moved to the upper and lower drawers. The transfer period on such files is sometimes six months or often once a year.

Some files are highly specialized, such as case files kept by attorneys or collection agencies. When the case has been completed, it is closed; and the file material can be transferred to an inactive file.

Destroying Files

The very last stage in the filing cycle is disposing of records that no longer serve a useful purpose. The decision about what files are to be destroyed must be made by the management of a business since the decision is determined by legal considerations—some tax records will never be destroyed—and the special needs of the business. The management of every company should establish some plan for the periodic destruction of useless files.

THE MANAGEMENT OF NONPAPER RECORDS

The tremendous increase in the number of records to be stored, resulting from the introduction of such business technology as data and word processing, has created the need for new types of nonpaper storage, such as cards, tapes, disks, and microforms.

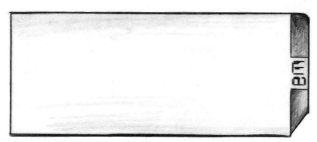

Fig. 107. Magnetic card

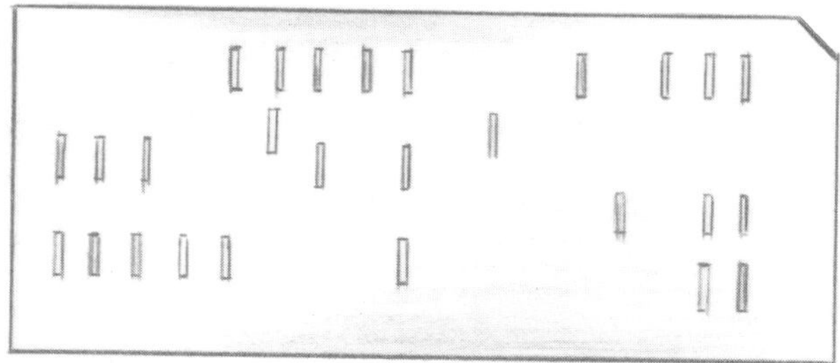

Fig. 108. Punched card

Data are stored on cards by keystroking punched holes in paper cards and electronic impulses on magnetic cards.

Fig. 109. Tape *Fig. 110. Disks*

Data are also stored on tapes and disks by keystroking electronic impulses. However, the storage capacity of tapes and disks is significantly greater than the storage capacity of cards. This fact produces a substantial savings for business in both storage space and storage costs.

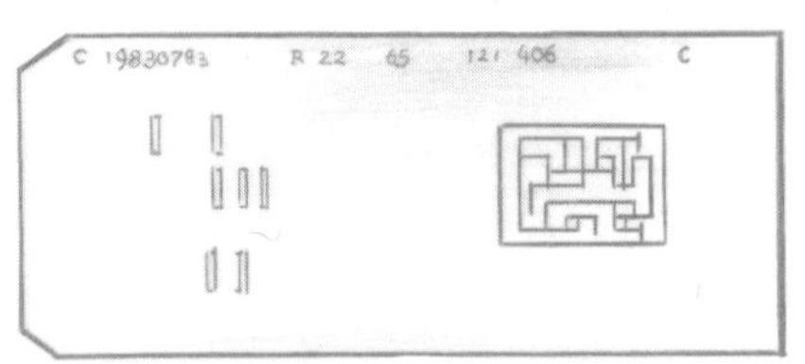

Aperture Card

Microfiche

Microfilm

Fig. 111. Microforms

Microforms are another type of storage media consisting of microfilm, microfiche, and aperture cards. Data are stored on microforms by reducing the size of the original document photographically. Because one microform has the capacity to store a large number of documents (or records), microforms also produce savings for business in space and storage costs.

Storing Nonpaper Records

Files, cabinets, holders, and bins are the types of equipment used to store and protect nonpaper records.

Commonly used files for disks are album files and rotary files. Both types of files use rigid pockets to provide support for pliable disks and to protect disks from dust, moisture, and excessive changes of temperature.

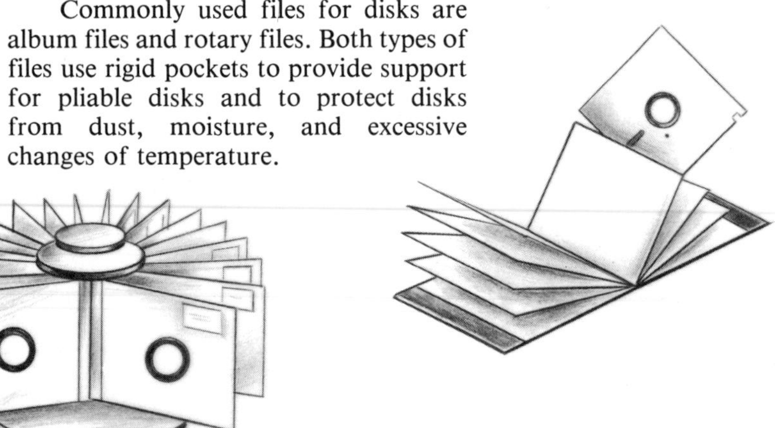

Rotary File

Fig. 112. Disk files

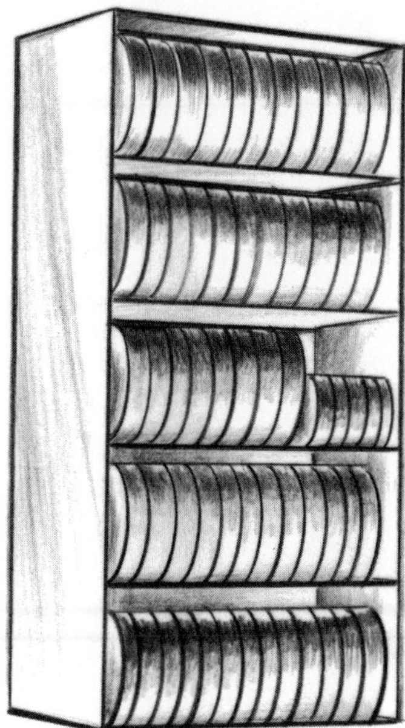

Fig. 113. Magnetic tape cabinet

Magnetic tapes and reels are housed in metal or plastic canisters and then placed on grooved shelves in storage cabinets that are similar to bookcases. The canisters protect the tapes from dust, moisture, and excessive changes in temperature.

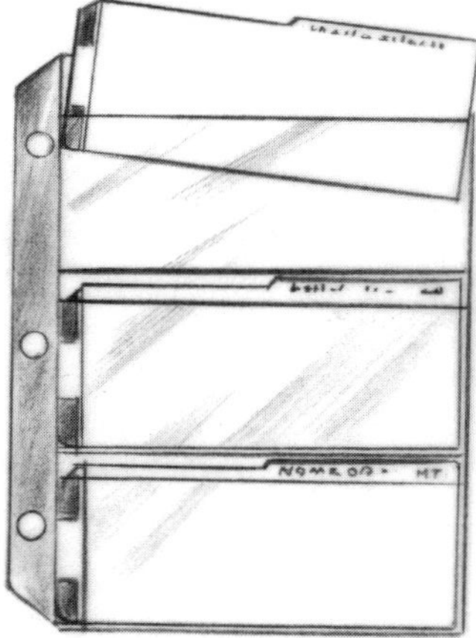

Fig. 114. Magnetic card holder

Magnetic cards are first placed in sleeves (or envelopes) which are then placed in clear plastic ("see-through") pockets that are mounted on rigid-backed pages. The pages are stored in ring binders.

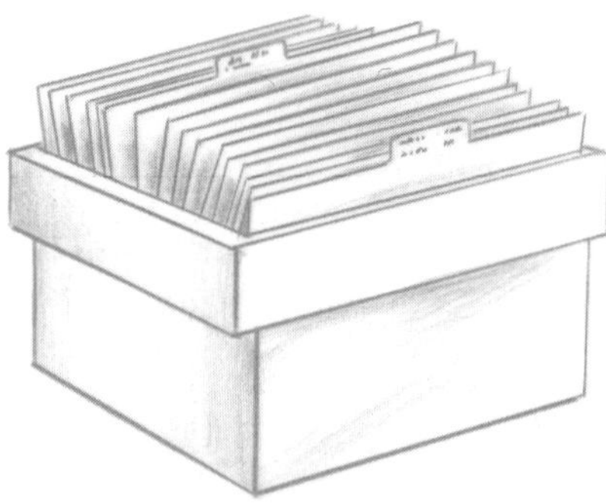

Fig. 115. Microfiche bin

Microfiche are usually placed in paper envelopes for protection and stored in desk-top bins containing dividers. Other methods of storing microfiche include ring-binder albums with pockets and pockets in rotary files.

Labeling Nonpaper Records

The purpose of storing records is to ensure that they can be found quickly and easily when they are needed. To make this possible, proper labeling and identification of records are essential.

Fig. 116. Disk label

Each disk includes a label on which the contents of the disk are identified by a description in words or numbers. Disks may be filed alphabetically (by subject or name) or numerically (by job contract, department, or client number). The numeric method of filing disks requires a supplemental alphabetic index file.

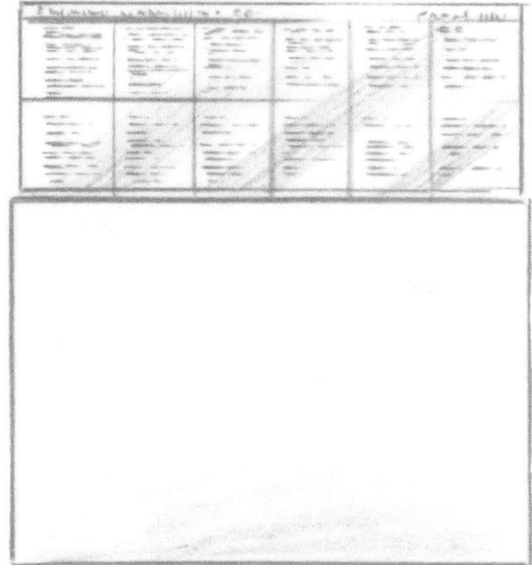

Fig. 117. Microfiche label

A filing code and other information called a "header" are lettered across the top or bottom margin of the fiche. This information, which can be read without the use of a reader/viewer, is used for identification of the fiche.

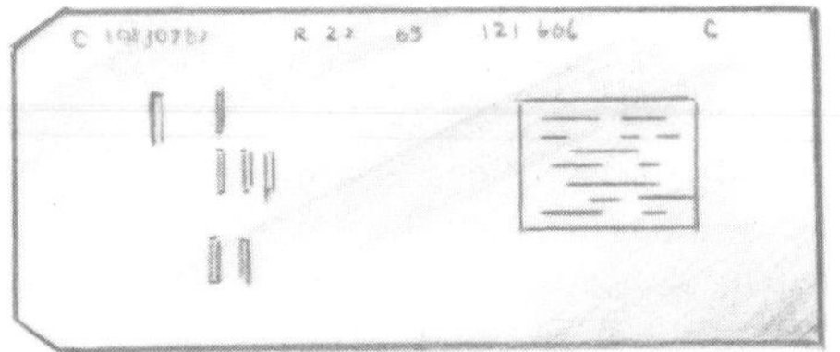

Fig. 118. Card labels

Punched cards with a micro image (called aperture cards) are labeled with printed names and/or numbers at the top of the card as the card is being punched.

Magnetic cards are placed in envelopes (or sleeves) for protection. Labeling is handwritten on the envelope in the form of words and/or numbers, or the information is typed on pressure-sensitive labels that are affixed to the envelope. No labeling can be put directly on the magnetic card.

Fig. 119. Tape label

Since it is not practical to put a label directly on magnetic tape, tapes are placed in metal and plastic canisters; and a label containing identification in the form of words and/or numbers is affixed to the container.

Retention of Nonpaper Records

Stored records are retained for varying periods of time based on the value of the information and legal considerations. Records stored on electronic media and microforms can be stored in considerably less space than paper records.

Retrieving Data Stored On Nonpaper Records

With the technology that is available today, many stored records can be retrieved electronically with a reader device.

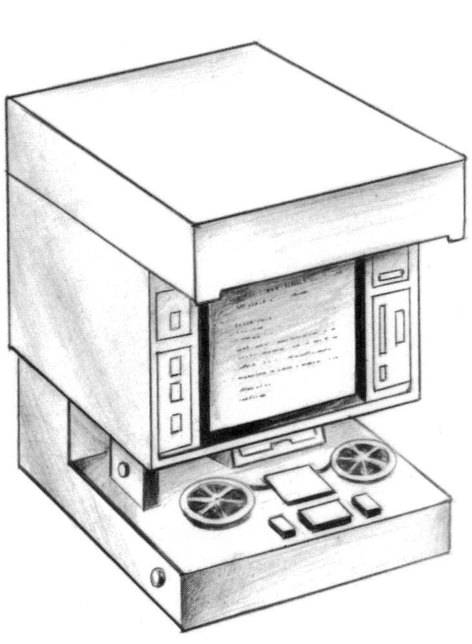

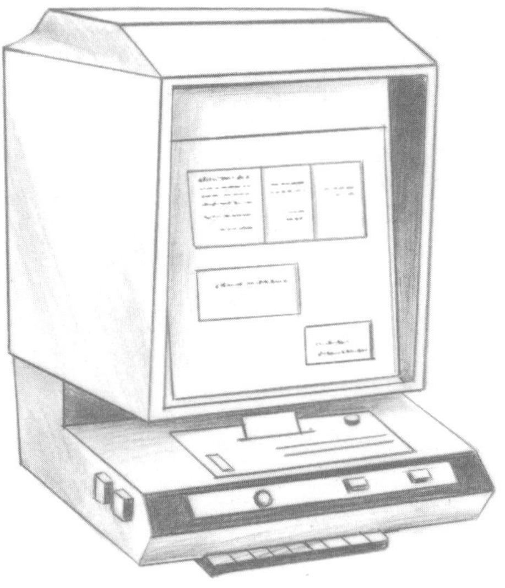

Fig. 120. Microfilm/microfiche readers

Since microfilm and microfiche are records that have been greatly reduced in size, a reader is used to enlarge to its original size, an image stored on these media. By using a reader/printer, a hard (or paper) copy of a microdocument can be produced.

Fig. 121. CRT console

A word processing operator recalls a stored document from a **disk** by keyboarding a code for the document desired. The document appears on a television-like screen on the console. By using a separate printer, a hard (or paper) copy of the document can be produced.

Fig. 122. Computer console with printer

A computer operator recalls a stored record from a **tape or a disk** by keystroking the code for the document desired. The document then appears on the screen of the computer console; and, by means of a printer that is attached to the computer, a hard (or paper) copy of the document can be produced.

Some computers are equipped with microfiche printers that allow stored data to be produced in the form of microfiche rather than hard copy. The microfiche is then placed on a reader for viewing. This process saves a tremendous amount of paper. Later, if it is required, a hard copy can be processed from the microfiche by using a reader/printer.

One of the early forms of storing word processing data was a magnetic card. Data stored on a magnetic card is retrieved by playing it out in the form of hard copy on a Mag Card (magnetic card) Typewriter.

Fig. 123. Mag Card unit

The Future Of Records Management

What does the future hold for records management?

Information is the most important tool and the greatest need of modern business. As business, industry, and government strive toward "the paperless society," the management of electronic and photographic records will become more and more important.

Trained personnel **skilled in the technologies of records management** will have opportunities for challenging and useful careers. Mastering the tools of modern technology and combining them with the creative management of resources will give business access to information when it is needed at a cost that can be justified.

TYPES OF FILING METHODS

Here is a listing of the various types of filing methods that are used in most businesses and the characteristics of those methods. Revised ARMA (Association of Records Managers and Administrators) rules for alphabetic indexing—a frequently used filing procedure—follow a brief description of subject, geographic, and numeric filing.

Subject Filing

Records are usually filed by subject under the following conditions:

1. When all of the records about one product or activity are likely to be needed in one place at one time.
2. When the records (such as inventory records) do not refer to the name of a person or an organization.
3. When it is likely that records will be requested by subject.
4. When records would become so subdivided they would be difficult to find if they were not filed by subject.

Geographic Filing

Geographic filing is used when there is a need to look for the records filed according to some geographic area such as a state, a country, a town or city, or a section of a town or city. Guides and folders in the file drawers and labels on nonpaper records are arranged according to the geographic division required by the business. Businesses that have a particular need for geographic files are real estate firms, public utilities, and mail-order businesses.

Numeric Filing

In numeric filing, records are coded with a number. Because all the records have a coded number, they do not have to be placed in alphabetical order in the files. For that reason, closely related records can be placed near each other in the files. Numeric files are easy to expand because new records are inserted at the end of the existing files, and they do not have to be fitted into existing space. Numeric files require an alphabetic index showing a code number under which each type of record is filed. This index must be checked when coding new material or looking for materials already filed. From that point of view, numeric filing is said to be an indirect filing method.

ARMA RULES FOR ALPHABETIC FILING

The Association of Records Managers and Administrators, located in Prairie Village, KS, is a group of national experts who have made an effort to reconcile differences in alphabetizing systems currently in use. Here are the rules they suggest for standardizing alphabetic filing systems.

Rule 1: Individual Names

Names of individuals are transposed. The surname is the key indexing unit; the first name is the 2nd unit; and the middle name is the 3rd unit.

Name	File as		
	Key Unit	2nd Unit	3rd Unit
Robert Francis Johnson	Johnson	Robert	Francis

1a. Nicknames: File under surname if surname is known; otherwise, file as written.

1b. Prefixes: File surname prefixes such as Da, de, De, Del, Des, Du, La, Les, Mac, Mc, San, Van, Von, Von der, etc., as one unit regardless of whether they are written as one or two words. These units are filed alphabetically. For example, McDonald is filed between Ma and Me:

Massachusetts Mutual Life Insurance
Mayflower Delicatessen
McAllister, George Associates
McDonald Auto Repair
Mead's Restaurant

1c. Titles/Degrees: Disregard titles and degrees such as Dr. or Princess. Exception: When a title is followed by only one name, such as Queen Elizabeth, file as written.

1d. Name Endings: Jr., Sr., 2nd, and III are considered indexing units.

1e. Married Women: Index by surname followed by first name and either maiden or middle name.

1f. Foreign Names: If you can't decide which name is the last name, file as written.

Name	File as		
	Key Unit	2nd Unit	3rd Unit
John Barrymore, Jr.	Barrymore	John	Junior
Dr. Mary Anne Malone	Malone	Mary	Anne (Dr.)
Michael L. McNamara	McNamara	Michael	L.
Mrs. John Moreland (Sandra Anne)	Moreland	Sandra	Anne
Princess Anne	Priness	Anne	
Red Baron	Red	Baron	
Von Ritter, Jerome	VonRitter	Jerome	
Yuen Chi Kui	Yuen	Chi	Kui

Rule 2: Company Names File business names in the sequence in which they are written unless the business name contains the complete name of an individual. In this case, transpose the individual name and use the surname as the indexing unit. Exception: Do not transpose the name of a business when the individual name is so well known it would lead to confusion.

Name	File as		
	Key Unit	2nd Unit	3rd Unit
General Wheel Corporation	General	Wheel	Corporation
Eugene Haviland Associates	Haviland	Eugene	Associates
Montgomery Ward	Montgomery	Ward	

2a. Nicknames: File company names as incorporated, not by nicknames.
2b. Endings: Endings such as Corporation, Company, and Bros. are considered filing units.
2c. Trade names: File as one unit.
2d. Subsidiary companies/divisions: File by name used on letterhead, invoices, purchase orders, and other business forms.

Name	File as			
	Key Unit	2nd Unit	3rd Unit	4th Unit
Brown Brothers	Brown	Brothers		
Green Arrow Mead Company	Green	Arrow	Mead	Company
IBM	International	Business	Machines	
Sure Foot Wax Company	SureFoot	Wax	Company	

Rule 3: Single Letters/ Single Words

Index single letters in company names separately even if they are written together without spaces, such as radio and television call letters.

File a single name before an identical name followed by initials or other words and letters.

Name	File as			
	Key Unit	2nd Unit	3rd Unit	4th Unit
ABC Forms	A	B	C	Forms
L L Cleaners	L	L	Cleaners	
Smith	Smith			
John Smith	Smith	John		
John Robert Smith	Smith	John	Robert	
WBIZ	W	B	I	Z

Rule 4: One Word Or Two

Names that may be written either as one word or two should be indexed as one unit.

Name	File as		
	Key Unit	2nd Unit	3rd Unit
Inter State Milk Company	Interstate	Milk	Company

4a. Hyphenated words: Hyphenated **surnames** are indexed as one unit. Hyphenated **business names** are indexed as two units.
4b. Compound Geographic Names: Index these as separate units. Exception: When the first part of a compound word is foreign, file the two words as one.
Example: Del Rio is indexed as DelRio.
4c. Compass Point Words: Each compass point word (north, south, west, east) is a separate unit.

Name	File as			
	Key Unit	2nd Unit	3rd Unit	4th Unit
Boat-Plane Freight Company	Boat	Plane	Freight	Company
Del Rio Chili Company	DelRio	Chili	Company	
Mary Ruth Leed-Smith	LeedSmith	Mary	Ruth	
New York Times	New	York	Times	
Northeast Upholsterers	North	East	Upholsterers	

Rule 5: Abbreviations

File all abbreviations as though the word were written out in full. Single letters other than abbreviations are considered as separate indexing units.

Name	File as			
	Key Unit	2nd Unit	3rd Unit	4th Unit
Ft. Worth Cattle Company	Fort	Worth	Cattle	Company
Jill St. John	SaintJohn	Jill		
Wm. Smith	Smith	William		

Rule 6: And's, The's, Of's, A's, For's and 'S

The's, and's, &, of's, a's, for's and apostrophes in elisions are disregarded in filing.

Exception: File foreign articles (a, an, the) as written in foreign firm names.
Example: El Paso Real Estate.

Name	File as			
	Key Unit	2nd Unit	3rd Unit	4th Unit
The Federal Bank of New York	Federal	Bank	New	York(of)
Top of the Mountain Motel	Top(of the)	Mountain	Motel	
What's Happening Records	Whats	Happening	Records	
El Paso Real Estate	ElPaso	Real	Estate	

Rule 7: Governments

U.S. and Foreign Government Names: The key indexing unit is the name of the federal government or the foreign government. Subdivide by title of the department and then by bureau, division, commission, or board.

State/Local Agencies: Index by the name of the state, county, or city government. Subdivide with names of organizational units.

Name	File as					
	Key Unit	2nd Unit	3rd Unit	4th Unit	5th Unit	6th Unit
Dade County Department of Public Welfare	Dade	County(of)	Public	Welfare	Department (of)	
Michigan Department of Highways	Michigan	State(of)	Highways	Department (of)		
Interstate Commerce Commission	United	States	Government	Interstate	Commerce	Commission
Republic of Uruguay Department of Agriculture	Uruguay	Republic (of)	Agriculture	Department (of)		

Rule 8: Numbers*

File numbers as though spelled out. Three and four digit numbers are read as hundreds. Five or more digits are read as thousands.

If a number contains two numbers, such as 18-21, file by the lowest number.

Name	File as		
	Key Unit	2nd Unit	3rd Unit
Dock on 22nd Street	Dock(on)	Twenty-second	Street
18-22 Club	Eighteen Twentytwo	Club	
The 42nd Street Theater	Fortysecond (The)	Street	Theater
1776 Apartments	Seventeen Hundred Seventysix	Apartments	

*An alternative practice in number filing is to place all names starting with numbers at the beginning of the alphabetic file. Numbers already spelled out should be filed alphabetically.

Example: 42nd Street Theater
1776 Apartments
Aaron, Ann
Abell, Daniel

Rule 9: Identical Names

When the same name appears with different addresses, file first by name, then by city, state, and street name. Example:

Big Discount Stores Stamford, CT 1 Washington Blvd.	Fit Right Shoes Rome, Nebraska
Big Discount Stores Stamford, CT 22 Washington Blvd.	Fit Right Shoes Rome, New York

Rule 10: Institutions

Churches, hospitals, newspapers, periodicals, hotels, and motels: Index as written. Exception: Reverse names beginning with "hotel" or "motel" so that the distinctive name is first.

Colleges, schools** financial institutions, libraries, and chambers of commerce: Index under the distinctive name. When further description is needed, follow by city, state, and branch. Individual names used as distinctive names of institutions are not inverted.

**Telephone books disagree on this one. They file schools under the name of the town where the school is located and then file the name of the school under Public School.

Name	File as				
	Key Unit	2nd Unit	3rd Unit	4th Unit	5th Unit
Hotel Biltmore	Biltmore	Hotel			
University of Bridgeport	Bridgeport	University (of)			
First National Bank, New York	First	National	Bank	New	York
The Houston Post	Houston(The)	Post			
North Street School, Greenwich, CT	North	Street	School	Greenwich	CT
Presbyterian Hospital of New York	Presbyterian	Hospital	New	York(of)	
Reader's Digest	Readers	Digest			
Theodore Roosevelt Library, New York	Theodore	Roosevelt	Library	New	York

The preceding rules cover **most** questions about alphabetic filing. Occasionally a highly specialized filing situation requires a particular alphabetic twist, but this is rare according to ARMA. They suggest **making a rule** if none of the preceding rules work. They also caution that it is of vital importance to **BE CONSISTENT.** By being consistent, you will always be able to find what you are looking for in the files—that's what alphabetizing is really about!

FOR REVIEW AND DISCUSSION

1. Discuss the four key ingredients of a good filing system.
2. Explain the terms Centralized Files and Decentralized Files.
3. Explain the responsibilities of the File Department personnel.
4. Explain the purpose of a File Index.
5. Discuss the seven steps to be taken in preparing materials to be filed.
6. Discuss the ways materials may be requested from the files.
7. Discuss the use of an Out Card.
8. Explain the term, Cross Reference.
9. Discuss the steps that can be taken to find lost file records.
10. Discuss the transferring of filed materials.
11. Discuss the final destruction of file records.
12. Explain the four types of storage of nonpaper records.
13. Explain how disks are stored. Explain how microfiche are stored.
14. Explain how cards are labeled. Explain how tapes are labeled.
15. Explain how records stored on microfilm and microfiche are retrieved. Explain how records stored on disks are retrieved.
16. Explain the term, "the paperless society."
17. Name and explain briefly the four methods of filing described in this chapter.

Turn to your workbook and complete Student Project 18.

CHAPTER 12

Financial Records

OBJECTIVE

After studying Chapter 12 you will understand the importance of and functions of such financial records as:

- Income Statement
- Balance Sheet
- Budget
- Payroll Records
- Petty Cash Records
- Bank Deposits

JOB-RELATED VOCABULARY

Gross Pay—Salary or wages before any deductions are taken.

Inclusive Dates—The from/to dates indicating when something (such as a business trip) began and when it ended.

Replenished—Built up again. (The petty cash fund is replenished when money is added to it to replace what has been spent.)

Denomination—Value or size (the value of or amount of money).

Without Recourse—Without the right to come back to hold the maker or a previous endorser liable for a negotiable instrument (such as a check).

Magnetic Ink—Electronically sensitive ink that can be "read" or detected by electronic data processing equipment.

Computation—Mathematical figuring.

It is of vital importance for every employee of a business to understand the value of keeping accurate financial records. The executives of a company interpret the growth and development of a business and plan for the future as a result of studying the financial records the company keeps.

The financial records described in this chapter are the basic records that most office workers may expect to encounter in the course of their work.

FINANCIAL STATEMENTS AND THEIR USES

There are two financial statements that every office worker should understand: the Income Statement and the Balance Sheet.

The Income Statement

The Income Statement (sometimes called the Statement of Income and Retained Earnings) is a financial report of the income, the expenses, and the net profit or loss from operating a business over a given period of time, such as a month, a three-month period, or a twelve-month period (sometimes referred to as a fiscal period). An Income Statement usually contains five parts or five items:

1. **Income**—revenue from the sale of products or services less the returns and allowances on those sales.
2. **Cost of Goods Sold**—the **cost** of inventory on hand at the beginning of the accounting period, plus the **cost** of goods produced, less the **cost** of the finished goods inventory on hand at the end of the accounting period.
3. **Gross Profit on Sales**—the difference between the Income and the Cost of Goods Sold. (Profit before the expenses of doing business are deducted.)
4. **Operating Expenses**—the amount expended for doing business during the accounting period.
5. **Net Income or Net Loss**—If the **Gross Profit** is larger than the Operating Expenses, a Net Profit results. If the **Operating Expenses** are larger than the Gross Profit, a Net Loss results.

MORGAN GLASS CORPORATION

Statement of Income and Retained Earnings

Year Ended June 30, 19--

Income		
Sales	$4,562,551	
Returns & Allowances	23,850	
Net Sales		$4,538,701
Cost of Goods Sold		
Inventory on hand July 1	360,000	
Cost of Goods Manufactured	2,618,671	
Total Goods Available for Sale	2,978,671	
Inventory on hand June 30	259,068	
Cost of Goods Sold		2,719,603
Gross Profit on Sales		1,819,098
Operating Expenses		
Selling Expenses:		
Sales Salaries	$ 179,500	
Sales Supplies & Expenses	566,552	
Total Selling Expenses		746,052
Administrative Expenses:		
Officers' Salaries	$ 155,320	
Office Salaries	205,573	
Administrative Expenses	200,000	
Bad Debts Expense	11,906	
Total Administrative Expenses		572,799
Total Operating Expenses		1,318,851
Net Income Before Taxes		500,247
Provision for Income Taxes		225,000
Net Income After Taxes		275,247
Retained Earnings July		445,699
Retained Earnings June 30 (to Balance Sheet)		$ 720,946

Fig. 124. Statement of Income and Retained Earnings

The Balance Sheet

The Balance Sheet is an itemized list of the assets (property owned by the business), the liabilities (the obligations the business has incurred), and the equity (the difference between the assets and the liabilities—representing owners' rights) of a business at a given date. The balance sheet is prepared in two parts:

1. Assets
2. Liabilities and Equity

The totals of both parts of the Balance Sheet must be exactly the same. The basic accounting equation, Assets = Liabilities + Proprietorship (or equity), therefore, applies to the Balance Sheet. By studying the Balance Sheet of the Morgan Glass Corporation in Fig. 125, you will quickly see that the total assets ($2,329,875) are equal to the total liabilities and Stockholders' equity as of June 30, 19 ____. You will also notice that the Stockholders' equity is three times total liabilities of the company. This fact indicates that Morgan Glass Corporation is in an extremely favorable financial position.

MORGAN GLASS CORPORATION

Balance Sheet

June 30, 19--

Assets

Current Assets			
Cash in Bank			$ 288,702
Accounts Receivable		$ 584,369	
Allowance for Bad Debts		13,616	570,753
Inventories			
Raw Materials		234,000	
Work in Progress		189,000	
Finished Goods		367,200	790,200
Prepaid Expenses			
Prepaid Insurance		27,450	
Supplies on Hand		2,250	29,700
Total Current Assets			1,679,355
Fixed Assets			
Land		93,600	
Plant & Equipment	747,000		
Accumulated Depreciation	190,080	556,920	
Total Fixed Assets			650,520
Total Assets			$2,329,875

Liabilities and Stockholders' Equity

Current Liabilities		
Accounts Payable	274,409	
Wages Payable	8,100	
Payroll Taxes Payable	21,420	
Income Taxes Payable	225,000	
Total Liabilities		$ 528,929
Stockholders' Equity		
Common Stock	1,080,000	
Retained Earnings	720,946	
Total Stockholders' Equity		1,800,946
Total Liabilities and Stockholders' Equity		$2,329,875

Fig. 125. Balance Sheet

The Budget

The budget is an estimate of the income and expenses of a business for a given period of time (usually a year). Although the budget is not usually considered a financial statement, it is important for office workers to understand what constitutes a good budget. A good budget should meet the following criteria:

1. It should reflect the past performance of the company and anticipate future trends.
2. It should provide the management personnel responsible for making the budget work with some means of control.
3. The budget should be restricted enough to demand good performance without asking for the impossible.
4. The budget should be reviewed by management before it is adopted.
5. The budget should provide for periodic reports to compare actual income and expenses with those budgeted.

PAYROLL RECORDS

Payroll records are extremely important, because they are the basis on which each employee of the business pays his/her income taxes. Because of this fact, payroll records are subject to constant scrutiny by the Internal Revenue Service (IRS) and by state and city income tax departments.

Social Security Numbers

Each person who wants to work must obtain an employee account number from the Social Security Administration. To obtain an account number, it is necessary to complete an SS 5 Form (available at the local post office or social security office). If the social security account number card which will be sent to the applicant is lost, it may be replaced by writing to the Social Security Administration. If the holder of a social security account number changes his/her name, the change must be reported on Form OAAN-7003 (Request for Change in Social Security Records).

Withholding Exemption Certificate

When a new employee is hired by a firm, the employee must complete an Employee's Withholding Exemption Certificate (Form W-4). The form includes the employee's social security number and the number of exemptions he/she claims. The usual exemptions are as follows:

- An exemption for the employee (unless he/she is already being claimed on another certificate)
- An exemption for a spouse (unless he/she is already being claimed on another certificate)
- An exemption for each dependent (unless he/she is claimed on another certificate)

Payroll Deductions

Each employee who is a regular employee of a business is subject by law to payroll deductions from his/her gross pay. Payroll deductions include the following:

F.I.C.A. Tax—Under the Federal Insurance Contribution Act, both the employee and the employer are subject to taxes of the same amount based on gross pay (before deductions). The amount is collected from the employee by the employer and forwarded (with his/her own contribution) to the district Director of Internal Revenue or an authorized bank at the end of each calendar quarter or more frequently if sums exceed a designated amount.

Withholding (Income Tax) Deductions—The Federal Government requires **most** employers to withhold from the compensation paid to employees (wages, salaries, commissions, bonuses, and vacation pay) a certain amount (based on the amount of the gross pay and the number of dependents the employee claims) as advance payment on the employee's Federal income tax.

In addition, some states and some cities tax personal income. The rates of tax vary with the states and the cities.

Besides the deductions required by Federal and state law, employees frequently have deductions for such things as:

- Hospital Care Insurance
- Group Life Insurance
- Stock or Bond Purchases
- Savings through Company Credit Unions

These deductions are usually voluntary, and they usually may be canceled at the employee's option.

Wages And Salaries

The term **wages** indicates a rate per hour, and the term **salaries** indicates a rate per week or per month. Ordinarily, production employees are paid on an hourly (wages) basis; and office employees are usually paid on a salary basis.

Most hourly and salaried employees come under the provisions of the Fair Labor Standards Act which sets a minimum hourly wage and requires that employees be paid time and a half (50 percent greater than the regular hourly rate) for all hours over 40 hours a week. For that reason, employers must keep a detailed record of the hours each employee works; and those records must be made available to the Government examiner (of the Wage and Hour Division of the Department of Labor) at any time he/she wants to review them.

Professional workers and executives are excluded from the provisions of the Fair Labor Standards Act.

Tax-Related Records

All records of hours worked and wages paid to each employee of a business along with all other appropriate computations and memorandums must be kept **indefinitely.** These materials should be stored in a safe place, and they should be labeled so that they are instantly accessible.

Every employee of a business who travels for business purposes must keep a detailed record of the expenses he/she incurs for business travel (tips, transportation, hotels, meals, parking, convention registration fees). It is always a good idea to get receipts for cash expenses and to make them a part of expense reports. Each expense report should indicate the reason for the trip and the inclusive dates of the trip; and it should provide a detailed accounting of the expenses incurred day to day.

When clients or customers are entertained for business purposes, it is important to give a complete report of the entertainment expense. The report should contain the following:

- Date of the entertainment
- Name of the guest(s) and the company or firm he/she represents
- An explanation of the entertainment including the type of entertainment, the place where the entertainment took place, and a brief explanation of the purpose of the entertainment
- The total cost of the entertainment

It is a good idea to attach a cash receipt or a credit card receipt to the entertainment report.

All papers and records related to payroll and tax matters are highly confidential in nature. For that reason, the utmost care must be taken to protect this information and to keep it safe from the prying eyes of persons who are not concerned with it!

PETTY CASH RECORDS

Payments of small amounts in cash are frequently made from a petty cash fund. Both the size of the total fund and the maximum amount that can be paid from the fund for one transaction vary greatly from company to company. The petty cash fund—frequently administered by a secretary or an office clerk—should be kept in a safe place that can be locked when the person administering the fund is away from his/her desk.

Petty Cash Receipt

Every person requesting money from the Petty Cash Fund should fill out a Petty Cash Voucher (receipt), containing: the amount of money disbursed, the date, the purpose for which the money was used, the name of the person or firm that received the money, and the signature of the person who received the money. No money should ever be disbursed from the Petty Cash Fund unless a Petty Cash Voucher is completed first.

Periodically, the Petty Cash Fund will need to be replenished as it gets low. When the fund is to be replenished, the person responsible for it should prepare a Petty Cash Report (see Fig. 127) for the Accounting Department, which will issue a check to replenish the fund.

PETTY CASH VOUCHER NO. 11

FOR	AMOUNT
Stamp Pad	$1.25

Received from MORGAN GLASS CORPORATION

By Karl Thomas Date 5/7/--

Approved By Helen Louis Date 5/7/--

Fig. 126. Petty Cash Voucher

Petty Cash Report

May 15, 19--

Balance on hand (4/12/--)		$25.00
Expenditures:		
Postage	$3.78	
Heart Fund	8.00	
Collect Telegram	4.50	
Taxi	5.40	
Book	3.25	24.93
Balance on hand (5/15/--)		$ .07
Amount to be replenished		$24.93

Fig. 127. Petty Cash Report

Preparing Bank Deposits

By following an established procedure for making bank deposits, you can save yourself time and costly errors.

Preparing Cash For Deposit

When large quantities of cash are to be deposited, banks prefer to have both the coins and the bills being deposited wrapped in money wrappers that the banks furnish.

Bills of each denomination are made into packages of $50, $100, $200 and up. The bills are laid face up with the picture on each bill facing the same direction. Each group of all-of-a-kind bills is wrapped tightly with a money wrapper (a narrow strip of paper with the total amount of the group of bills printed on the top). The person preparing the money for deposit prints the name of the company (or individual on a personal account) making the deposit. Extra bills that are not enough to make a package should be counted and placed right side up with the largest denomination at the bottom and the smallest on the top. The entire stack of bills to be deposited (both in wrappers and loose) should be bound with an elastic band to keep them together.

Preparing Checks For Deposit

Checks should be inspected to be sure they are made payable to the company, to be sure the amount in writing and the amount in figures agree, and to be sure that they are properly signed. Following this inspection, checks should be endorsed. (Note: Many companies follow the procedure of endorsing incoming checks "For Deposit Only" as soon as they arrive. In that way, it is difficult, if not impossible, for anyone except a company official to cash the checks—a real protection if they are stolen.)

Here are a few of the endorsements commonly used:

Restrictive Endorsement (an endorsement containing a special condition)—It is commonly used when checks are being deposited. When a check is endorsed "For Deposit Only," it can be **deposited** only to the account of the company or person whose name appears in the endorsement.

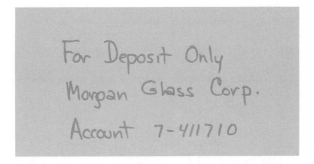

Fig. 128. Check with a restrictive endorsement

Blank Endorsement (the signature of the payee—the person to whom the check is made payable)—A blank endorsement makes the check payable to **any** holder. For that reason, a blank endorsement should not be used except at the bank immediately before the check is being deposited or cashed.

Fig. 129. Check with a blank endorsement

Endorsement in Full (the name of the specified payee and the endorser's signature)—A check containing an endorsement in full specifies the bank, person, or company to whom the check is being made payable; and it must also contain the signature of the person to whom the check was originally made payable. If the bank, person or company to whom the check was endorsed wanted to transfer the check to someone else, it must be endorsed again.

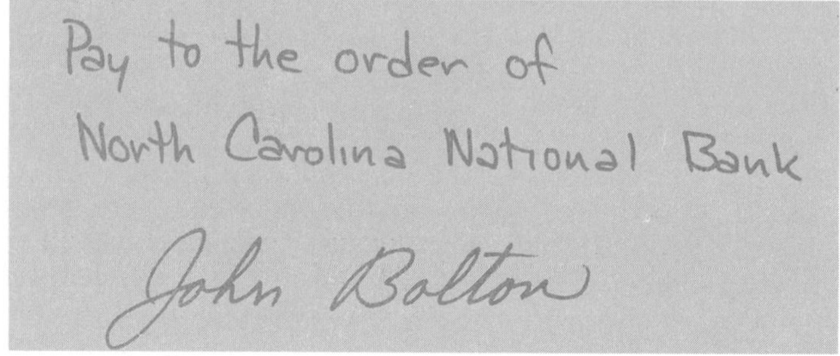

Fig. 130. Check with an endorsement in full

Another type of endorsement, called a **qualified endorsement,** can also be used under special conditions. Such an endorsement contains the name of the bank, person, or company to whom the check is being made payable; the signature of the person to whom the check was originally made payable; and the words "without recourse." A qualified endorsement passes title to the check without holding the endorser responsible if the maker refuses to pay or is unable to pay. **Usually, a bank will not accept a check containing a qualified endorsement** for deposit from a regular depositor. The decision to put a qualified (without recourse) endorsement on a check would usually rest with the company controller or the company attorney, not with a clerical person preparing a bank deposit.

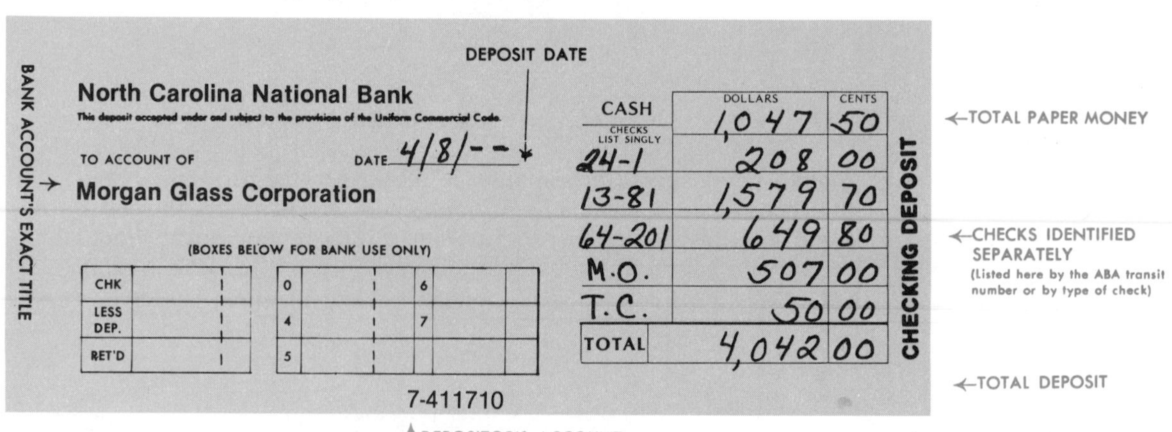

	DOLLARS	CENTS
CASH	1,047	50
CHECKS LIST SINGLY		
24-1	208	00
13-81	1,579	70
64-201	649	80
M.O.	507	00
T.C.	50	00
TOTAL	4,042	00

Fig. 131. Completed deposit slip

Preparing A Deposit Slip

Although there are many different types of deposit slips in use today, it is common practice for most banks to use deposit slips designed for use with some type of automated equipment. Figure 131 shows a deposit slip prepared by an accounting clerk for the Morgan Glass Corporation. Each part of the deposit slip has been labeled to indicate its purpose. The following is a description of the key items in a deposit:

Account Number—Banks identify their depositors by account numbers. Sometimes, the account number is printed on the deposit slip with magnetic ink. If it is not, it must be written on the deposit slip when a deposit is being prepared. Deposits to and withdrawals from accounts are posted by the account number rather than by the account name.

Bank Transit Number—Every bank in the United States has been assigned an American Bankers Association (ABA) Transit Number. A transit number is usually printed in the upper right hand corner of each check drawn on a particular bank. The transit number identifies the bank for clearinghouse functions. Here is an explanation of a typical transit number:

$$\frac{1\text{-}2}{210}$$

1 city or state code
2 specific bank code

2 Federal Reserve District Code
1 Code for the branch in the district
0 Number of days required to clear the bank

Ordinarily checks to be deposited are listed on the deposit slip using the top two ABA Transit Numbers (1-2 in the preceding example). It is equally acceptable to list the check by the name of the maker (a person or a company). The point to keep in mind is that the depositor must be able to identify the check in order to have the maker stop payment on it and issue a new check if the original check is lost during the bank's collection procedures.

List of Checks—Most banks prefer to have each check being deposited listed separately. Money orders and travelers checks should be listed individually as "Post Office Money Order," "Bank Money Order," "American Express Money Order," or "American Express Travelers Cheque."

Night Depository

Even though many banks have established branches that stay open after traditional banking hours, some depositors have need to deposit large amounts of cash late in the evening after all banks are closed. For that reason, most banks maintain a night depository. A depositor completes a regular deposit slip and places it in a bank deposit bag along with the cash and checks to be deposited. The bag is locked and dropped into the night deposit slot on the outside of the bank. During the next business day, a bank teller opens the bag and completes the deposit. The depositor then stops by the bank to pick up the deposit bag and the deposit receipt. The depositor can also arrange to have the deposit bag remain locked at the bank until he/she goes in person to make the deposit. The main purpose of a night depository is to keep money and checks safe overnight in the bank vault until they can be deposited.

Deposit By Mail

Deposits made by mail have become very popular in recent years because they save the depositor from having to stand in line at the bank waiting to make a deposit. The depositor completes a deposit slip and endorses all checks "For Deposit Only" or "Pay To The Order Of (name of bank)" and places the checks and the deposit slip in a heavy duty envelope (usually provided by the bank) for mailing to the bank. Currency should never be deposited by mail unless registered mail is used. The bank will process the deposit; and many banks will send the depositor a receipt, a new deposit slip, and a new envelope by return mail.

THE COMPANY CHECKING ACCOUNT

Preparing Check Stubs

The first step to be taken when a check is to be written is to prepare the stub. If the check stub is not prepared first, the data could be forgotten (and often is), making it impossible to keep an accurate checkbook record. The check stub usually calls for the following information: the date, the name of the payee, the amount for which the check was written, and an adequate description of the purpose of the check. If the check covers several different items, each item should be shown individually with a final total for all the items. If a check is written to pay an insurance premium, the name of the insured and the policy number should appear on the check stub. Keeping carefully detailed records can pay rich dividends if the checkbook is audited by an auditing firm or by the Internal Revenue Service.

The amount of each check should be deducted immediately from the previous balance, and the new balance should be recorded in the proper place on the check stub. Deposits should be entered on the check stubs on the same day on which they are made.

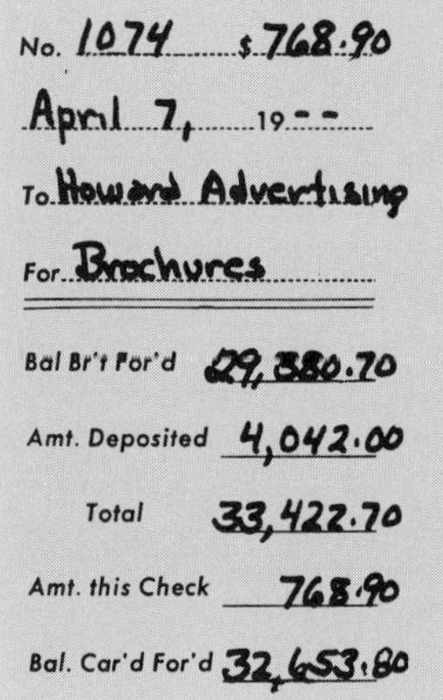
No. 1074 $ 768.90
April 7, 19--
To Howard Advertising
For Brochures
Bal Br't For'd 29,380.70
Amt. Deposited 4,042.00
Total 33,422.70
Amt. this Check 768.90
Bal. Car'd For'd 32,653.80

Fig. 132. Completed check stub

Preparing Checks

After the stub has been completed, a handwritten check would be prepared in the following order: (**Note:** Some checks are not prenumbered. In that instance, the check number would be entered first.)

1. **Date**—Even though a check is not dated, it is still valid. However, for your own protection, it is important to put the correct date on the check. Checks may be dated on a Sunday or a holiday (contrary to popular belief), but checks should not be dated with a future date. Banks are not authorized to pay postdated checks.
2. **Payee**—Checks should be made payable to a specific person or company (the payee). It is not a good idea to make checks payable to "Cash," "Order," or "Bearer" because such checks can be cashed by anyone.
3. **Amount**—A person should write the amount of the check in figures and then spell it in words. (If there is a difference between the amount in figures and the amount that is spelled, the spelled amount is considered to be correct.) To prevent alterations, begin the figure right next to the dollar sign and start the written amount at the extreme left edge of the line. Also, fill in the line after the amount written in words up to the word "dollar" with a wavy line as illustrated in Fig. 133. If the check is written for an amount less than $1, draw a circle around the amount written in figures. Precede the amount written in words with the word "only" and cross out the word "Dollars" that is printed at the end of the line. Some companies use

a check protector to fill in the amount in words. As it imprints the amount, it perforates the check paper so that the amount cannot be changed.

4. **Signature**—The signature on a check must agree exactly with the signature on file at the bank for the account. Never write over a signature on a check to correct it. Mark the check "VOID" and write a new one. And, above all, never sign a blank check.

A typewritten check should be prepared in the same careful manner (see Fig. 134). In addition to checks prepared by the general office staff, companies that write a large number of checks usually have an automated check writing system. A machine operation writes, dates, imprints, and signs checks at high speeds. In addition, the machine provides a list of checks written on a particular date and a total of the amount of money disbursed by check daily.

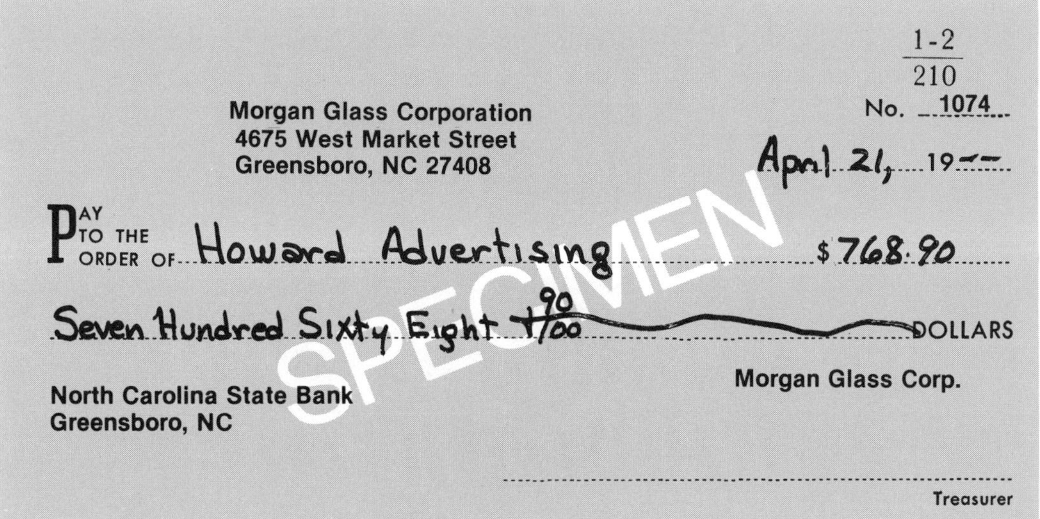

1-2/210

Morgan Glass Corporation
4675 West Market Street
Greensboro, NC 27408

No. 1074

April 21, 19--

PAY TO THE ORDER OF Howard Advertising $768.90

Seven Hundred Sixty Eight 90/100 DOLLARS

North Carolina State Bank
Greensboro, NC

Morgan Glass Corp.

Treasurer

SPECIMEN

Fig. 133. Properly completed handwritten check

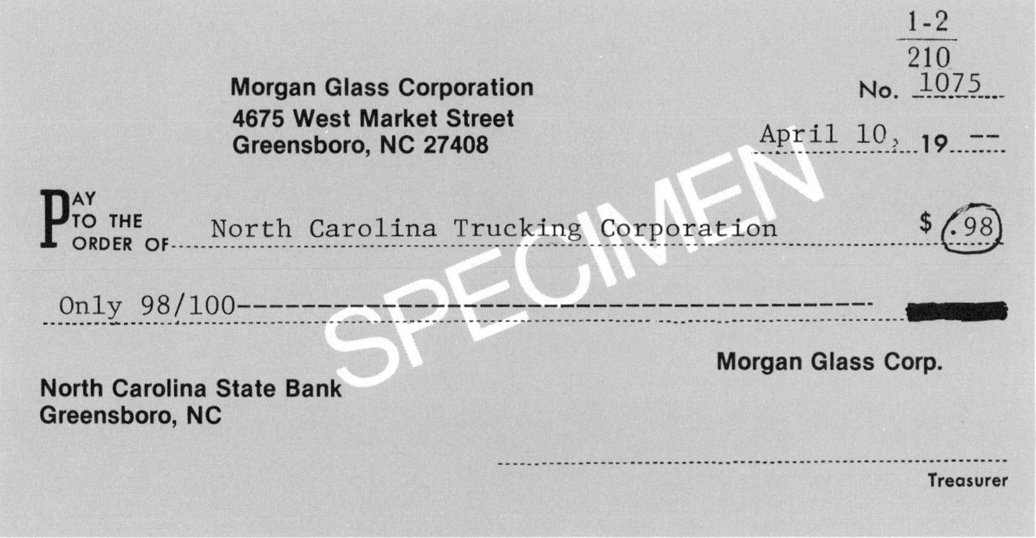

1-2/210

Morgan Glass Corporation
4675 West Market Street
Greensboro, NC 27408

No. 1075

April 10, 19 --

PAY TO THE ORDER OF North Carolina Trucking Corporation $ .98

Only 98/100--

North Carolina State Bank
Greensboro, NC

Morgan Glass Corp.

Treasurer

SPECIMEN

Fig. 134. Properly completed typewritten check showing an amount less than one dollar

Stopping Payment

If you need to stop payment on a check, you may do so by going to the bank to sign a Stop Payment Order. (**In some instances,** the bank will let you telephone a stop payment notice if you go into the bank within 24 hours to sign a Stop Payment Order.) You will need to give the bank the date of the check, the amount of the check, the name of the payee, and the reason payment is being stopped. If the stop payment request is received before the check is paid, the bank will make every effort to follow your instructions. Banks make a charge for this service that is deducted on the depositor's monthly bank statement.

RECONCILING THE BANK STATEMENT

Each month the bank sends each person or company that maintains a checking account the canceled checks the bank has paid during the month along with a statement listing the deposits, withdrawals, and service charges for the month. Everyone maintaining a checking account should reconcile the bank statement **as soon as the records are received from the bank** in order to bring the checkbook and the bank records into agreement. Many banks provide a form on the back of the monthly bank statement to help clients to reconcile their checking account. Following this procedure helps you to reconcile your bank balance:

1. Compare the amount of each canceled check with the amount shown on the bank statement. If the amounts agree, place a check mark next to each check listed on the bank statement as you do this.
2. Check the deposits listed on the bank statement with the deposits entered on the check stubs. Put a check mark (on both the check stub and the bank statement) beside each deposit that is entered correctly in both places.
3. Arrange the returned checks in numerical order.
4. Compare the checks with the check stubs. Put a check mark on the check stub next to each check that has been cleared (paid) by the bank.
5. From the checkbook stubs, make a list of the outstanding checks (those that have not yet been paid by the bank). For each outstanding check, show the check number and the amount. Total the outstanding checks.
6. To the bank balance (amount shown on the bank statement), add any **deposits in transit** (deposits entered on the checkbook stubs but not shown on the bank statement).
7. From this total, deduct the total of the outstanding checks. The result is the adjusted bank balance.
8. From the **checkbook balance** deduct the total of the service charges that appear on the bank statement and any other charges appearing on the bank statement **that were not previously entered in the checkbook.** At this point, the adjusted checkbook balance and the adjusted bank balance should be the same.

If the two adjusted balances (bank and checkbook) do not agree, you will need to take the following steps to find the error:

1. Go over the computation on the reconciliation to be sure there is no error.
2. Go through the check stubs and the bank statement to be sure that every check has been accounted for either as cleared by the bank or outstanding.
3. Go through the check stubs and the bank statement to be sure all deposits have been accounted for either as entered or in transit.

4. If the error has not been found, go over the computation on each check stub from the time of the last reconciliation. If an error is found, identify it as follows: "Error—Should be $.....; corrected on Stub #....."

5. If the error still has not been found, chances are the bank made an arithmetical error in the statement; and the bank should be asked to check its records.

When the bank reconciliation is completed, it should be initialed and dated by the person who prepared it and filed in a file folder (latest reconciliation on top). The outstanding checks listed on the reconciliation will need to be checked at the beginning of the next month when the new bank statement arrives.

Canceled checks and financial statements should be filed for future reference. Although procedures on this vary, most companies keep bank statements, canceled checks, and bank reconciliations for a minimum of seven years.

June 19-- Bank Reconciliation

Morgan Glass Corporation

Bank Balance		$28,692.19
Plus Deposit in Transit		4,697.30
Total		33,389.49
Less Outstanding Checks:		
#1109	38.10	
#1128	367.80	
#1131	597.00	1,002.90
Adjusted Bank Balance		$32,386.59
Checkbook Balance		$32,413.06
Less:		
Service Charges	10.47	
Other Charges	16.00	26.47
Adjusted Checkbook Balance		$32,386.59

Fig. 135. Bank Reconciliation

FOR REVIEW AND DISCUSSION

1. Why is it important for every employee of a business to understand the necessity of keeping accurate financial records?
2. Explain briefly the purpose of an Income Statement.
3. Explain briefly the purpose of a Balance Sheet.
4. Explain briefly the purpose of a Budget.
5. Why are well-kept payroll records particularly important to a company?
6. What two payroll deductions are **all** regular employees of businesses in the United States subject to by law?
7. Explain the terms "wages" and "salaries."
8. Explain the purpose of a Petty Cash Fund.
9. How should checks be listed on a deposit slip?
10. What is the first step to be taken when a check is to be prepared?
11. What four essential parts must be completed on a check?
12. Explain briefly the procedure for stopping payment on a check that has already been issued.
13. Why is it important to reconcile a bank statement as soon as it arrives from the bank?
14. What are the steps to be taken (in order) if the bank reconciliation does not balance?

Turn to your workbook and complete Student Project 19.

CHAPTER 13

Business Reports And Legal Papers

OBJECTIVE

After studying Chapter 13 you will understand the procedures for preparing and typing reports, the procedures for various types of legal papers, and the procedures for minutes and resolutions.

JOB-RELATED VOCABULARY

Logical Sequence—Logical order; from one step to the next in progressive order.

Notarized—Sworn or attested to as containing the legal signature(s) of the maker(s).

Business reports are the means by which ideas, instructions, plans, minutes, resolutions and data are transmitted. When reports are properly prepared, they contain the basic ingredients for planning and decision making. For that reason, all reports should be accurate, complete, concise, clear, and conclusive.

PREPARING BUSINESS REPORTS

The careful, step-by-step procedure a report writer uses to gather and present the information in a report will determine, in large measure, how well received the report will be. To prepare a report that will be informative, accurate, and well received, follow these six steps:

1. Plan and outline the report subject by subject, topic by topic.
2. Research every possible source of information for the topic you are reporting. Take notes from each source, and identify the source in the notes (for future reference).
3. After the report has been planned and researched, type it in rough-draft form. Make margins one inch wide or wider and double or triple space the material. These procedures allow plenty of space for corrections, additions, and revisions. (One well-known expert on report writing suggests typing the draft copy on the upper half of each page and leaving the bottom half of the page blank for corrections, additions, and revisions.)
4. The rough-draft copy should be checked carefully for completeness, organization, style, word choice, and the mechanics of writing (grammar, punctuation, spelling and sentence structure). At this point, the report should also be checked for effective organization to be sure the material develops in logical sequence. The beginning statements should be read carefully to assure that they are clear and interesting and to be sure they encourage the reader to continue reading. The concluding statements need to be read carefully, too, to assure that they re-emphasize the most important points in the report.
5. The next step is the preparation of the revised manuscript, taking into consideration all of the changes and corrections that have been made. The goal here is to prepare a report that is accurate, eye appealing, and easy to read.
6. The final steps in the preparation of a report are proofreading the revised copy before it is presented to the person (or group) who will examine it and the preparation of a letter of transmittal (letter of explanation) if one is to accompany the report.

Typing A Report In Final Form

Even though a report is well written, it must be typed so it is free of errors and so it will look good to the person or group who will review it. Otherwise, it will not get the attention it deserves. Here are some simple directions for typing a report in a professional manner:

1. **Stationery**—The final copy of a report should be typed on good quality 8½ by 11 bond paper of medium weight (about 16-pound weight).
2. **Margins**—Here is a chart that will help you to determine the margins that should be used depending on whether the report will be unbound, topbound, or leftbound:

Margins	Unbound	Topbound	Leftbound
Top Margin:			
First Page	Line 10	Line 13 (pica) Line 16 (elite)	Line 10
Other Pages	Line 7	Line 10	Line 7
Side Margin:			
Left	1 inch	1 inch	1½ inches
Right	1 inch	1 inch	1 inch
Bottom Margin:	1 inch	1 inch	1 inch

3. **Spacing—**
   A. Single Space: all display typing such as headings that will take two lines, all quotations that will fill more than four typed lines, footnotes, and listings.
   B. Double Space (leave one blank line): the body of a report unless there is a special need to save space or materials.
   C. Triple Space (leave two blank lines): **after** the heading on any page and **before** any major subheading.
   D. Quadruple Space (leave three blank lines): to set off a table or chart from the rest of the report.

4. **Pagination**—Page numbers should be added after the report has been completely typed and just before it is to be bound. (If the report is a long one, it is a good idea to indicate page numbers with a soft lead pencil as you go along in order to keep the report in proper sequence.) Pages in the preface or introduction to a report are numbered with small Roman numerals that are centered one inch from the bottom edge of the page. The page number on the first page of a manuscript is typed at the center point one-half inch from the bottom of the page. The page number on second and succeeding pages is typed on Line 4 for unbound and leftbound manuscripts; and on topbound manuscripts, the page number is typed at the center point one-half from the bottom of the page.

5. **Footnotes**—Footnotes are numbered and typed at the bottom of the page **ending** approximately one inch from the bottom of the page. (It is suggested that a numbered page-line guide be used for footnote placement.) A light pencil mark may be used at the right edge of the page one inch from the bottom and another mark about one-fourth inch above the one inch mark. The marks will guide the typist in placing the footnote properly on the page.

[1]Harry R. Moon, OFFICE PROCEDURES (Bronx, NY:
Milady Publishing Corporation, 19--), page 56.

Fig. 136. Footnote for a book reference

The footnote in Fig. 136 is an illustration of a **book** reference. It includes the author's name (first name, initial, last name), the title of the book (in capitals or underlined), the place of publication and the name of the publisher (in parentheses), and the page(s) on which the quoted material is found.

[2]Susan M. Ruffin, "Teaching Business Subjects To Special Needs Students," Journal of Business Education, (October, 19--), pp. 16-21.

Fig. 137. Footnote for a magazine reference

The footnote in Fig. 137 is an illustration of a **magazine** reference. It includes the author's name (first name, initial, last name), the title of the article (in quotation marks), the title of the magazine (underlined), the month and year of publication (enclosed in parentheses), and the page(s) on which the quoted material is found.

6. **Bibliography**—The references used in the report are also listed on the bibliography page. They are typed in alphabetical order according to the author's last name. If a periodical does not include the author's name, the first word in the title of the article serves as the alphabetic indicator. The first line of each reference is typed at the left margin. Second and all succeeding lines are indented five spaces from the left margin. Each reference entry is single spaced with a double space between entries.

   A. **Unbound Reports**
   The bibliography of an unbound report begins on **Line 10** (the same top margin as page one). The title "Bibliography" is centered horizontally and typed in capital letters. There is a triple space (two blank lines) after the title. Side and bottom margins remain one inch. The page number is typed on Line 4 even with the right margin.

   B. **Leftbound Reports**
   The bibliography of a leftbound report begins on **Line 10** (the same top margin as page one). The title "Bibliography" is centered horizontally and typed in capital letters. There is a triple space (two blank lines) after the title. The left margin is one and one-half inches; the right margin is one inch. The page number is typed on Line 4 even with the right margin.

   C. **Topbound Reports**
   The bibliography of a topbound report begins on **Line 13** if the report is typed on a **pica** typewriter and on **Line 16** if the report is typed on an **elite** typewriter (the same margins as page one). The title "Bibliography" is centered horizontally and typed in capital letters. There is a triple space (two blank lines) after the title. Side and bottom margins remain one inch. The page number is typed one-half inch from the bottom of the page.

BIBLIOGRAPHY

Carty, Richard. VISUAL MERCHANDISING PRINCIPLES AND PRACTICE. Bronx, NY: Milady Publishing Corporation, 19--.

Frazier, Lois E., and Moon, Harry R. GUIDE TO TRANSCRIPITION. Bronx, NY: Milady Publishing Corporation, 19--.

Frye, Marianne E.; Kline, Geraldine A.; Hubbard, Kay A.; and Moon, Harry R. MEDICAL SECRETARY-RECEPTIONIST SIMULATION PROJECT. Bronx, NY: Milady Publishing Corporation, 19--.

Mayer, Kenneth R. "Teaching Students To Become Better Postal Consumers," Business Education Forum (January, 19--), pp. 21-22.

Moon, Harry R. OFFICE PROCEDURES. Bronx, NY: Milady Publishing Corporation, 19--.

Ruffin, Susan M. "Teaching Business Subjects To Special Needs Students," Journal of Business Education (October, 19--), pp. 16-21.

Tolman, Ruth. FASHION MARKETING AND MERCHANDISING. Bronx, NY: Milady Publishing Corporation, 19--.

Fig. 138. Bibliography page

7. **Copies**—In these days of electronic copying machines, it is usually more practical (and more economical) to make machine copies of the original pages of a report that has been typed and paginated than it is to prepare carbon copies at the typewriter. The primary requirement is that all **copies** of a report be neat and readable.

PRESENTATION OF FIGURES THROUGH TABLES AND CHARTS

Tables and charts are frequently used to make reports more interesting and more informative. To be effective, tables and charts must be easy to read; and the information in them must be arranged in logical sequence.

Preparing A Typewritten Table Or Chart

Clarity and simplicity must be the primary concerns of anyone who is preparing a typewritten table or chart. Before trying to type a table or chart, it is a good plan to prepare a "dummy" table or chart in pencil on a sheet of paper. In that way, you will be able to present the material in the sequence that will emphasize the facts you are stressing in the report. Here are some additional points to remember when you are preparing a table or chart:

1. **Title**—The title of a table or chart should describe clearly what the table or chart represents. The first letter of each important word in the title may be capitalized or the entire title may be typed in caps. The entire title should be centered over the table or chart.
2. **Column Headings**—The column headings should describe specifically (in as few words as possible) what information is contained in the column. The first letters of all words in the column headings are usually typed with capital letters. The column headings should be centered over the columns they represent.

3. **Chart or Table Placement**—The table or chart should be placed in the report in such a way as to enhance the readability and clarity of the report. It is a good idea to place a table or chart as soon as possible after reference has been made to it.

MORGAN GLASS CORPORATION
Directory of Offices

Name	Title	Office Location
Bolton, John	Director of Personnel	145B
Carlton, Mildred	Dealership Divison Director	206
Conover, Wilma C.	Interviewer	144
Davidson, T. L.	Marketing Division Center	210
Grosswald, Hyman T.	Chairman of the Board	300
Hendricks, William	Secretary to J. Bolton	145A
Lewis, Helen	Chief Accountant	208
Mendez, Manual	Vice-President/Operations	304
Stein, Ann C.	Director of Public Information	110
Thomas, Helen D.	President	310
Thomas, Karl	Head/Order Department	212
Trembly, Jean	Office Administrator	200

Fig. 139. Handwritten "dummy"

MORGAN GLASS CORPORATION

Directory of Offices

Name	Title	Office Location
Bolton, John	Director of Personnel	145B
Carlton, Mildred	Dealership Division Director	206
Conover, Wilma C.	Interviewer	144
Davidson, T. L.	Marketing Division Director	210
Grosswald, Hyman T.	Chairman of the Board	300
Hendricks, William	Secretary to J. Bolton	145A
Lewis, Helen	Chief Accountant	208
Mendez, Manual	Vice-President/Operations	304
Stein, Ann C.	Director of Public Information	110
Thomas, Helen D.	President	310
Thomas, Karl	Head/Order Department	212
Trembly, Jean	Office Administrator	200

Fig. 140. Table typewritten in final form

LEGAL PAPERS AND PROCEDURES

As an office worker, you may be asked to help prepare legal papers either from a rough draft or from dictation. Among the legal papers you may be asked to help prepare are: a contract, power of attorney, affidavit, acknowledgment, or a will. While each legal document has its own requirements, there are some general procedures that are usually agreed upon by people who prepare legal papers:

1. **Margins**—Most legal documents are typed on legal size paper which is 8½ by 14 inches. The left margin on legal paper is ruled (printed) with a double line 1⅜ inches from the left edge of the paper. The right margin is ruled (printed) wih a single red line ⅜ of an inch from the right edge of the paper. Legal papers typed on legal size stationery are bound at the top in a legal back (to be explained in No. 6).

2. **Paragraphs and Spacing**—Paragraphs of legal documents are usually indented ten spaces. Either single or double spacing may be used, but double spacing is usually preferred.

3. **Erasures and Corrections**—Erasures on **key details,** such as names, amounts, and dates are forbidden in most states. If an error is discovered, the entire page must be retyped; and if the legal document has already been signed, the changes on that page must be initialed by the signers.

4. **Number of Copies**—Usually the person for whom you are preparing a legal document will indicate the number of copies to be prepared. Some companies have a standard rule about the number of copies to be prepared, such as: one original and three copies (two for distribution and one for the file). The person preparing the document should indicate on the file copy (upper right-hand corner) how the original and the other copies are distributed.

5. **Signatures and Seal**—A line for each signature should be typed. Three blank lines should be left between signatures. Immediately below each signature line, you should type the complete name of the person who will sign on that line followed by the word (Seal) or the abbreviation (L.S.).

   Examples:

. . . . (Seal)
Ellen T. Smythe
. . . . (Seal)
Harold G. Greenwood
. . . . (L.S.)
Marilyn C. Tower
. . . . (L.S.)
Otis F. Carlton

   Usually, legal documents are either notarized before a notary public, or they are signed in the presence of witnesses. Therefore two lines for the witnesses' signatures should be typed flush with the left margin with two lines between them preceded by the word "WITNESS:" typed in caps.

   Example:

WITNESS:
. . . .
. . . .

(NOTE: If you are ever asked to witness the signatures on a legal document, be sure the signatures are **actually signed** in your presence.)

6. **Legal Back**—Typed legal documents are usually bound in a legal back measuring 9 by 15½ inches. The legal back is heavier, wider, and longer than the legal document itself. The cover side provides space for an endorsement—a description of the document it contains and the names of the parties to the document.

BILL OF SALE

KNOW ALL MEN BY THESE PRESENTS:

THAT I, Louise Ellen Hunt of 3840 Glenwood Avenue, Raleigh, North Carolina, of the first part for and in consideration of the sum of Five Thousand Dollars ($5,000) lawful money of the United States, to me in hand paid, at or before the ensealing and delivery of these presents by Morgan Glass Corporation, of 4675 West Market Street, Greensboro, North Carolina, Guilford County, State of North Carolina, of the second part, the receipt whereof is hereby acknowledged, have bargained and sold, and by these presents do sell, grant and convey unto said party of the second part, its executors, administrators and assigns my design and model of handcut crystal tableware in the "Fantasia" pattern.

TO HAVE AND TO HOLD the same unto the said party of the second part, its executors, administrators and assigns forever. And I do for me and my heirs, executors, and administrators, covenant and agree, to and with the said party of the second part, to warrant and defend the sale of the aforesaid design hereby sold unto the said party of the second part, its executors, administrators and assigns, against all and every person and persons whomsoever.

IN WITNESS WHEREOF, I have hereunto set my hand and seal the tenth day of August in the year one thousand nine hundred and ________ ________.

Louise E. Hunt (L.S.)
Louise Ellen Hunt

Sealed and Delivered
in the Presence of

Karl Smith

Donald R. Rich

Fig. 141. Bill of sale typed on legal paper with printed margins

Dale T. Henson
4791 West Market Street
Greensboro, NC 27408
241-7915

To Greenberg, Carlson, and Taylor
Attorney(s) for Louise Ellen Hunt

Service of a copy of the within Bill of Sale **is hereby admitted.**
Dated, August 10, 19-- ________________

Fig. 142. Completed legal back

MINUTES

Minutes are the **official records** of meetings that show what action was taken during the meeting. Since minutes are frequently used for reference, every detail included in the minutes should be complete and accurate.

Preparing

If you are asked to take the minutes for a meeting, you should have the following information **before** the meeting begins:

- The name of the organization
- The date, place, and time of the meeting
- The agenda (or schedule of business to be covered during the meeting)

In addition, you should get a list of persons who attend the meeting so the minutes show who was present and who was absent. (Some groups ask for a motion that absent members be excused. If that is done, the minutes should show members "present" and "excused.") You should also have available the minutes of previous meetings (particularly those of the last meeting) in case they need to be consulted during the meeting. (The person taking minutes during a meeting should not leave the meeting to gather information unless the chairperson asks him/her to do so.)

Taking Minutes

As the meeting progresses, take notes about the points that you think are important and interesting. Identify each topic that is discussed and show the names of the people who participate in the discussion. Motions and resolutions, whether they are passed or not, should be recorded **word for word.** This is very important because future proceedings will be governed by the interpretation of the wording in the minutes.

Typing Minutes

The minutes of an **informal meeting** should be brief, and they should cover only the essential points of the meeting. The minutes of a **formal meeting** are typed in detail. Minutes of a meeting should include the following items:

1. The name of the group
2. The time, date, and place of the meeting and whether it is a regular or a special meeting
3. The names of the presiding officer, the secretary, and those present and those absent. (NOTE: During the meeting of a **large organization,** only names of the **members present** are recorded in order to prove that there was a **quorum**—the minimum number of members necessary in order to be able to conduct business for the group.)
4. A statement that the minutes of the previous meeting were read and that those minutes were approved, amended, or corrected
5. Reports of committees or persons who were previously assigned special responsibilities (The Treasurer's Report, for example)
6. A statement about unfinished business (from previous meetings) that was discussed and the action that was taken
7. A statement about new business that was brought up during the meeting, the discussion that took place, and the action that was taken
8. The date, time, and place of the next meeting
9. The time of adjournment
10. The signature of the person responsible for the minutes

Approving Minutes

To be officially acceptable, minutes will need to be approved (or amended or corrected) at the following meeting. If the minutes need to be **corrected** before they are approved; and if only a few words or lines are affected, lines may be drawn through the incorrect words and the proper insertions may be made above them. If more than a few words or lines are affected, lines may be drawn through the sentences or paragraphs to be corrected; and the corrections may be written on a new page. The page number of the page where the correction appears should be indicated on the original minutes.

The chairperson usually proofreads the minutes before they are distributed to the group to be sure there are no omissions or errors. The minutes should not be rewritten after they are approved by the group.

RESOLUTIONS

A **resolution** is an **official written statement that expresses the opinion, wishes, or intent of a group.** A resolution may be written to honor, to show appreciation, to indicate that action has been taken, to offer congratulations, to express regret, to commemorate, or to present a program of action.

Such introductory terms as WHEREAS, RESOLVED, and RESOLVED FURTHER are frequently used in formal resolutions. The word **resolved** is typed in italics or underlined, and it is followed by a comma. The first word **after any of the introductory terms** is capitalized.

RESOLUTION
Adopted, July 10, 19--

Whereas, Helen T. Lewis, the Chief Accountant at Morgan Glass Corporation, is a faithful, dedicated, and loyal employee; and

Whereas, She has recently been awarded the designation of Certified Public Accountant (CPA) by the State of North Carolina; and

Whereas, She received the Distinguished Business Graduate Award from her Alma Mater, Meredith College in Raleigh, North Carolina; therefore, be it

Resolved, That the Management Club at Morgan Glass Corporation expresses appreciation to Helen T. Lewis for her leadership, dedication, loyalty, and creativity on behalf of the company; and be it

Resolved, That a copy of this resolution be placed in the company reception area for all to see

John Bolton, Secretary

Ann C. Stein, Chairperson
Management Club

Fig. 143. Typed Resolution

FOR REVIEW AND DISCUSSION

1. What is the purpose of a business report?
2. Describe the steps to be taken (in logical order) when you are preparing a report.
3. Describe the seven procedures that need to be considered when you are ready to type a report in final form.
4. Describe the three procedures that should be considered when a typewritten table or chart is to be a part of a report.
5. Describe the six procedures that need to be considered when you are typing legal papers.
6. What is the purpose of minutes of a meeting?
7. What names need to be included in the minutes of a **large** organization? Why?
8. What is a resolution? For what purpose is a resolution written?

Turn to your workbook and complete Student Projects 20 and 21.

CHAPTER 14

Purchasing And Selling For The Office

OBJECTIVE

After studying Chapter 14 you will understand the procedures for purchasing and selling for the business office, and you will understand the uses of drafts and promissory notes and the meanings of some basic shipping terms.

JOB-RELATED VOCABULARY

Depleted—Completely used or exhausted in the course of doing business.

Negotiable—Transferable from one person to another so title passes to the receiving party.

f.o.b. (or FOB)—Free on board (a term used in shipping).

If a business office functions efficiently, there must be ample supplies at hand to take care of the operation of the business. As an office worker (in a small office), you may have the responsibility of dispensing office supplies as necessary, keeping an inventory of office supplies on hand, and seeing that those supplies are reordered before the existing supply is depleted.

PURCHASING IN A LARGE OFFICE

Most large companies have a stockroom where all office stationery and supplies are kept. When an office worker needs supplies, he/she completes a Stock Requisition and delivers it to the Stock Clerk in the stockroom. Either the supplies requested are given to the employee, or they are delivered to him/her at a later time by a messenger. It is also the job of the Stock Clerk to keep a running inventory of stationery and supplies on hand and to reorder materials **before** the supply is exhausted.

Purchase Requisition

When an employee needs stationery or supplies or a piece of office equipment or supplies that are not already in stock, he/she completes a Purchase Requisition for those materials. The Purchase Requisition is sent to the Purchasing Agent; and the purchasing procedure is begun for those items. A Purchase Requisition contains the following information:

1. The name, department, and telephone extension of the person making the request for the supplies.
2. The current date.
3. A brief description of the item being ordered, including the quantity needed.
4. The date on which the supplies are needed.
5. The name (or code) of the department that will use the supplies.
6. The name, department, and telephone extension of the person to whom the supplies should be delivered.

PURCHASE REQUISITION

FROM:

Name Marlene S. Samson Department Operations

Date October 10, 19-- Telephone Ext. 15 Charge to Account No. 473.01-4 (Accounting Use Only)

QUANTITY	DESCRIPTION-USE SEPARATE LINE FOR EACH ITEM	ACCOUNTING USE ONLY		
		UNIT COST	TOTAL	COST
2 reams	MGC Letterheads in stock LD			
2 boxes	No. 10 Envelopes (MGC) in stock LD			
1 box	Manila File Folders in stock LD			
9	Micro Cassettes (for Dictaphone Dictating System) Order # 877179 (box of 3)	$11.80	$35	40

Deliver To: Marlene Samson Department Operations

Telephone Ext. 15 For Use By Operations Department

Date Needed ASAP

Approved for Purchase L. C. Daniels
Purchasing Agent

Fig. 144. Purchase Requisition

Purchase Order

In most large companies the Purchasing Agent issues a numbered Purchase Order to a particular company after he/she has received a purchase request on a Purchase Requisition. A Purchase Order usually contains the following information:

1. The name and complete address of the company **placing** the order.
2. The name and complete address of the company **receiving** the order.
3. The current date.
4. A description of the merchandise being ordered, including the quantity, the catalog number, and the price.
5. The method of shipment requested.
6. The date needed.
7. The terms of payment.
8. The signature of the Purchasing Agent.

Ordinarily, copies of a Purchase Order are distributed to the following departments:

1. Receiving Department (so that the merchandise delivered can be compared to the Purchase Order)
2. Stockroom (so the Stock Clerk will know that the supplies have been ordered)
3. Purchasing Department (as a record that the supplies have been ordered)

It is important to remember that purchasing procedures vary considerably from company to company. The procedures described here are typical of those used in most large companies. The purpose of the procedures is to **control** the **purchase and distribution** of office supplies.

MORGAN GLASS CORPORATION
467 West Market Street
Greensboro, NC 27408

Purchase Order No. 8460

This Purchase Order Number must appear on all invoices and packages.

TO: Dictaphone Corporation
2610 Feberal Highway
Greensboro, NC 27408

Greensboro, NC October 11, 19--

QUANITY	CATALOG NUMBER	DESCRIPTION	PRICE
3 boxes	877179	Micro Cassettes for Dictaphone Dictating System	$35.40

Needed by ASAP

Ship Via Your Truck

Terms 2/10, Net 30

MORGAN GLASS CORPORATION

by L. C. Daniels

NOTE: Please send an acknowledgment of this order by return mail giving an approximate shipping date.

Fig. 145. Purchase Order

PURCHASING IN A SMALL COMPANY

In small companies, the purchase and distribution of stationery and supplies are handled by a member of the general office staff or by a secretary. Supplies are ordinarily ordered either by telephone or by letter. (Usually small companies don't use Purchase Requisitions or Purchase Orders.) When a member of the office staff needs supplies, he/she goes to the person who has the responsibility for distributing supplies and requests the supplies needed. (The person who distributes supplies should keep a simple, accurate record of supplies on hand and supplies dispersed so supplies can be reordered before they run out.) When supplies are getting low, it would be that employee's responsibility to reorder.

Ordering By Telephone

If an order for supplies is placed by telephone, it is extremely important to make a list of items being ordered to include the following:

1. Name of item, quantity being ordered, catalog number, price
2. Name and telephone number of the company from whom the items are being ordered
3. The date the items are needed
4. The method of shipment you desire

When you have given the entire order and the name and address of your company to the clerk in the other company's Order Department, ask him/her to repeat it so you can check to be sure all the details of the order are correct. Finally, keep the sheet on which you write the details of the order so you can check the shipment you receive with the order you placed.

Ordering By Letter

When you place an order by letter, you would, of course, use the company letterhead. The letter (see Fig. 146) should contain the following details:

1. The current date
2. The name of the item being ordered, quantity ordered, catalog number (if known), and price
3. The method of payment
4. The method of shipment
5. The date by which the items are needed

The copy of the letter can be used to check the shipment you receive with the order you placed.

Whether you place an order by telephone or by letter, it is a good idea to "shop around" for the best price consistent with quality merchandise and service. This procedure involves contacting several firms that handle the materials you need to order to find out which one can quote you the best price. Keep in mind that quantity, delivery time, and credit terms (along with quality merchandise and good service) can make a difference in what is a "good buy."

The purpose of standardized order and distribution procedures for a small company is the same as for large companies: To control the **purchase and distribution** of office supplies.

SELLING FOR THE OFFICE

Since the basic purpose of any business in a free-enterprise system is the purchase and sale of goods to make a profit, it is essential that every employee of a business think in terms of **sales** and **profits.**

In small companies particularly, the members of the general office staff will be involved with company sales by taking telephone orders, filling orders sent to the company by mail, and by servicing all orders. For that reason, each employee needs to be prepared to meet his/her responsibilities. Here are some suggestions:

1. Study your company's catalog and price list so you will know what they offer to buyers.

MORGAN GLASS CORPORATION
4675 West Market Street
Greensboro, NC 27408-1925

November 14, 19--

Dictaphone Corporation
2610 Federal Highway
Greensboro, NC 27408

Gentlemen:

Please have your installer deliver the following items, described in your current catalog:

2	3892	DCX III Dictaphone Transcribers	$1,390.00
2	3251	Dictamite MX	650.00
2 boxes	877179	Micro Cassettes (for Dictamite)	23.60
			$2,063.60

Our Purchase Order No. 8601 is attached. Please include this number on all papers referring to this order.

We would like to have this equipment as soon as possible, because we have just opened a new office.

Sincerely yours,

MORGAN GLASS CORPORATION

L. C. Daniels

Lawrence C. Daniels
Purchasing Agent

em

Enclosure

Fig. 146. Order letter

2. Learn all you can about your company's products and services and how they are sold.
3. Learn all you can about the customers to whom your company sells. Try to understand each customer's personality, his/her needs, likes, and dislikes.
4. Have a copy of the company catalog, price list, and order blank close by for telephone orders, so you will be "ready for action" when an order is telephoned to you.
5. Always double check every detail of **every** order so the order can be completed accurately and quickly.

Remember: Quality merchandise and prompt, courteous service are the framework on which good business relationships are built.

INSTRUMENTS OF CREDIT

Most firms that buy materials on open account can pay the invoice for the materials within the selling company's regular billing cycle (usually 30 days from shipment). For those companies that are not able to pay within the regular billing cycle, the use of a draft or a promissory note is rather common.

Drafts

A draft is an unconditional **order** in writing by one person to another. It is signed by the person giving it, and directs the person to whom it is addressed to pay on demand or at a fixed or determinable future time a sum of money.

Bank Draft—A bank draft is really a bank check drawn on funds the bank has on deposit in another bank. To purchase a bank draft, the buyer gives the bank an amount equal to the amount of the desired draft plus a service charge.

Commercial Draft—A commercial draft is a demand by one party (drawer) for payment by another party (drawee) to a third party (payee—usually a bank). The commonly used commercial drafts are the following:

Sight Draft—A demand for payment of a specific amount of money on sight of the draft. (A sight draft must be accepted by the drawee before it becomes a promise to pay.)

March 18, 19-- No. 29

At Sight

Pay to the order of Morgan Glass Corporation $3000.00

Three Thousand---Dollars

To: Howard Hotel/Restaurant Supply Company
Nashville, TN

Fig. 147. Sight draft

Time Draft—A demand for payment at a fixed future time (30 days, 90 days, 6 months, 1 year from the date of the draft). (A time draft must also be accepted before it becomes a promise to pay.)

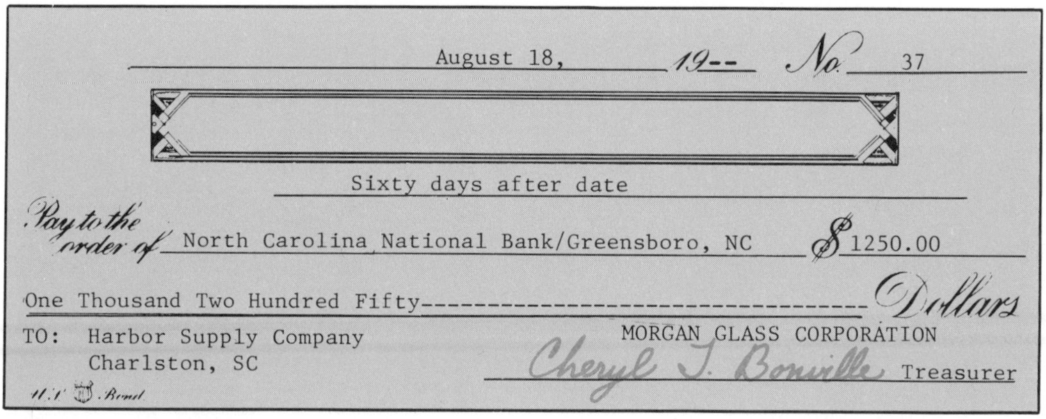

August 18, 19-- No. 37

Sixty days after date

Pay to the order of North Carolina National Bank/Greensboro, NC $1250.00

One Thousand Two Hundred Fifty---------------------------------- Dollars

TO: Harbor Supply Company
Charlston, SC

MORGAN GLASS CORPORATION
Cheryl T. Bonville Treasurer

Fig. 148. Time draft

Trade Acceptance—A demand for payment limited to transactions arising from the purchase and shipment of goods. When a trade acceptance is accompanied by an order bill of lading, a carrier will not release a shipment of merchandise to the purchaser until the purchaser signs the trade acceptance. The trade acceptance is then presented for payment on its maturity date. (A trade acceptance must always be accompanied by a bill for goods sold.)

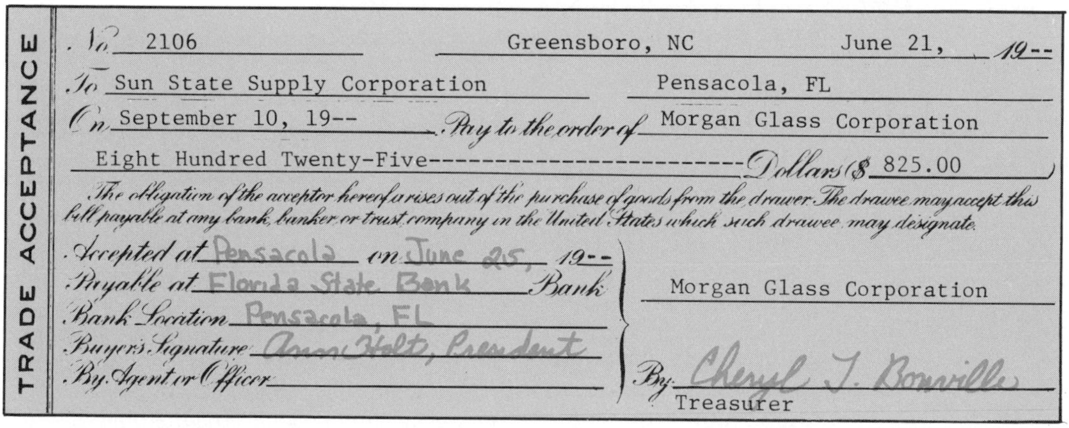

TRADE ACCEPTANCE

No. 2106 Greensboro, NC June 21, 19--

To Sun State Supply Corporation Pensacola, FL

On September 10, 19-- Pay to the order of Morgan Glass Corporation

Eight Hundred Twenty-Five------------------------ Dollars ($ 825.00)

The obligation of the acceptor hereof arises out of the purchase of goods from the drawer. The drawee may accept this bill payable at any bank, banker or trust company in the United States which such drawee may designate.

Accepted at Pensacola on June 25, 19--
Payable at Florida State Bank Bank
Bank Location Pensacola, FL
Buyer's Signature Ann Holt, President
By Agent or Officer

Morgan Glass Corporation
By: Cheryl T. Bonville
Treasurer

Fig. 149. Trade acceptance

Promissory Note

A promissory note is an unconditional **promise** in writing to pay a specified sum of money at a fixed or determinable future time. The person to whom a promissory note is made is called the **payee.** The person who signs a promissory note is called the **maker.** A promissory note is negotiable, and it may be transferred from one person to another if it contains the following:

1. Date
2. Unconditional promise to pay
3. Sum of money expressed in both figures and words
4. Due at a fixed or determinable future time
5. Payable to the bearer of the note or his/her order
6. Must be in writing
7. Rate of interest stated (if the note is interest bearing)
8. Signature of the maker

$ 10,000.00 December 10, 19--

Ninety days---------------------- after date we promise to pay to

the order of Morgan Glass Corporation

Ten Thousand-- Dollars

at North Carolina National Bank, Greensboro, NC

Value received Harper Restaurant Supply Company

No. 106 Due March 10, 19-- J. L. Harper President

AD 41

Fig. 150. Promissory note

SHIPPING TERMS

Anyone who handles orders and shipments for a company needs to be aware of some key shipping terms in order to handle orders correctly.

f.o.b. Destination

The **seller** agrees to pay all shipping charges to get the merchandise to the buyer.

Example: Morgan Glass Corp. in Greensboro, NC orders 70,000 catalogs from Vicking Press in Minneapolis, MN. The shipping terms are **f.o.b. destination.** Therefore, **Vicking Press will pay** to get the catalogs from their dock in Minneapolis to the Morgan Glass Corporation warehouse in Greensboro, NC.

f.o.b. Shipping Point

The seller agrees to pay to get the merchandise **to the shipper designated by the buyer.** From that point on, the buyer pays the shipping charges. These terms usually mean that the buyer will pay the entire shipping costs since the shipper usually picks up the merchandise at the seller's warehouse dock.

Collect

The buyer agrees to pay the amount of the invoice for the merchandise plus shipping charges before he/she takes delivery of the shipment. Only a limited number of companies will ship merchandise "collect."

Net 30 or Net 60

The net amount of the invoice (cost of merchandise plus shipping charges less a discount—if one applies) must be paid by 30 or 60 days after the shipping date.

FOR REVIEW AND DISCUSSION

1. Describe the usual procedures for purchasing and dispersing office stationery and supplies in a large office.
2. Describe the function of the Purchase Requisition and the Purchase Order.
3. Describe the usual procedures for purchasing and dispersing office stationery and supplies in a small office.
4. Explain the information that must be had by members of the general office staff of a small company who will be involved with sales.
5. Explain the function of the following instruments of credit: Bank Draft, Sight Draft, Time Draft, Trade Acceptance, and Promissory Note.
6. Explain the following shipping terms: f.o.b. destination, f.o.b. shipping point, collect, net 30.

Turn to your workbook and complete Student Project 22.

CHAPTER 15

The Electronic Calculator

OBJECTIVE

After studying Chapter 15, you will understand how electronic calculators operate and you will understand some of the features electronic calculators frequently possess, including:

- The numeric keyboard to:
  - Add
  - Subtract
  - Multiply
  - Divide
- Decimal point selector
- Subtotals
- Correction techniques
- Repeat adding and subtracting
- Memory register

JOB-RELATED VOCABULARY

Calculator—An electronic (or mechanical) device for performing mathematical calculations automatically.

Vertical—Perpendicular to the plane of the horizon.

Horizontal—Parallel to the horizon or to a base line.

Visual Display—Lighted numbers showing the answers to problems performed on an electronic calculator.

Printing Calculator—A calculator on which answers to problems are printed on a paper tape.

Accumulated—Collected—as in the accumulated (or collected) subtotals of several problems.

Clear—To remove—as to remove (or clear) previous entries from a calculator.

Memory Register—The part of a calculator that retains (or "remembers" or stores) previously entered figures or calculations.

A recent study of office operations shows that the electronic calculator is one of the most popular office machines being used by members of management support staffs (secretarial and clerical workers). In order to perform job functions productively and efficiently, every office worker should be able to perform basic functions on an electronic calculator by using the "touch" method without looking at the keyboard.

There are many different types of calculators with a wide variety of features. However, most calculators have basic standard features that are similar. Before you begin calculating, you must determine how to turn on the calculator you will be using and how to clear the calculator of all previous entries. (Some calculators clear automatically when they are turned on. Others have a separate key to clear an amount entered on the keyboard and another key to clear an amount stored in the memory.)

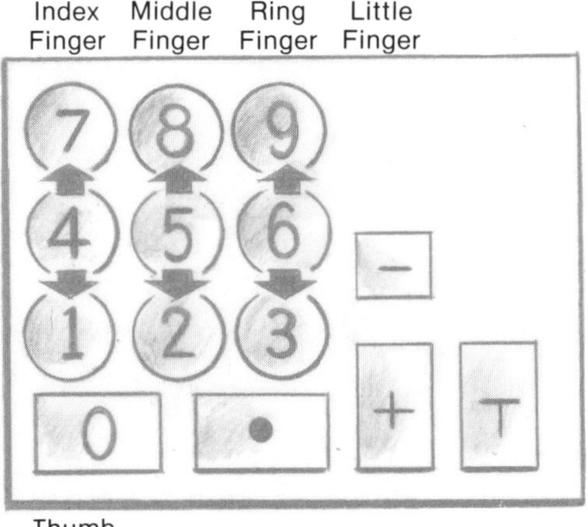

Fig. 151. Keyboard of an electronic calculator

Operating The Numeric Keyboard To Add

The keyboards of **most** electronic calculators are arranged similar to the keyboard shown in Fig. 151. (However, variations on this arrangement do exist.) The keys on the first vertical row (the row to the **far** left of the keyboard) are operated with the **index finger** on the right hand. The center row of (vertical) keys is operated with the **middle finger,** and the row of (vertical) keys on the far right of the keyboard is operated with the **ring finger** (of the right hand). The horizontal row of keys in the center of the keyboard (the 4, 5, and 6 keys) are considered the "home" position. Keep your fingers on those keys and reach for the other keys by moving the appropriate finger up or down. After you have pressed (or tapped) a number, always return that finger to its home position before you enter the next number. When the decimal key is located under the far right [vertical] row of keys, it is operated with the **ring finger.** When the decimal key is located under the middle (vertical) row of keys, it is operated by the **middle finger.** The plus, minus, and total keys are operated by the **little finger** on the right hand. (Sometimes the plus key is located under the far right (vertical) row of keys. In that situation, the plus key is operated by the **ring finger**.)

Keys on an electronic calculator should be operated with a light "tapping" motion.

$$\begin{array}{r} 472 \\ +\ 386 \\ \hline =\ 858 \end{array}$$

To keyboard the preceding problem, an operator "taps" the 4 and the 7 keys with the index finger, the 2 key with the middle finger, and the plus key with the little finger. Next, the operator taps the 3 key with the ring finger, the 8 key with the middle finger, the 6 key with the ring finger, and the plus and the total keys with the little finger. (Common symbols on the total key are *, T, and =.) The total (858) will appear in the lighted display or on a printed tape (or both).

Fig. 152. Total shown in lighted display

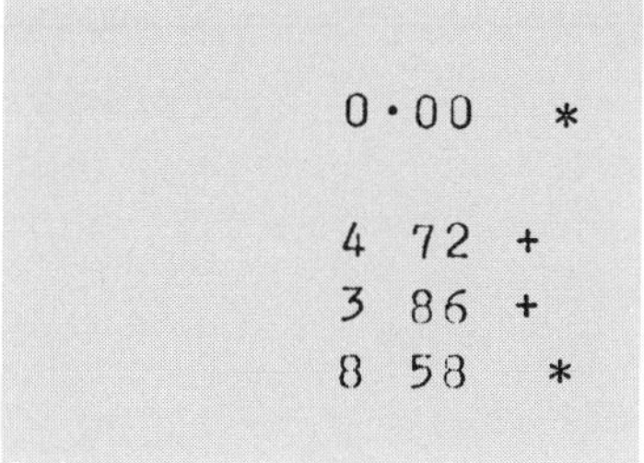

Fig. 153. Total shown on a printed tape

The Decimal Point Selector

Most electronic calculators are equipped with an automatic decimal point selector which can be set to the number of decimal places desired (or to no decimal places). On some calculators, the add mode (or +) automatically provides two decimal places for every amount entered. Still other calculators have a DS (decimal selector) Key. To select a decimal setting on a calculator equipped with a DS Key, depress that key, and then enter the desired number of decimal places on the numeric keyboard. (For example, if three decimal places are needed, tap the number three.) Then proceed with the calculation, and the decimal point will appear in the correct place. Be sure to study carefully the machine you are using so you will understand which procedure to use.

Subtracting With An Electronic Calculator

The procedure for subtracting on an electronic calculator is very similar to the procedure for adding.

$$\begin{array}{rr} & 647.28 \\ - & 106.29 \\ \hline = & 540.99 \end{array}$$

On most desk calculators, the preceding problem is entered as follows: (Be sure to set the decimal point selector on two.) First, tap 6, 4, 7, 2, 8, plus (or add); now tap 1, 0, 6, 2, 9, minus (or subtract). (On some **small calculators,** an operator enters amounts exactly as they are read, so you would enter the minus or subtract key **before** you enter the last set of digits.) Now tap the total key, and the correct answer (540.99) should be showing in lighted display and/or on a printed tape.

An electronic calculator will display an answer in a negative (or credit) amount by showing a minus sign on the display and/or tape. If a negative answer appears, be sure to include the minus sign when you record your answer.

CAUTION: Some electronic calculators include an **algebraic** minus key (or a change-sign key) along with the regular minus (or subtract) key. The algebraic minus key **sometimes** shows the minus sign in parentheses (−), and this key is used to reverse negative amounts to their positive equivalents (or vice versa). Do not use this key for subtraction problems.

Finding Subtotals

If you are using a calculator with a visual display, the amount shown after each entry is a subtotal. If you are using a printing calculator that does not have a visual display, tap the subtotal key each time you want a subtotal (after a minimum of two numbers have been entered).

Some printing calculators do not have a subtotal key. To get a subtotal on those calculators, tap the total key. Doing this **totals the numbers** to that point and **clears the machine.** Therefore, to continue calculating, you must **re-enter the subtotal** before you proceed with the calculation. (Remember, though, when you are using a printing calculator **with a subtotal key,** it is **not necessary** to re-enter the subtotal because the **subtotal key does not clear the machine.**) The following illustration shows a calculator tape with subtotals from a machine that **does not** have a subtotal key. (The subtotals on the tape have been marked with the letter "s.")

```
      0·00  *

    432·14  +
    278·10  +
    710·24  *(s)

    710·24  +
    791·86  +
  1,502·10  *(s)

  1,502·10  +
    301·77  +
  1,803·87  *(T)
```

Fig. 154. Subtotals on a tape from a calculator without a subtotal key

Correcting Errors In Entering Amounts

To remove an amount that has been entered on the keyboard but **not yet calculated** (added, subtracted, multiplied, or divided) push the **clear (C)** or the **Clear Entry (CE)** key; then enter the correct amount and continue calculating.

Some machines have a backspace key (—►) which removes single digits without removing the entire amount.

On some display calculators an E or the word ERROR will appear in the display if two keys are depressed at the same time. If this situation occurs, depress the clear or clear entry key, and re-enter the amount.

If you discover an error **after** pushing the add key, cancel the entry by **subtracting** the same amount. If you discover an error **after** pushing the subtract key, cancel the entry by **adding** the same amount.

Repeat Adding and Subtracting

```
27
27
27
38
38
12
12
──
```

Notice in the preceding problem that each amount is to be added more than once. When you are using most **display** calculators, it is not necessary to re-enter the same amount several times. (Most printing calculators also have an automatic repeat adding feature.) Simply enter the amount once, then tap the **add** key for the number of times you want to add the number. To complete the preceding problem, enter 27; and tap the add key three times. Enter 38, and tap the add key two times; then enter 12 and tap the add key twice. After each succeeding tap, the accumulated subtotal will be displayed. The last amount shown will be the total (181).

The same procedure that applies to repeat addition also applies to repeat subtraction. The only difference is that you tap the **subtraction key** as many times as you wish to subtract an amount.

$4,687.50
– 127.50
– 127.50
– 127.50
– 35.00
– 35.00
– 21.10
– 21.10

To complete the preceding problem, enter $4,687.50 and tap the **add** key once. Enter $127.50 and tap the **subtract** key three times. Enter $35.00 and tap the subtract key twice. Enter $21.10 and tap the subtract key twice. The last amount showing in the display is the final total ($4,192.80).

On **small** display calculators, it is usually necessary to enter and add or subtract each amount separately.

Multiplying

On most electronic calculators, multiplication problems are entered **exactly as they are read.**

46
× 15

To enter the preceding problem, which is read "forty-six times fifteen equals":

Tap 46
Tap the multiplication (×) key
Tap 15
Tap the equals (=) key
The answer (690) should appear in the display and/or on the printed tape.

It is not necessary to clear the calculator after each multiplication. The calculator clears automatically when the operator enters the next amount.

9 × 5 × 6 × 8 =

The preceding problem shows multiple factors to be multiplied. Enter the multiplication exactly as you read it. Each time you tap the multiplication key, the product is obtained and included as a factor in the continued multiplication. For the problem shown above, the **display** would show the following:

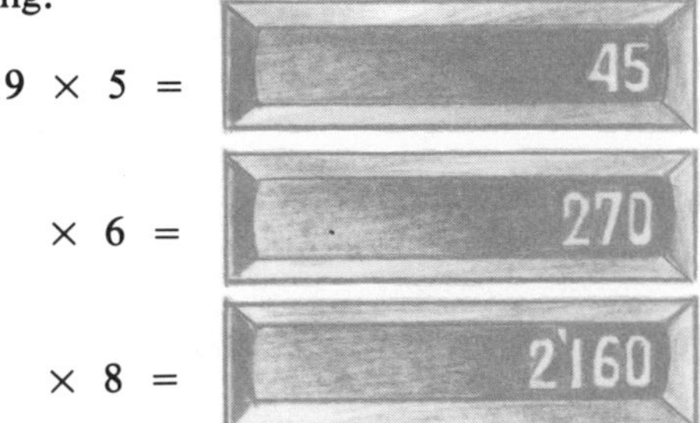

Fig. 155. Displays for multiplication problem

A **printed tape** of the problem shown above would look like this:

```
       0·  CA
       9·  x
       5·  =↑
   45·00

      45·  x
       6·  =↑
  270·00

     270·  x
       8·  =↑
2,160·00
```

Fig. 156. Printed tape for multiplication problem

Dividing

Enter division problems on the calculator **as they are read.** To enter the problem 1675 ÷ 25:

Tap 1675
Tap the division (÷) key
Tap 25
Tap the equals (=) key

The total showing in the display and/or on the printed tape should be 67.

After regular division problems, it is not necessary to clear the calculator. Entering the next division problem automatically clears previous entries.

Many calculators have a constant feature that automatically retains any amount entered after the divide key (÷) is depressed. To divide by a constant factor on a machine with this feature, enter the first problem as it is read. Thereafter, enter only the dividend and tap the equals key. The divisor will be held as a constant until you enter a new divisor.

Dividend		Divisor
6,428	÷	21
4,127	÷	21
3,901	÷	21

To complete the preceding problem when you are using a calculator **with the constant feature:**

Tap 6428
Tap the divide (÷) key
Tap 21
Tap the equals (=) key
Tap 4127
Tap the equals key
Tap 3901
Tap the equals key

Each time you tap the equals key, the correct quotients (306, 196, 185) will appear in the display and/or on a printed tape.

The Memory Register

Many electronic calculators have a **memory register.** Some calculators even have more than one memory register, and numbers or Roman numerals are used to designate keys for the different memory registers. The following symbols are frequently used to designate keys associated with memory register:

CM	Clear Memory
M* or *M	Memory Total and Clear
M M	Results Keys
RM MR RCL M	Memory Recall (subtotal)
STR STO M=	Store Key

If a display calculator does not have an automatic repeat add feature, the memory feature can be used for repeat adding.

15
15
15
27
27

The preceding problem could be added by using the memory feature as follows:

Tap 15
Tap M+ M+ M+
Tap 27
Tap M+ M+
Tap M* (Memory Total)

The total amount recalled from the memory should be 99.

When you have a series of problems in which the same figure is added and subtracted several times, you can also use the memory feature. In the following problems 1575 is repeated.

1575	1575	1575	1575
486	2101	− 387	− 218

To complete the preceding problems using the memory feature:

Tap 1575
Tap Store Key
Tap MR+ 486+*
Tap MR+ 2101+*
Tap MR+ 387−*
Tap MR+ 218−*

To remove a constant, clear the memory or enter another figure as a constant.

Remember, not every calculator is equipped to solve the foregoing problem using the memory register. If the calculator you are using is not so equipped, treat the problems as regular additions and subtractions.

Some calculators have an **automatic** constant which does not need to be activated. This feature retains any amount entered with the plus (+) or minus (−) keys. To work the preceding problems on a calculator with an automatic constant:

Tap 1575 +
Tap 486 + (2061 should show in display)
Tap − (to restore constant)
Tap 2101 + (3676 should show in display)
Tap − (to restore constant)
Tap 387 − (1188 should show in display)
Tap + (to restore constant)
Tap 218 − (1357 should show in display)

The discussion in this chapter has been designed to acquaint you with the basic operations that electronic calculators perform and the capabilities they possess.

FOR REVIEW AND DISCUSSION

1. What are the first steps an operator should take when he/she begins working with an electronic calculator?
2. Why is it important for an operator to learn the "touch" method of calculator operation?
3. What are the "home" keys on the calculator keyboard?
4. What is the correct stroking technique when using an electronic calculator?
5. What is the function of a decimal point selector? a DS Key? How does a DS Key work?
6. How does the algebraic minus key (or change-sign key) differ from the subtract key?
7. How does an operator remove an amount entered on a calculator keyboard but not yet manipulated by the calculator? How does an operator remove an amount that has been added? subtracted?
8. How does an operator repeat add or repeat subtract on an electronic calculator?
9. Explain the sequence for entering a multiplication problem or a division problem in an electronic calculator.
10. How does an "automatic constant" feature on an electronic calculator work?

Turn to your workbook and complete Student Project 23.

CHAPTER 16

Reprographics

OBJECTIVE

After studying Chapter 16 you will understand the functions of the following duplicating processes:

- Direct duplicating
- Stencil duplicating
- Offset duplicating
- Photocopy duplicating

You will also understand how to choose the best duplicating process for the job to be done, and how to collate materials that have been duplicated.

JOB-RELATED VOCABULARY

Collate—Assemble pages in proper order and fasten them into sets.

Criteria—The standards on which judgment about something may be based.

Eject—Send out.

Master—A device used to produce a printed page by means of carbon (dye) transfer in the direct duplicating process.

Porous Fibers—Fibers on a stencil that allow liquid (ink) to pass through.

Burnishing Tool—A device for making a stencil shiny by rubbing, in order to close up the porous fibers when an error has been made.

Original—That material (such as written or drawn material) from which a copy can be made.

Reprographics—All procedures and machines involved in reproducing printed material.

The successful communication of business facts and statistics requires literally billions of duplicate copies each year. The duplicating process that should be used will depend upon what is to be duplicated, how it will be used, and when it will be needed. In this chapter you will study direct, stencil, offset, and photocopy (contact) duplicating. In addition, you will consider the criteria that determine which of the duplicating methods should be used.

Large companies frequently have separate duplicating departments. If you have materials to be duplicated, you send those materials (along with a master or stencil) to the duplicating department. It is also necessary to supply the duplicating department with complete details of what is needed. The duplicating department makes the copies, collates them (if necessary), and returns the finished work to you. In a small office, however, you may be responsible for the entire duplicating pro cess.

DIRECT DUPLICATING PROCESS

Fig. 157. Direct process duplicator

The direct duplicating process produces copies by means of a master prepared with direct-process carbon paper. The dye from the carbon paper is transferred to the back of the master as a result of pressure from a typewriter key or from a pen (used for drawing or tracing). When the master is placed on the duplicating machine, the carbon side is up so the carbon will come in contact with sheets of fluid-moistened paper. As the fluid-moistened paper passes through the duplicating machine under pressure, it actually picks up a small deposit of the carbon from the master.

Copies produced in purple are easiest to read, but copies can also be produced in blue, green, red, and black. Masters can be saved and reused up to 400 copies if they are carefully prepared.

The direct duplicating process, also called the liquid, fluid, or spirit process, is widely used for inside-office distribution because it is a very economical method of duplicating.

STENCIL DUPLICATING PROCESS

Fig. 158. The stencil duplicator

The stencil duplicating process produces copies by means of a stencil and an inked drum. A stencil is a piece of thin tissue that is coated with a waxy substance that is impervious to ink. When the stencil is drawn, written, or typed, the wax coating is pushed aside and the porous fibers are exposed. The stencil is placed on the inked drum of the duplicating machine. When the paper comes in contact with the drum under pressure, the ink flows through the porous fibers onto the paper to make the copy.

Fig. 159. Stencil duplicating process

Stencils can be saved and reused, but they must be cleaned (of ink) before they are stored. Most stencils can be expected to produce five thousand copies. High-quality stencils can produce up to ten thousand copies.

Different color inks can be used with stencils; and by using a special multicolor ink pad, as many as five colors can be reproduced at the same time.

ELECTRONIC STENCIL OR MASTER MAKERS

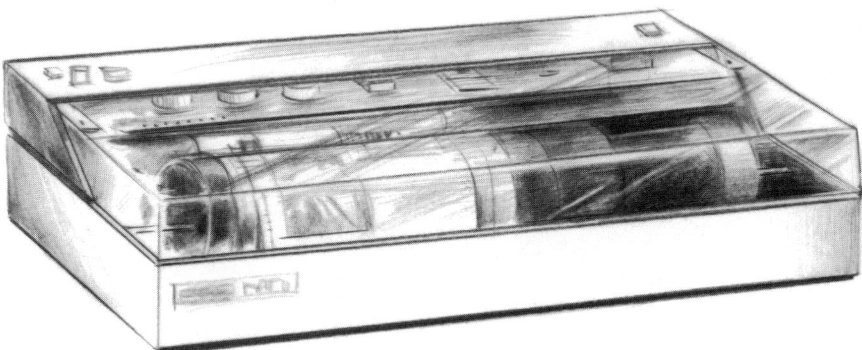

Fig. 160. Electronic stencil/master maker

Many offices now have electronic machines that will make offset masters, stencils, and fluid masters from typewritten, printed, drawn, or handwritten copy. The original copy is wrapped around one cylinder of the machine; and the offset master, stencil, or fluid master is wrapped around a different cylinder. When the machine is started, both cylinders revolve. A beam of light scans the original copy and "burns" the image picked up from that copy into the stencil or master. A stencil or master maker produces a master or stencil much faster than you could type one manually. A stencil or master maker also eliminates the need to proofread the finished master or stencil, because the copy (from which the master or stencil is made) is proofread before it is put on the stencil or master maker.

Fig. 161. Offset duplicator

OFFSET AND PHOTOCOPYING PROCESSES

The offset duplicator is used extensively for catalogs, bulletins, booklets, and company newspapers. The offset duplicator is especially useful for jobs requiring a fine quality of reproduction. The offset duplicator can reproduce thousands of copies of materials that have been typed, drawn, or traced directly on a master sheet or plate with grease-base ribbon or ink. Photographs, charts, diagrams, and previously printed matter may be reproduced by pasting the materials on a layout sheet and photographing them. The photo image is then reproduced on an offset plate or master.

Offset masters may be plastic, paper, or metal plate. Usually paper masters are used for short runs and plastic masters for medium runs. Metal plates are used for long runs or for printing that requires extremely high quality. Like direct process masters (paper), offset masters (sometimes of an entire printed page) may be made by using one of several office copiers. Different color inks are usable with offset masters and copies may be printed in several colors. However, to print in several colors requires a separate master for each color and a separate run through the press.

Typing An Offset Master

In many ways, typing an offset master is easier than typing a stencil or a direct-process master. The only special requirement is a typewriter ribbon with a grease-base ink. (In fact, an offset ribbon can be used for all office typing.) A plastic-backed ribbon usually produces the sharpest image. A fiber ribbon that has been used repeatedly may not reproduce well. Care must be taken when typing the master that the paper-bail rolls on the typewriter do not ride over the area that is to be reproduced. It is important, too, to hold the master along the edges because fingerprints on the printing surface will reproduce. Some authorities suggest that it is a good idea to allow about an hour between typing of the master and the printing to permit the image to set.

Here are some suggestions for making corrections on an offset master:

1. Erase an error with a special eraser for correcting offset masters. (Any soft, nongritty eraser will also work.) Use only a few **light** erasing strokes. Be sure to clean the eraser by rubbing it on a clean paper after **each erasing stroke** to prevent the ink on the eraser from rubbing into the surface of the master. (The "shadow" that remains after the error has been erased will not reproduce.)
2. Type the correction on the spot you have just erased, using a normal touch. (Remember, a second correction cannot be made on the same spot.)
3. If it is necessary to remove a master from the typewriter before you have finished typing it, put a plain sheet of white paper over it before you reinsert the master to prevent the typewriter roller from smudging the type.

Offset masters may be stored and rerun if they are properly cleaned. Clean masters with a cotton pad moistened with water. Rub the masters gently to remove any traces of ink or solution. When the master has been cleaned, it should be sprayed with a thin coating of preservative. After the preservative has dried, the master should be placed in a plain (non-oily) paper folder and stored in a file drawer.

Many offset machines use a photographed master (plate) that is made from an ordinary typewritten or printed page or from a drawing.

Fig. 162. Photocopy machine

Photocopying (Or Contact) Process

Sometimes an exact (facsimile) copy is needed. In those instances, photocopying machines are used. One big advantage of photocopying machines is the ease with which copies can be made. Another advantage is that originals can remain safe in the office while exact copies can be sent to people who have need for them. There are a great many copying machines used in business offices today. Copiers are classified as pass-through or flat-bed-type copiers. With a pass-through copier, the original is inserted in an opening in the copier. Rollers inside the copier draw the original through the copier and eject both the original and the copy.

With a flat-bed copier, the original is placed on a sheet of glass (material to be copied facing down) on the top of the copier. The original remains on the glass while it is being copied. A flat-bed copier permits copying the pages of a bound book by placing the open book face down on the glass.

Photocopy machines produce copies through a variety of processes. The processes you will use most frequently in an office are the **electrostatic** and the **infrared** processes.

Electrostatic Process

Electrostatic copiers are the ones most frequently used in business offices. Many people call this type of copier a "Xerox" because that is the brand name of a well-known manufacturer of electrostatic copiers. Electrostatic copiers produce dark copy that looks very much like the original. Corrections on the original, if they are made carefully, will not show on a copy made by the electrostatic process. (Liquid correction fluid works well for making corrections on materials to be copied by the electrostatic process.)

Infrared Process

The infrared process requires special paper, and the material to be copied (the original) must contain carbon. Therefore, images made with ballpoint pens will not reproduce with this process; and some colors (particularly red, blue, and green) will not reproduce. Fluid masters, offset masters, and transparency masters can be prepared on an infrared copier. An infrared copier, sometimes called a "Thermofax," can make copies in as little as five seconds.

Duplicating Costs

If the method of preparing the master is similar, if similar methods of purchasing supplies and paper are used, and if the length of the run is about the same, the direct duplicating method is the least expensive. The stencil method is the next, and the photocopy and offset methods are the most expensive methods of duplicating.

CHOOSING A DUPLICATING PROCESS

What is to be copied, the quality of copy required, the number of copies required, the speed with which the copies are needed, and the cost per copy help determine which duplicating process should be used. It is important to keep in mind, too, that duplicating equipment is being improved constantly. Therefore, before purchasing equipment, it is important to study your needs carefully to determine what equipment will meet them best.

USING THE PROPER COPYING OR DUPLICATING PROCESS

Process	Used primarily for
Electrostatic copier	Quick copies; few copies; excellent quality
Infrared copier	Quick copies; few copies; quality not important
Offset duplicator	Many copies; excellent quality
Stencil	Many copies; good quality; moderate cost
Fluid	Quick copies; low cost; quality not important

Certain things, such as money, postage stamps, driver's licenses, automobile registrations, U.S. passports, and copyrighted material (except under carefully controlled conditions), must not be copied.

COLLATING

A copy job (or a printing job) that has two or more pages requires collating (assembling pages in proper order and fastening them into sets). To collate **small amounts** of material, place the copies of each page (in correct order) in separate stacks on a table. Lift the top page from each stack until you have assembled a complete set. Fasten complete sets together by stapling the pages in the upper left-hand corner or by surrounding each complete set with a paper band.

When **large amounts** of material need to be collated, mechanical collating machines can be used. The pages of a job to be collated are stacked in separate compartments of a collator. On each stack rests a rubber-tipped metal rod that pushes a single page out of each compartment as a foot control is depressed (or as a preset timing switch is automatically activated). The extending pages are gathered in sets and crisscrossed for stapling or binding when the collating has been completed.

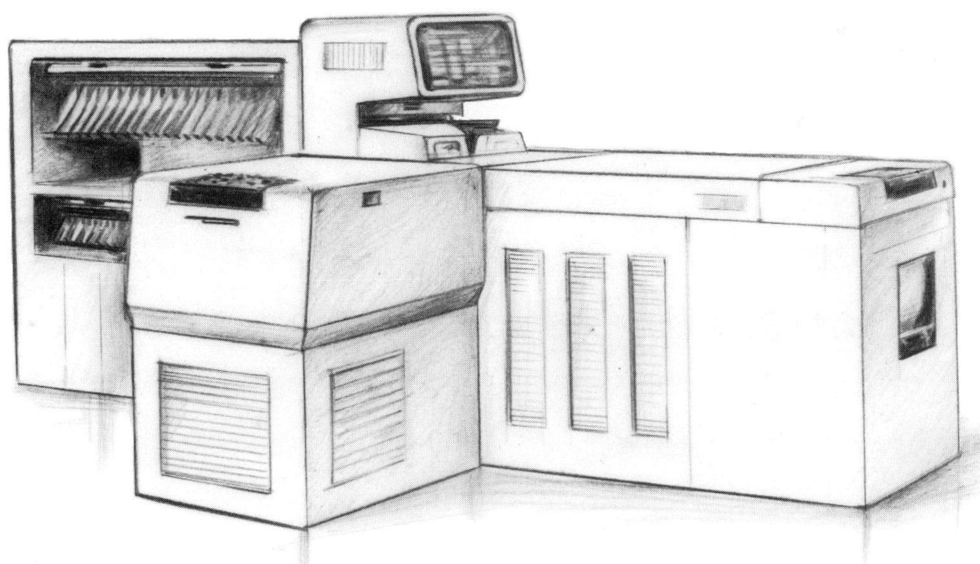

Fig. 163. Collator attached to a copying machine

Some copying machines are equipped with collators that mechanically gather pages together and bind them into sets.

FOR REVIEW AND DISCUSSION

1. Explain how the direct duplicating process works.
2. Explain how the stencil duplicating process works.
3. What is an electronic stencil or master maker? How does it work? What are the advantages of using an electronic stencil or master maker?
4. Explain the advantages of the photocopying process.
5. What factors determine the type of duplicating process that should be used?
6. Describe the types of materials that should not be duplicated using the photocopying process.
7. What are the two photocopying processes used most frequently in business offices?
8. What is collating? How should you collate a **small** amount of material? a **large** amount of material?

Turn to your workbook and complete Student Project 24.

CHAPTER 17

Planning Meetings And Conferences

OBJECTIVE

After studying Chapter 17 you will understand what is required to plan and produce smooth-running business meetings and conferences. You will be particularly aware of:

- Initial planning
- Meeting requirements
- Follow-up reports and letters
- Meeting evaluation

JOB-RELATED VOCABULARY

Meeting—A group of people coming together to hear speakers and view audio-visual presentations.

Conference—A group of people coming together to exchange views and receive reports.

Facilities—The meeting rooms, food service setup, lighting facilities, guest-room accommodations, and audio-visual equipment available at a hotel or convention center.

Confirmation—A written statement describing arrangements that have been made for a meeting, a conference, or a banquet.

Verbatim Notes—A word-for-word statement describing exactly what was said during a meeting or a conference.

Resolutions—Formal expressions of opinion, of will, or of intent voted by an official group.

More and more companies are holding meetings and conferences of various types. Such meetings and conferences help companies to plan for growth and development by bringing together carefully chosen experts who share their knowledge and pool their talents. For that reason, these meetings and conferences serve a very useful management function. The success of such meetings depends very much upon having a responsible person to plan and check the details from the time the decision is made to hold the meeting or conference until every detail resulting from the meetings has been taken care of. That person could be YOU! For that reason, study the following information carefully.

INITIAL PLANNING

The keys to the success of a meeting or conference are careful, detailed planning and a selection of a competent person to take primary responsibility for the success of the meetings **from an arrangements point of view.** The success of the overall meeting will depend, of course, on the program. Here are some suggestions that will help you to plan a successful meeting or conference:

1. As soon as the date(s) for the meeting or conference has (have) been set, contact the hotel or conference center where the meeting will be held. Hotels and conference centers that cater to meetings and conferences are very busy. In fact, some of them are completely booked a year or more in advance! To get the dates your company wants, book your meetings as far in advance as possible. For most meetings, allow **at least** six months. For large meetings and conferences, bookings should be made two or three years in advance.
2. Here is a list of the information that you will need to give the director of sales (at a hotel) or the director (at a conference center) when you are booking a meeting or conference:
   A. The inclusive (from/to) dates.
   B. The approximate number of participants.
   C. The number of meeting rooms that will be needed.
   D. The times (each day) the meetings will be in session.
   E. The number of hotel guest rooms that will be required (if applicable).
   F. The food-service functions (luncheons, dinners, cocktail parties, banquets, coffee breaks) that will be required and the approximate number of people to be served.
   G. The special equipment you will require for the meetings (overhead projector, slide projector, cassette player, 16mm projector, screen, chalkboard).
   H. The name, address and telephone number of the person from your company who will be responsible for the meeting arrangements (perhaps you!).

   If it is possible to do so, go in person to make meeting arrangements. In that way, you can see for yourself the facilities that are available; and you can determine if they would suit your needs. If you cannot go in person to make arrangements for a meeting, write a **detailed** letter describing your needs. (Use the suggestions A through H above as an outline for your letter.) If you **must** make arrangements for a meeting or a conference by telephone, be sure to write a detailed letter to the person with whom you make the arrangements as a confirmation of your conversation.
3. As soon as the date and the place for a meeting or conference have been established, send an announcement about the meeting (containing dates, cost—if any, sample program, names of meeting leaders, and the meeting place) to everyone who is expected to participate. By doing this very early (try for six months in advance of the meeting), you will be encouraging a better attendance; and you will be helping others to plan their schedules more intelligently.

   In the announcement about the meeting or conference, encourage participants to register early and to make their hotel reservations (if applicable) early. Doing this will enable you and the hotel or conference center to plan for the meetings more realistically.

MEETING REQUIREMENTS

At least 60 days in advance of a meeting or conference, you should send the hotel or conference center the **specific arrangements**, such as the meeting-room setup (session-by-session, day-by-day) and the food-service setup your meeting will require. Allowing 60 days for the hotel or conference center to make final arrangements for your meeting will enable them to serve your group more professionally.

Many hotels and conference centers have a Meeting Requirements Form that they ask meeting sponsors to complete for each day a meeting is in session. Figure 164 is a Meeting Requirements Form that has been completed for a meeting to be held by Morgan Glass Corporation at the Holiday Inn—Four Seasons in Greensboro, North Carolina.

MEETING REQUIREMENTS FORM

Holiday Inn—Four Seasons
Greensboro, NC

Name of Group Morgan Glass Corp. – Dealership Division

Address 4675 West Market Street / Greensboro, NC 27408

Name of Person in Charge Charles Gunder Telephone (919) 272-1672 Ext. 171

Day/Date of Meeting Friday, October 10, 19--
(Complete a separate form for each day of the meeting)

Billing Procedure Direct Bill to company – Attention: Charles Gunder

Meeting Function – Morning (list all requirements) (Registration 8 a.m. to 9 a.m.)

Time 9:00 a.m. to 12 noon (Pine Room)
Schoolroom Style (40 people)
Chalkboard/Chalk/Eraser
Projection Screen
Overhead Projector
Ashtrays (one side of the room only); water pitchers and glasses at each table
Lectern with light and microphone front of room
Table for supplies (covered) front right of room

Meeting Function – Afternoon (list all requirements)

Time 1:30 p.m. – 4:30 p.m. (Pine Room)
Same set up as morning
Freshen ashtrays, water pitchers, and glasses
Slide projector

Meeting Function – Evening (list all requirements)

Time ....
None

Fig. 164. Meeting Requirements Form (front)

Food Service Functions – Morning (list all requirements)

Time 10:15 a.m. to 10:30 a.m. (40 people)
Coffee/Tea/Sanka
Assorted Danish
Cream/Sugar/Lemon Slices

Food Service Functions – Afternoon (list all requirements)

Time 12:15 p.m. to 1:30 p.m.
Luncheon – Oak Room (45 people)
Cream of Potato Soup (cup)
Garden Salad
Chicken Kiev
Rice
Vegetable Medley
Apple Cobbler/Whipped Cream
Coffee/Tea/Milk

(Four Round tables of 10 each/Head table for five)

Food Service Functions – Evening (list all requirements) (Carolina Room)

Time 6:00 p.m. to 7:30 p.m. (Please serve only during these hours.)
Cocktail Party (Company Sponsored) 45 people
Highballs/Mixed Drinks/Beer
Potato Chips/Pretzels/Mixed Nuts
Dip: Onion, Clam, Chive
Assorted Cheeses and Crackers

Note: Admission to the cocktail party will be by conference name badge only. Please have someone tend the door to check.

Will you require food service to an organization sponsored hospitality suite in addition to the above?
☐ Yes ☑ No

(back)

On The Day Of The Meeting

The person who has responsibility for the meeting should plan to arrive at the hotel or conference center **well in advance** of the time the meeting is scheduled to start to check on final details and to be sure that arrangements are progressing satisfactorily. (Often some last-minute decisions will have to be made no matter how carefully you have planned.)

Registration For The Meeting

You will need to make arrangements for someone to take care of registration of meeting participants in an area of the hotel or conference center near where the meeting is to be held. (A hallway outside the meeting room is a good place for registration, but be sure that bulletin boards in the main foyer direct participants to the room and floor where the meeting is to be held.) Registration is much easier if the name badges and kits of material for participants are prepared in advance. In that way, each participant comes to the registration table, gives his/her name, and he/she receives a name badge and a kit of materials without delay. If for some reason you must register meeting participants "on the spot," have **several** people available to help with registration so it can be handled quickly and efficiently. (Nothing gets a meeting off to a poor start like a long wait in a registration line.)

Additional Helpers

It is very important for the person who has responsibility for a meeting or conference to be free during the meetings to answer questions of hotel or conference center staff, to take special telephone calls about the meeting, and to greet and direct meeting participants and speakers to the proper places. For that reason, you should plan to have one or two people present to run errands, answer telephones, and to take meeting notes. By arranging for additional people to assist in this way, you will be providing for a smooth-running, well-organized meeting or conference.

The person who takes notes will need to prepare an accurate summary of the discussion that takes place during each phase of the meeting or conference. In addition, he/she will need to take verbatim notes on resolutions (see page 149) that are adopted or on major decisions that are made. It is the responsibility of the person taking notes to prepare the follow-up report of the meeting.

FOLLOW-UP REPORTS AND LETTERS

When the meeting or conference is over, it will be the responsibility of the person who has managed the meeting to see that a summary of the details of the meeting is sent to every meeting participant.

The person who takes notes during the meeting prepares the notes in typewritten form and delivers them to the person who managed the meeting. The person who managed the meeting has the report duplicated and sends it to each meeting participant along with a letter of explanation (usually composed by the person responsible for the meeting program).

It is also the responsibility of the person who managed the meeting to write thank-you letters to the members of the hotel or conference center staff who serviced the meeting and to the people who helped with registration, running errands, and taking notes. (It is the program chairman's responsibility to write thank-you letters to speakers and to meeting participants.)

MGC **MORGAN GLASS CORPORATION**
4675 West Market Street
Greensboro, NC 27408-1925

October 14, 19--

Mr. Alton C. Ward
Convention Services Director
Holiday Inn - Four Seasons
3121 High Point Road
Greensboro, NC 27407

Dear Mr. Ward:

I take this opportunity to thank you for the outstanding job you and your efficient staff did for our Dealership Division Meeting at the Holiday Inn - Four Seasons on Friday, October 10.

The meeting room setup crew, the food-service staff, and the Food-Service Manager all did an outstanding job of helping us to make our 15th annual Dealership Conference a huge success.

I overheard the Director of our Dealership Division, Ms Mildred Carlton, comment that the Holiday Inn - Four Seasons has an efficient staff and superb meeting facilities.

You may be sure we shall return to your hotel when we have another meeting in Greensboro.

Sincerely yours,

MORGAN GLASS CORPORATION

Charles S. Gunder

Charles S. Gunder
Meeting Coordinator

em

Fig. 165. Thank-you letter

EVALUATION As soon as a meeting or conference is over, the person in charge of arrangements and the program chairperson for the meeting should evaluate the results of the meeting. By evaluating while the details are still clear, they should be able to make valuable suggestions that will help in planning and conducting a similar meeting or conference. Here are some questions that should be answered during an evaluation session:

1. Did the hotel or conference center have enough advance time to plan adequately for the meeting?

2. Did the meeting participants get enough advance notice so they could work the meeting into busy schedules?
3. Were the meeting rooms satisfactory from the following points of view:
   A. Room size?
   B. Room setup?
   C. Special equipment required?
   D. Ventilating and lighting?
   E. Noise control?
4. Were the hotel or conference center guest rooms satisfactory for the meeting participants? (if applicable)
5. Were the food-service functions satisfactory from the following points of view:
   A. Promptness?
   B. Service?
   C. Quality of food?
   D. Physical arrangements?
   E. Cost?
6. Did the registration of meeting participants progress smoothly?
7. Were there enough company employees on hand to ensure a smooth-running program?
8. Was the follow-up report sent to meeting participants promptly?
9. Did the meeting or conference accomplish the purpose for which it was held?

By evaluating each of the preceding nine areas carefully and honestly, meeting planners will have a valuable reference when another meeting or conference is to be planned.

FOR REVIEW AND DISCUSSION

1. Why do company-sponsored meetings and conferences serve an important management function?
2. What are the keys to the success of a meeting or conference?
3. Explain the steps that need to be taken to plan a successful meeting or conference.
4. Why is it a good idea to go **in person** to a hotel or conference center to make meeting arrangements?
5. How far in advance should you plan to make **detailed arrangements** (room setup, food service) for a meeting or conference with a hotel or conference center? Why?
6. Explain the function of a Meeting Requirements Form.
7. What is the best way to handle registration for a meeting or conference?
8. What kinds of helpers should be present during a meeting or conference to be sure the person who has primary responsibility for the meeting or conference can be free to handle important last-minute details?
9. What should a follow-up report for a meeting or conference contain and whose responsibility is it to prepare and send such a report?
10. To whom should the person responsible for meeting arrangements write thank-you letters?
11. Who is responsible for evaluating a meeting or conference? What factors should be evaluated?
12. Of what value is the meeting or conference evaluation?

Please turn to your workbook and complete Student Project 25.

CHAPTER 18

Planning Business Travel

OBJECTIVE

After studying Chapter 18 you will understand:
- How to book airline reservations
- How to book hotel/motel reservations
- How to book rental car reservations
- How to use professional travel services
- How to use traveler's checks and credit cards
- How to prepare an itinerary

JOB-RELATED VOCABULARY

Destination City—The city which is a passenger's final stop on a flight.

Origin City—The city in which a passenger begins a flight.

Accessibility—The quality of being easy to find or locate.

Note: An additional glossary of job-related vocabulary will be found on pages 192-193 of this chapter.

Today's office worker is often called upon to make travel arrangements for his/her employer and for other executives within the company for which he/she works.

This chapter will deal with the office worker's role in arranging successful business travel through air travel reservations, hotel reservations, rental car reservations, and other travel-related information.

Some companies rely on travel agencies to make travel arrangements for their personnel, while other companies have their own Travel Department to handle all travel arrangements. However, typically an employer will say to his/her secretary or assistant: "I need a flight to Los Angeles on Friday." The executive will then rely upon his/her secretary to make all travel arrangements. He/she will expect you to ask the appropriate questions—"What day will you be returning?" "Will you need a hotel reservation?" "Will you need to rent a car while you are in Los Angeles?"—and then proceed to make the proper travel arrangements.

THE OFFICIAL AIRLINE GUIDE (OAG)

The main section of the OAG lists flight departure and arrival times, classes of service available, type of aircraft, meals served, and the stops the flight makes (if any) en route between the origin city and the destination city. The OAG is also a fast, easy way to check supplementary flight information, such as fares, availability of ground transportation, and minimum connecting times.

Airline Reservations

If executives from your company travel for business, the company should have one or two hotel information reference books, such as Hotel Red Book and a copy of the Official Airline Guide (OAG), Quick Reference, North American Edition. The OAG contains airline flight schedules for all flights throughout the United States and Canada.

Airline Codes, City Codes, Service Codes, and Air-Transportation Terms

It is important to learn a few of the words, terms, and codes used in the air-travel industry. The speed of air travel and the demand for rapid customer service require fast, concise, efficient communication among airline employees and airline companies. The representatives of air transportation companies have spent many years developing and standardizing a suitable language of codes and terms to be used by all air carriers in order to meet their needs for speed and efficiency.

As a potential office worker who will probably be making airline reservations, you should be familiar with a few of these codes and terms. Here is a partial list of **two-letter airline codes:**

U S Air	AL
American	AA
Continental	CO
Delta	DL
Eastern	EA
Northwest	NW
Ozark	OZ
Pan American	PA
Piedmont	PI
Republic	RC
Trans World	TW
United	UA
Western	WA

Here is a list of **three-letter city codes** for major cities:

Atlanta	ATL
Boston	BOS
Chicago	CHI
Cincinnati	CVG
Cleveland	CLE
Dallas	DAL
Denver	DEN
Detroit	DET
Houston	HOU
Kansas City	MKC
Los Angeles	LAX
Miami	MIA
Minneapolis	MSP
New Orleans	MSY
New York City	NYC
Philadelphia	PHL
Phoenix	PHX
Pittsburgh	PIT
San Francisco	SFO
St. Louis	STL
Seattle	SEA
Washington, DC	WAS

Here are some codes designating **types of service:**

Classes of Service:

C Jet Business Coach
F Jet First Class
FN Jet Night Coach First Class
K Jet Economy
S Jet Standard—one class
Y Jet Coach
YN Jet Night Coach

Food Service Designator:

B Breakfast
L Lunch
D Dinner
S Snack
* An asterisk in the meal column of the OAG indicates that a remark concerning food service follows flight listing.

Note: A "/" symbol shown with the food service designator indicates meal service differs depending on class of service. Normally a food service indicator to the left of the "/" symbol indicates service applicable to the First Class compartment of the aircraft. A food service indicator to the right of the "/" indicates food service applicable to the Coach.

EXAMPLE: L/S
First Class passengers receive Lunch
Coach Class passengers receive a Snack

EXAMPLE: S/
First Class passengers receive a Snack
Coach Class passengers receive NO food service.

Here are the **three-character codes** designating the **types of jet aircraft** being used for a flight:

B72 Boeing 720
DC8 McDonnell Douglas DC8 Jet
DC9 McDonnell Douglas DC9 Jet
DC10 McDonnell Douglas DC10 Jumbo Jet
D8S and D9S McDonnell Douglas DC8 and DC9 that are longer (stretch) and carry more passengers
L10 Lockheed L1011 Jumbo Jet
SSC Supersonic Concorde
707 Boeing 707 Passenger Jet
727 Boeing 727 Passenger Jet
737 Boeing 737 Passenger Jet
747 Boeing 747 Passenger Jumbo Jet
767 Boeing's 767 Passenger Jet (Wide Body)

All domestic flights operate daily unless some other schedule is indicated in the OAG. Exceptions to daily operation of a flight are explained as follows:

1 Monday
2 Tuesday
3 Wednesday
4 Thursday
5 Friday
6 Saturday
7 Sunday
X Except

POCKET FLI

Freq.	Leave	Arrive			Flight	Class	Eq	Ml	S
To DALLAS/FT. WORTH, TEXAS								**CST**	**DFW**
D-DFW (DALLAS/FT. WORTH)									
F-FTW (MEACHAM FIELD/FT. WORTH)									
H-JDB (DOWNTOWN HELIPORT/FT. WORTH)									
L-DAL (LOVE FIELD-DALLAS)									
From **AMARILLO, TEXAS**								**CST**	**AMA**
X67	6:30a	7:30a	L	WN	500	S	737		0
6	6:30a	7:30a	L	WN	500	K	737		0
	7:00a	8:00a	D	AA	84	FYBQM	72S	S	0
	7:20a	8:15a	D	DL	1635	FYBMV	D9S	S	0
X67	9:20a	10:20a	L	WN	163	S	737		0
67	9:20a	10:20a	L	WN	163	K	737		0
	11:05a	12:08p	D	AA	127	FYBQM	72S	S	0
X67	11:20a	12:20p	L	WN	49	S	737		0
67	11:20a	12:20p	L	WN	49	K	737		0
	12:59p	2:04p	D	AA	472	FYBQM	72S	S	0
X67	1:20p	2:20p	L	WN	65	S	737		0
67	1:20p	2:20p	L	WN	65	K	737		0
	2:00p	2:55p	D	DL	1464	FYBMV	D9S		0
X67	3:20p	4:20p	L	WN	507	S	737		0
67	3:20p	4:20p	L	WN	507	K	737		0
	5:20p	6:15p	D	DL	1666	FYBMV	D9S	S	0
X67	5:20p	6:20p	L	WN	193	S	737		0
67	5:20p	6:20p	L	WN	193	K	737		0
	6:01p	7:07p	D	AA	292	FYBQM	72S	S	0
	7:20p	8:20p	L	WN	113	K	737		0
57	9:20p	10:20p	L	WN	521	K	737		0

Fig. 166. Southwest Airlines (WN) Flight 500 from Amarillo, TX to Dallas, TX operates daily except Saturday and Sunday (X67). Southwest Airlines Flight 163 operates only on Saturday and Sunday (67).

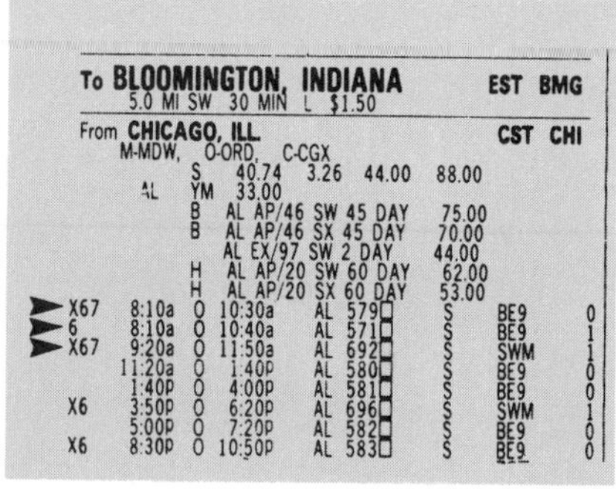

To BLOOMINGTON, INDIANA **EST BMG**
5.0 MI SW 30 MIN L $1.50

From **CHICAGO, ILL.** **CST CHI**
M-MDW, O-ORD, C-CGX
S 40.74 3.26 44.00 88.00
AL YM 33.00
B AL AP/46 SW 45 DAY 75.00
B AL AP/46 SX 45 DAY 70.00
AL EX/97 SW 2 DAY 44.00
H AL AP/20 SW 60 DAY 62.00
H AL AP/20 SX 60 DAY 53.00

Freq.	Leave		Arrive		Flight	Class	Eq	
X67	8:10a	O	10:30a	AL	579☐	S	BE9	0
6	8:10a	O	10:40a	AL	571☐	S	BE9	1
X67	9:20a	O	11:50a	AL	692☐	S	SWM	1
	11:20a	O	1:40P	AL	580☐	S	BE9	0
	1:40P	O	4:00P	AL	581☐	S	BE9	0
X6	3:50P	O	6:20P	AL	696☐	S	SWM	1
	5:00P	O	7:20P	AL	582☐	S	BE9	0
X6	8:30P	O	10:50P	AL	583☐	S	BE9	0

Fig. 167. U S Air, Flight No. 579 from Chicago, Illinois to Bloomington, Indiana operates every day X67 (except Saturday and Sunday). U S Air, Flight No. 571 operates 6 (only on Saturday). U S Air, Flight No. 692 operates every day X67 (except Saturday and Sunday).

Here is a glossary of frequently used air-transportation terms:

1. Booking (or Reservation)—A space held by a passenger on a flight.
2. Connecting City—A city into which a passenger holds a reservation on one flight and out of which the same passenger holds a reservation on another flight in order to fly between the point of origin and the point of destination. (If both flights are on **the same airline,** the connection is an "on-line connection." If the flight into the connecting city and out of the connecting city are on **different airlines,** the connection is an "interline connection.")
3. Fare—The price for air transportation from an originating point to the point of destination.
4. Itinerary—All portions of a passenger's trip from beginning to end.
5. Cancellation—Notifying an airline on which you have booked a flight(s) that you will not be using the reservation.
6. Ticket (Standard Interline Passenger Ticket)—A form on which each portion (called a leg) of the passenger's complete itinerary is listed and on which the status of each flight is shown as follows:
   - OK— Flight booked and space confirmed
   - RQ— Space requested (at the time of ticketing the flight was booked to capacity—the airline has **requested** a reservation for the passenger in case there is a cancellation)
   - SA— Space available (used for military and youth fare stand-bys—the passenger will be boarded if space is available immediately prior to the departure of the flight)
7. Ticket Time Limit—The date by which the passenger agrees to be ticketed for a flight on which he/she holds a confirmed reservation. Many of the special fares now in use require that tickets be purchased a specified number of days before the flight.

8. Connecting Time—The minimum time necessary for both the passenger and his/her baggage to make a transfer from one flight to another in a connecting city. (Minimum connecting time for "on-line" connections is usually less than for "inter-line" connections.)
9. Non-Stop—Flight makes no stops between originating and destination city.
10. Direct Flight—A flight from the origin city to the destination **without a change of aircraft**, but the flight stops en route.
11. Connecting Flight—A flight from the origin city to the destination city **with a change of aircraft** (and sometimes a change of **airlines**) at an intermediate city en route.

Here is a lists of **ground transportation codes:**

L	Limo	R	Rental Car
T	Taxi	A	Air Taxi

The following is a complete list of **Time Zones and Time Zone Codes:**

		Hours from Greenwich Mean Time (GMT)	
Time Zone	**Code**	**Standard Time (S)**	**Daylight Time (s)**
Atlantic	A	−4	−3
Alaska	A	−10	−9
Bering	B	−11	−10
*Central	C	−6	−5
*Eastern	E	−5	−4
Hawaiian	H	−10	Daylight Time does not apply
*Mountain	M	−7	−6
Newfoundland	N	−3½	−2½
*Pacific	P	−8	−7
Yukon	Y	−9	−8

*Starred items are the time zones within Continental United States.

EST refers to Eastern Standard Time; PDT refers to Pacific Daylight Time, and so on. Daylight time does not apply in the Hawaiian Time Zone.

Greenwich Mean Time refers to the time standard on which all time zones are based.

Example: If it is 10 a.m. Greenwich Mean Time it is 5 a.m. Eastern Standard Time (minus 5 hours) and 6 a.m. Eastern Daylight Time (minus 4 hours).

Using The Official Airline Guide (OAG)

To use the OAG, find the destination (TO) city first. The destination city is printed in bold type and destination cities are listed alphabetically. Under the destination city you will find the origin (FROM) cities listed in alphabetical order in slightly smaller type. If the city from which you want a flight (origin city) is not listed under the destination city, there are no **direct flights from the origin city to the destination city and a connecting flight must be constructed.**

Category 1

By studying Category 1, Destination (TO) City Data in Fig. 168, you will see the destination city in this listing is Dallas/Fort Worth, that Dallas is on Central Daylight Time (CDT), and the city code is DFW. Also you will note there are two airports in the Dallas and the Fort Worth, Texas area:

D—DFW (Dallas/Fort Worth International Airport)
L—DAL (Dallas Love Field Airport)

Category 2

By studying Category 2, Ground Transportation Data in Fig. 168, you will see that Dallas Love Field Airport is seven (7) miles north of downtown Dallas and takes about 35 minutes by L (airport limo). The cost of the limo is $2.50 per person one way. The code R/A indicates car rental service is also available at the airport.

"Between 430 & 615P 40 MIN" indicates that during rush hour traffic, between the hours of 4:30 p.m. and 6:15 p.m., a passenger should allow a minimum of 40 minutes to drive or to take an airport limo into Dallas.

"DFW/Dallas" indicates Dallas/Fort Worth International Airport—which is the main airport in Dallas. As Fig. 168 indicates, it is 17 miles west of downtown, and takes about 35 minutes by limo. The cost of the limo is $2.50 per person one way.

Category 3

Origin (FROM) City Data gives flight information from Washington, D.C. to Dallas, Texas. You will notice that Washington, D.C. is on EST (Eastern Standard Time) and the three-letter city code is WAS. There are three airports in the Washington, D.C. area that have flights to Dallas:

D—IAD (Washington, D.C.—Dulles Airport)
N—DCA (Washington, D.C.—National Airport)
I—BAL (Baltimore—Maryland Airport)

Category 4

Direct Flight Fares Data shows fares for **direct flights** from origin cities to destination cities. Figure 169 (detailed explanation of Category 4 in Fig. 168) shows fares for all classes of service between Washington, D.C., and Dallas, Texas. As you can see, the first class fare, "F," is $150 one way plus an 8% tax of $12, for a total of $162 one way. Round trip is $324 (just double the one way fare). Coach class, "Y," is $100 one way plus an 8% tax of $8, for a total of $108 one way.

Figure 169 also shows you "YM" fares for military personnel traveling with confirmed reservations. The regular "YM" fare is $81 including tax; however, Eastern Airlines (EA) charges $82 for the same service.

All types of special round trip excursion fares or discount fares are indicated by "B." These fares are often referred to by the airlines as "Super Savers" or "Peanuts." Since there are numerous restrictions on these fares, they will probably not be used by a person traveling for business. These promotional fares are to encourage family vacation travel by air rather than by automobile. When you make reservations for business travel, you will ordinarily use either "F" or "Y" class of service.

Category 5

Study the Direct Flights Schedule Data in Fig. 168. Direct flights are listed chronologically from the first flight of the day to the last. All times shown in Fig 168 are local time in Washington (origin city) for departure of the flight and local time in Dallas (destination city) for the arrival of the flight. The first flight shown in Fig. 168 reads as follows:

8:52a D 11:13 D AA 93 FYB 707 B O

Interpretation:

The flight leaves Washington, D.C., at 8:52 a.m. from "D" (Dulles Airport) and arrives at 11:13 a.m. Dallas time at "D" (Dallas/Fort Worth Airport). The airline "AA" is American and the Flight Number is 93. The passenger has a choice of "F" (First Class) or "Y" (Coach Class) or "B" (Special Fare). The aircraft used is a Boeing

SAMPLE LISTING

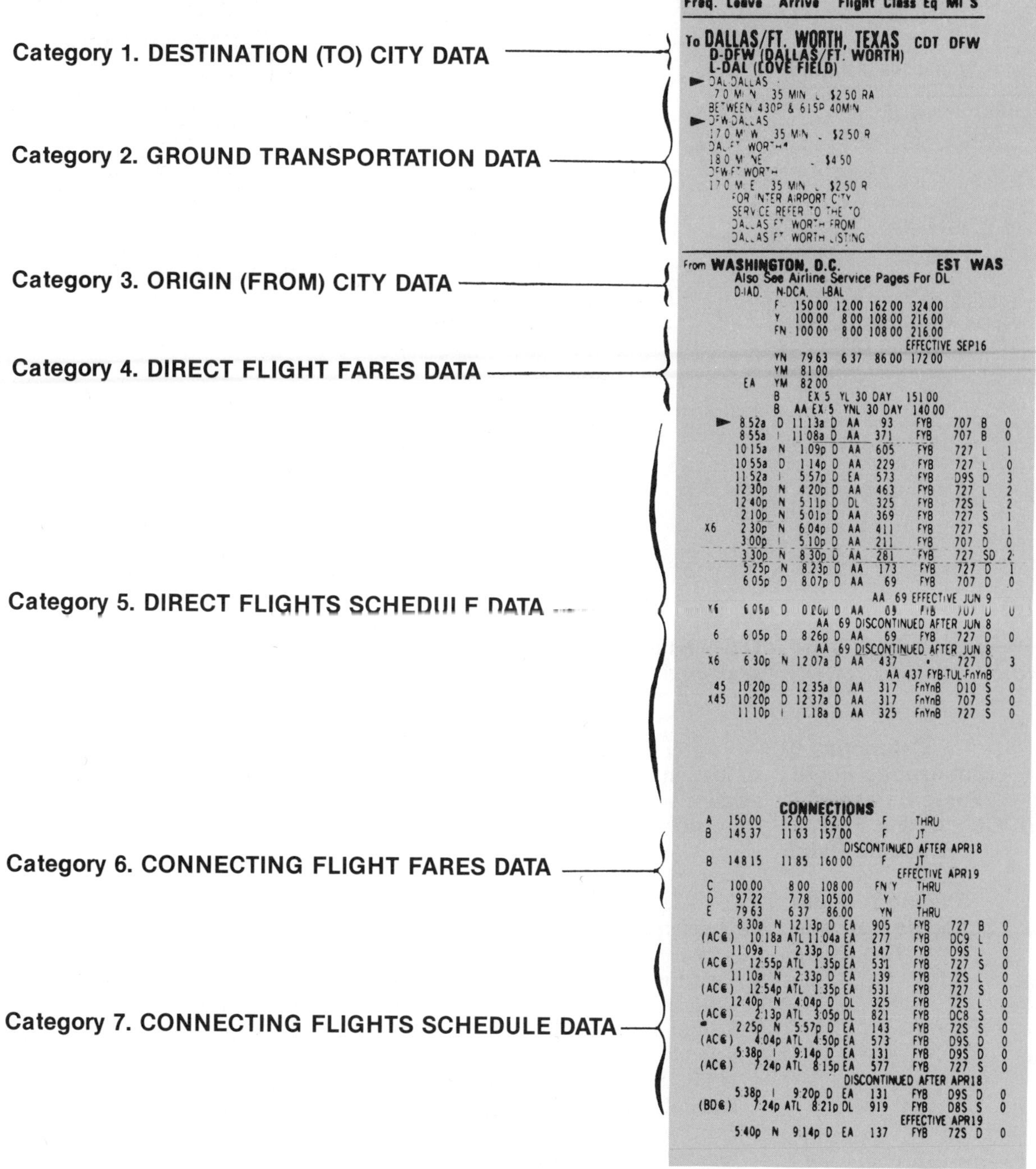


```
Freq. Leave  Arrive  Flight Class Eq MI S

To DALLAS/FT. WORTH, TEXAS  CDT DFW
   D-DFW (DALLAS/FT. WORTH)
   L-DAL (LOVE FIELD)
 ► DAL-DALLAS
   7.0 MI N   35 MIN L  $2.50 RA
   BETWEEN 430P & 615P 40MIN
 ► DFW-DALLAS
   17.0 MI W   35 MIN L  $2.50 R
   DAL-FT WORTH
   18.0 MI NE         L  $4.50
   DFW-FT WORTH
   17.0 MI E   35 MIN L  $2.50 R
      FOR INTER AIRPORT CITY
      SERVICE REFER TO THE TO
      DALLAS FT WORTH FROM
      DALLAS FT WORTH LISTING

From WASHINGTON, D.C.                 EST WAS
      Also See Airline Service Pages For DL
      D-IAD,  N-DCA,  I-BAL
            F   150.00  12.00  162.00  324.00
            Y   100.00   8.00  108.00  216.00
            FN  100.00   8.00  108.00  216.00
                                  EFFECTIVE SEP16
            YN   79.63   6.37   86.00  172.00
            YM   81.00
      EA    YM   82.00
            B      EX 5  YL 30 DAY   151.00
            B   AA EX 5  YNL 30 DAY  140.00
   ►  8.52a D 11.13a D AA  93  FYB  707 B  0
      8.55a I 11.08a D AA 371  FYB  707 B  0
     10.15a N  1.09p D AA 605  FYB  727 L  1
     10.55a D  1.14p D AA 229  FYB  727 L  0
     11.52a I  5.57p D EA 573  FYB  D9S D  3
     12.30p N  4.20p D AA 463  FYB  727 L  2
     12.40p N  5.11p D DL 325  FYB  72S L  2
      2.10p N  5.01p D AA 369  FYB  727 S  1
X6    2.30p N  6.04p D AA 411  FYB  727 S  1
      3.00p I  5.10p D AA 211  FYB  707 D  0
      3.30p N  8.30p D AA 281  FYB  727 SD 2
      5.25p N  8.23p D AA 173  FYB  727 D  1
      6.05p D  8.07p D AA  69  FYB  707 D  0
                        AA  69 EFFECTIVE JUN 9
X6    6.05p D  [illegible] D AA  69  FYB  707 D  0
                 AA  69 DISCONTINUED AFTER JUN 8
6     6.05p D  8.26p D AA  69  FYB  727 D  0
                 AA  69 DISCONTINUED AFTER JUN 8
X6    6.30p N 12.07a D AA 437   •   727 D  3
                        AA 437 FYB-TUL-FnYnB
45   10.20p D 12.35a D AA 317 FnYnB D10 S  0
X45  10.20p D 12.37a D AA 317 FnYnB 707 S  0
     11.10p I  1.18a D AA 325 FnYnB 727 S  0

                CONNECTIONS
  A  150.00   12.00  162.00   F    THRU
  B  145.37   11.63  157.00   F    JT
                     DISCONTINUED AFTER APR18
  B  148.15   11.85  160.00   F    JT
                         EFFECTIVE APR19
  C  100.00    8.00  108.00   FN Y THRU
  D   97.22    7.78  105.00   Y    JT
  E   79.63    6.37   86.00   YN   THRU
        8.30a N   12.13p D EA 905 FYB 727 B 0
(AC●)  10.18a ATL 11.04a EA 277 FYB DC9 L 0
       11.09a I    2.33p D EA 147 FYB D9S L 0
(AC●)  12.55p ATL  1.35p EA 531 FYB 727 S 0
       11.10a N    2.33p D EA 139 FYB 72S L 0
(AC●)  12.54p ATL  1.35p EA 531 FYB 727 S 0
       12.40p N    4.04p D DL 325 FYB 72S L 0
(AC●)   2.13p ATL  3.05p DL 821 FYB DC8 S 0
•       2.25p N    5.57p D EA 143 FYB 72S S 0
(AC●)   4.04p ATL  4.50p EA 573 FYB D9S D 0
        5.38p I    9.14p D EA 131 FYB D9S D 0
(AC●)   7.24p ATL  8.15p EA 577 FYB 727 S 0
                     DISCONTINUED AFTER APR18
        5.38p I    9.20p D EA 131 FYB D9S D 0
(BD●)   7.24p ATL  8.21p DL 919 FYB D8S S 0
                         EFFECTIVE APR19
        5.40p N    9.14p D EA 137 FYB 72S D 0
```

Fig. 168. An example of the types of information given for flight listings in the Official Airline Guide (OAG)

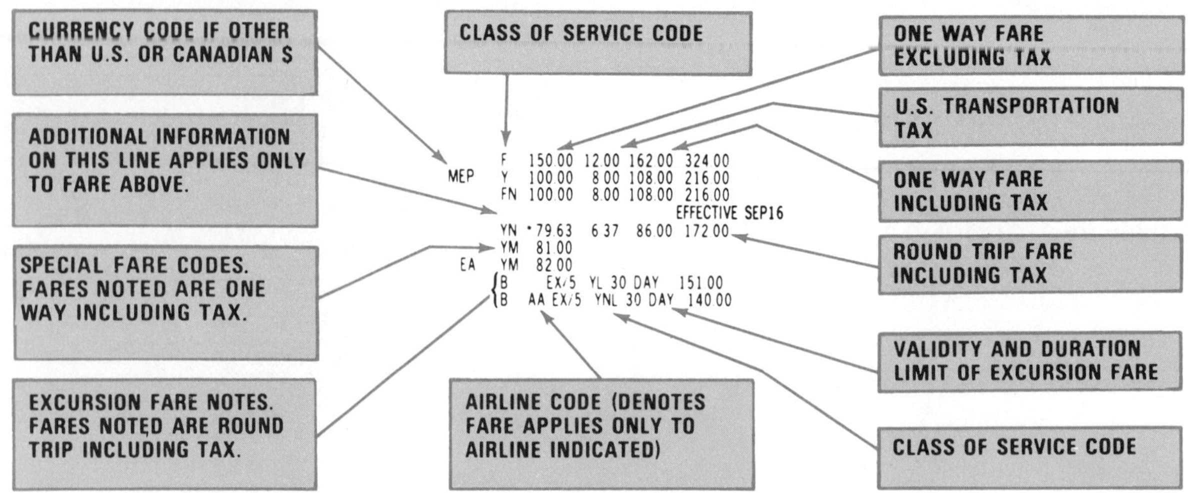

Fig. 169. Direct Flight Fares Data (detailed explanation)

CLASS OF SERVICE CODE

707. "B" shows breakfast will be served. The "0" indicates the flight will be nonstop between Washington, D.C., and Dallas, Texas. As you can see in Fig. 168, there are several flights daily between Washington, D.C. and Dallas, Texas; some are nonstop while others make 1, 2, or 3 stops en route. Remember "0" (or a nonstop flight) will be preferred by a person traveling for business.

Categories 6 (Connecting Flight Fares Data) and 7 (Connecting Flights Schedule Data)

Refer to Fig. 168 on page 191. Notice that the connecting fares information and the information about connecting flights is given immediately after the **Direct Flights Schedule Data.** (This concludes the discussion of the format of the OAG.)

Finding A Flight Schedule Between Two Cities

To select a flight between two cities, follow these steps after you have determined the time of day the passenger wants to fly and the class of service he/she will use:

1. Find the destination (to) city.
2. Under the destination city, find the origin (from) city.
3. Select the direct flight that best suits your time schedule from those listed.
4. If no direct flights are listed or if those listed do not suit your time schedule, select a connecting flight from those listed.
5. If no connecting flights are listed or if those listed do not suit your time schedule, arrange a connection of your own.

Booking A Flight With An Airline

After you have selected the flight(s) you want to book, you are ready to call the airline and make the reservation.

Mr. T.L. Davidson of Morgan Glass Corporation has asked you to get him a first-class flight from Greensboro to New York in the early morning on Tuesday, May 18. You have selected Delta Airlines Flight 370F leaving Greensboro at 7:35 a.m. (EDT) and arriving nonstop in

New York at 8:45 p.m. (EDT). Your conversation with the Delta Airlines reservations agent would be somewhat like the following:

Agent: "Delta Airlines, Mrs. Wilson."
Secretary: "I would like to book one reservation, first class, on Delta 370 on the 18th of May leaving Greensboro at 7:35 a.m. and arriving in New York at 8:45 a.m."
Agent: "I have confirmed one reservation on Flight 370, first class, on May 18. Breakfast will be served during the flight. Do you want to book a return flight?"
Secretary: "No, this will be a one-way flight."
Agent: "May I have the passenger's name, please."
Secretary: "Mr. T.L. Davidson."
Agent: "May I have a business and a home telephone contact for Mr. Davidson."
Secretary: "The business telephone is Area 919 272-1672, Ext. 4. Mr. Davidson's home phone is Area 919 273-1044."
Agent: "How would Mr. Davidson like to be ticketed?"
Secretary: "Mr. Davidson will pick up his ticket at the airport on the day of the flight and pay for it with his American Express Card."
Agent: "Fine, be sure to tell Mr. Davidson to pick up his ticket **at least** 45 minutes before flight departure time. May I help you with anything else today?"
Secretary: "No, thank you."
Agent: "Thank you for calling Delta."

The main point to keep in mind is that you will need to select your flight(s) and write the details **before** you call the airline to book a reservation. Doing this will enable you to make a booking accurately and quickly. Keep in mind, too, that airlines reservations agents are trained to help you to make air travel plans for a one-flight trip or for a 15-flight world tour. Ask for their help if you need it.

HOTEL/MOTEL RESERVATIONS

Another important duty a secretary or assistant performs for an employer who travels is to help him/her make hotel reservations. Making hotel arrangements is a very important responsibility when you consider that your employer may spend an hour with you planning a trip, a few more hours on an airplane; but he/she may spend days or even weeks as a guest at a hotel.

Many times a person who has traveled previously to a particular city will tell you where he/she has stayed and will ask you to book a reservation at that hotel. If your employer has no preference, it is your responsibility to find him/her a suitable hotel. The way you select a hotel and handle the reservation will surely have its effect on the traveler—for better or worse! To make a satisfactory hotel/motel reservation, you must understand the following:

1. Types of accommodations available
2. Hotel services available
3. Reservation and payment procedures

Types Of Accommodations Available

If you have had the opportunity to travel, either locally or around the world, you have undoubtedly noticed a wide variety of "places to stay." You may have seen modest motels in a midwestern town, high-rise beach hotels on the West Coast of the United States or in the Caribbean, stately tradition-filled hotels in Europe, and even youth hotels. Although there is no universal system of classifying hotels, the following three categories describe **most** of the accommodations available throughout the world.

A. Commercial Hotels
B. Resort Hotels
C. Motels

A. **Commercial Hotels**—Commercial hotels are the most common type of hotels. Although commercial hotels may vary from less than 100 rooms to well over 1,000 rooms, they do share some general characteristics. Commercial hotels are designed primarily to provide comfortable sleeping accommodations and food service. Accommodations and services range from a simple bedroom and a coffee shop to elegant suites and first class restaurants. Additional facilities are sometimes provided, but they are secondary to the sleeping accommodations and food service. Commercial hotels assume that their guests will spend most of their time outside the hotel. In larger cities the commercial hotels are **usually** near the downtown business district. A commercial hotel is ordinarily the type of hotel you would select for an employer who is traveling for business.

B. **Resort Hotels**—A stay at a resort hotel can be a vacation in itself. In addition to the standard facilities of a commercial hotel, resort hotels usually offer swimming pools (and/or private beaches), tennis courts and other recreational facilities, and sometimes entertainment by top stars. Although resort hotels can range from modest to elegant, most of them are located in an area known for scenic beauty, sightseeing potential, and recreational opportunities. (Examples: beach resorts, dude ranches, golf resorts, and ski lodges.) Most of the new hotels built within the last few years are a **combination** of resort and commercial hotels. Some of the larger hotel chains such as Sheraton, Hilton, Hyatt, and Marriott operate both commercial hotels and resort hotels.

C. **Motels**—Motor hotels, motor inns, and motels are both available and popular in the United States. The development and growth of these types of accommodations have been in direct proportion to the popularity of the "car trip." The principal characteristics of motels are accessibility and convenience for the motorist. Most motels are located on the fringes of cities near major highways. Although motels are built in many different designs, most often they are two-story buildings arranged in a quadrangle or a U-shape. Many motels provide the traveler with a swimming pool and a restaurant on the grounds. Holiday Inn, Howard Johnson, and Ramada Inn operate motels that offer such facilities.

Hotel Services Available

Hotel services depend upon the hotel selected and the amount of money the traveler wants to spend. Some hotels, especially those owned by the same hotel chain, are similar; but no two hotels are identical. Very few hotel chains offer every room or service in every hotel at the same rate. It is our intention here to discuss the services that **may** be available at a hotel. Because only a very few hotels have all of these services, you will need to determine which hotels offer which services before you make reservations.

Since a hotel guest will probably spend more time in his/her room than in any other part of the hotel, the size, decor, and comfort of the room are of primary importance. Hotel room rates are usually determined by the number of occupants in a room and by the size of the room. The most common terms describing hotel accommodations are the following:

HOTEL ACCOMMODATIONS

A. Single Room—A room for one person.
B. Twin Room—A room for two persons with two twin beds.
C. Double Room—A room for two persons with one double bed.
D. Double/Double—A room for one or more persons with two double beds.

In the United States all hotel rooms have a private bath (with either a bathtub and/or a shower).

In most hotels, the following **room services** are available to each guest:

1. The Housekeeping Department usually cleans, changes linens, and makes beds in each guest room daily. This service is usually included with the room rate.
2. Meals, ice, and beverages can be served to guests in their rooms. There is an extra charge for such service.
3. Laundry, dry cleaning, and shoe shining services are usually available for an extra charge.

Other Hotel Services

1. Meals **are not** usually included in the price of the room in hotels in the United States. However, the following meal plans may be available:
   A. European Plan (EP)—No meals included in the room rate.
   B. Continental Plan (CP)—Continental **breakfast** (coffee, rolls, or toast) included in the room rate.
   C. Full American Breakfast Only—Complete breakfast (for example: juice, eggs, bacon or sausage, toast, and coffee) included in the room rate.
   D. American Plan (AP)—Three complete meals a day included in the room rate.
   E. Modified American Plan (MAP)—Two complete meals a day (usually breakfast and dinner) included in the room rate.

Note: A guest on the American Plan or the Modified American Plan may usually choose any meal on the Table d'Hote Menu (complete meals). If the guest chooses to order from the A la Carte Menu (each item priced separately) and if the total ordered A la Carte exceeds the Table d'Hote price, the guest must pay the difference.

Example:

Total A la Carte Price	$ 12.75
Table d'Hote Price	10.50
Guest Charged	$ 2.25

   F. Full Pension (FP)—Same as American
2. Health Spas—Some hotels have complete health spas with gyms, handball courts, jogging tracks, swimming pools, and massage and steam bath services. Usually there is an additional charge for the use of health spa facilities.
3. Children's Recreation Areas—Some hotels (particularly in resort areas) have complete recreation areas for children with swings and other recreation equipment, handcraft materials, and a staff of trained counselors to work with the children of guests. Many hotels provide this service as part of the room rate.
4. Shopping Arcades—Some hotels (particularly commercial hotels in downtown locations) have shopping malls on the hotel premises. Hotel guests (and others) can buy a wide variety of items in these

shops. In some hotels, items purchased at the hotel arcade shops can be charged to the guest-room accounts.

5. Hairstylists—Many large hotels have both men's and women's hairstylists on the hotel premises. Usually those services can be charged to the guest-room accounts.
6. Airline Ticket Desks—Large hotels (particularly in downtown locations in major cities) frequently have ticket desks for the major air carriers serving the city in the hotel lobby. At these desks hotel guests (and others) can make airline reservations and purchase airline tickets.
7. Car Rental Desks—Many hotels (particularly in downtown locations and airport locations) have car rental services for the hotel guests (and others) available on the hotel premises.

Reservations And Payment Procedures

Reservations for hotel space can be obtained in the following ways:

1. Through a travel agency.
2. Through an airline reservations office.
3. By contacting the hotel directly on the telephone or by cable, telegram, or letter.
4. By calling a central reservations number ("800" number) operated by major hotel chains.

Whenever you make hotel reservations for an executive in your company, you will need the following information from the executive:

1. The type of room needed.
2. The day of arrival and the estimated time of arrival.
3. The day of departure.
4. The price range the executive is willing to pay for hotel accommodations.

   Note: If a hotel offers rooms with a price range—for example: a Double Room with a bath (DWB) from $45 to $65 a night—indicate the price range the executive wants—for example: Low, Medium, Superior, Deluxe, or Maximum. Avoid requesting a "Minimum Rate Room." Most hotels have only a few rooms at the minimum rate, and the rooms they have would probably not satisfy the executive.

5. The location in the destination city the executive wants to be near (airport, downtown, company).

The hotel should respond to your request for a reservation with the following information:

1. Confirmation of the FROM/TO dates.
2. The daily rate for the room requested.
3. The service charges and taxes to be added to the room rate.
4. Deposit required (if applicable) and a request for arrangements for paying for the room (usually the number of a major credit card—American Express, Diner's Club, Master Card, Visa—accepted by the hotel).

Never confirm a hotel reservation or a room rate to an executive unless you have received confirmation from the hotel (usually in writing). (Sometimes when you make a hotel reservation by telephone, the person making the reservation will give you a reservation number and his/her name for confirmation. The number should be written on a card and given to the traveling executive so it can be given to the front desk clerk at the hotel at the time the guest registers.)

When making hotel reservations, keep in mind that most hotel rooms are not ready for occupancy each day before 12 noon. (Earlier occupancy depends on early checkouts.) This fact can be frustrating to an executive who arrives at the hotel at 10 a.m. expecting a room. Also, if the executive plans to arrive late in the evening, the hotel should be told, because rooms are not usually held after 6 p.m. unless a Guaranteed Reservation (requiring a payment) is made. Under this agreement, the hotel will hold a room for the executive; but if he/she fails to check in and if the hotel has not been notified in advance that the executive will not use the room, the executive **must pay** one night's room rate or forfeit the deposit.

RENTAL CAR RESERVATIONS

The procedures for making rental car reservations are very similar to the procedures for making hotel reservations. Rental car reservations may be made in the following ways:

1. By calling the rental car agency directly or by contacting them by letter in advance.
2. By calling a central reservations number (''800'' number) operated by major rental car companies.
3. By calling a travel agency.
4. By calling **some** airline reservations offices.
5. By contacting a rental car agency booth at major airports or hotels.

When making rental car reservations, you will need to tell the agent:

1. The name and address of the person who will use the car.
2. The dates (from/to) he/she will need the car.
3. The place where he/she will pick up the car (the city and the location—the airport, a downtown hotel, a suburban rental center).

   Note: If the car is being picked up at the airport, you will need to give the car rental agent the name of the airline, the flight number, and the arrival time of the person who will rent the car.

4. The type of car he/she wants to rent (**Standard**—a full-size car; **Mid-Size**; a medium-size car; **Compact**—a small car).
5. The place where the renter will ''drop off'' the car.

Many car rental agencies advertise special rates (usually under special circumstances) from time to time. It is always a good idea to ask the car rental agent with whom you make a reservation if a special rate applies to the rental.

If the time between the time the reservation is made and the time the car will be picked up is long enough, the car rental agency will confirm the reservation by mail.

By following the procedures described here for making airline, hotel, and rental car reservations, you should be able to secure accommodations the executives from your company request. Do not hesitate to ask reservations agents for help if you need it, because they are well-trained professionals whose business it is to serve your travel needs.

USING TRAVEL SERVICES

Many companies that have a number of people traveling for business now have contracts with travel agencies to handle all of the company travel arrangements. In some instances, travel agencies have even established branch offices in company headquarters so they can provide for company travel needs more efficiently. There are two strong advantages to this arrangement:

- A company does not have the expense of an employee (or employees) who make travel arrangements for company employees who travel for business.

- All travel arrangements (flight reservations, hotel accommodations, rental car reservations, etc.) can be made through one agency (rather than have a secretary call an airline, a hotel, and a rental car agency individually).

A traveler **does not** pay an extra charge for making travel arrangements through a travel agency. A travel agency derives its income from commissions paid to the agency by airlines, hotels, rental car companies, cruise lines, and railroad companies.

Before you contact a travel agency to arrange travel for an executive for whom you work, it is important for you to **be prepared** with the proper information. The information you will need to give a travel agency is the same information you would need to give to an airline, a hotel, or a rental car agency (information that was discussed previously in this chapter). Before you call a travel agency to assist you with travel arrangements, be certain you have the following information:

- **Travel dates for each destination**
- **Travel time preferred** (either the time the executive prefers to leave his/her departure city or the time he/she wants to arrive in his/her destination city)
- **Destination(s)**
- **Type of airline service preferred** (coach or first class, and the type of aircraft if the executive has a preference)
- **Airline preferred** (if the traveling executive has a preference)
- **Hotel preferred** (including a specific hotel chain, the location of the hotel—downtown or near an office or factory, and the type of room accommodation—full-size bed, king-size bed, double, twin—if the executive has a preference)
- **Rental car preference** (including company, size of car, and the executive's automatic reservation number—with major car rental companies—if he/she has one)
- **Ticketing arrangements** (You will need to tell the agency how the traveling executive is to receive his/her tickets—by mail, agency will deliver, you will pick up.)
- **Form of payment information** (You will need to tell the agency how the traveling executive will pay for his/her travel accommodations. If a credit card is to be used, you will need to give the agency the credit card number, the type of card being used, and the expiration date.)

The need to have the preceding information organized and available **before** contacting a travel agency cannot be stressed too strongly.

TRAVELER'S CHECKS AND CREDIT CARDS

In recent years, it has become extremely dangerous for anyone to carry large sums of money on his/her person. For that reason, many executives who travel for business use traveler's checks and credit cards, both of which are **usually** acceptable to hotels, restaurants, airlines, and automobile rental agencies.

Traveler's Checks

American Express and Visa Traveler's Checks can be purchased from banks and travel agencies. American Express Traveler's Checks can also be purchased from vending machines at **some** airports and hotels. (Other types of traveler's checks are also available at travel agencies and financial institutions.) Traveler's checks, which are prenumbered, are sold in denominations of $10, $20, $50, and $100. The checks come in wallet-like envelopes. The person who will use the traveler's checks must sign each check when he/she purchases them. The checks must be signed again **in the presence of the person who cashes them. The comparison of signatures** helps to identify the person holding the checks even in a city where he/she is not known.

After an executive purchases traveler's checks, he/she should provide his/her secretary with a list of the check numbers and the amounts of each check. The secretary should then prepare a list for his/her files, and the executive should be given a list to carry in his/her briefcase. If the checks are lost or stolen, they can easily be replaced by going to **any agency that sells similar traveler's checks** in **any** city and by giving the office the numbers and amounts of the checks not used.

Credit Cards

Credit cards such as American Express, Diner's Club, Master Card, Visa, airline, rental car, hotel credit cards, and others permit a traveling executive to charge most of the services he/she will require while traveling, thereby relieving him/her of the need for carrying large amounts of cash. Most hotels will permit a registered guest who holds a major credit card to cash a personal check (up to a certain cash limit) without additional identification.

The credit card holder receives a monthly statement for each credit card, and that statement along with the credit card purchaser's receipt is helpful when expense reports are prepared and as proof for tax-deductible business expenses.

A secretary should prepare a list of credit cards and their numbers and the telephone numbers of the credit card companies for each credit card an executive carries. A copy of the list should be carried in the executive's briefcase, and the secretary should keep a list in his/her files. If the credit cards are lost or stolen, the credit card companies must be notified immediately (first by telephone, then by letter) to avoid liability for their misuse.

THE ITINERARY

A complete itinerary should be prepared for each executive who travels on business. The itinerary gives a complete day-by-day schedule of meetings, travel, and hotel contacts for the entire trip. The executive should have a copy of the itinerary; the executive's office should have a copy of the itinerary in case it needs to contact him/her; and the executive's family should have a copy of the itinerary.

An example of a well-prepared itinerary appears on page 200.

WHEN THE EXECUTIVE IS AWAY

It is a secretary's responsibility to keep the office running smoothly and productively in the absence of his/her employer. In addition to the routine matters that the secretary will handle alone when his/her employer is away, there will be special situations that will be beyond the secretary's knowledge or authority. It is a secretary's responsibility to arrange with his/her employer before he/she leaves on a business trip to have someone in the office handle those situations. Routine mail should be answered promptly. Mail requiring special attention should be put into a folder (the most urgent mail on the top) so that it can be discussed with the executive when he/she calls the office. If an executive is going to be away on an **extended** business trip, it might be helpful to him/her to have the secretary send a weekly digest of his/her correspondence. (The procedure for digesting mail was described in Chapter Six of this textbook.)

Usually, the office of an executive who is out of town on business has many requests for appointments with the executive when he/she returns to the office. It is unwise to make appointments for an executive too close to the date he/she returns to the office. The executive will need time to handle mail, prepare expense reports, and tend to other business matters that have accumulated during his/her absence before he/she is ready to receive office callers.

ITINERARY

Helen D. Thomas

(Atlanta, Columbia, Chicago, Philadelphia, Cleveland)

<u>Sunday, March 16</u>	Lv. Greensboro Airport, Eastern Airlines Flight 509, at 1:35 p.m., Ar. Atlanta Airport 2:39 p.m. Reservations: Atlanta Marriott (downtown) (404) 659-6500
<u>Monday, March 17</u>	All-day meeting at the Marriott with R. D. Thomas of Restaurant Supply Company of the South Lv. Atlanta Airport, Delta Airlines Flight 950, at 7:29 p.m., Ar. Columbia Airport 8:15 p.m. Reservations: Carolina Inn (Guaranteed) (803) 799-8200
<u>Tuesday, March 18</u>	Meeting 9 a.m. to 12 noon with Mr. Harold Sternberg, General Manager of Davidson's Department Store (at Mr. Sternberg's office) about a possible exclusive distributorship in South Carolina to handle the products of our Tableware Division Lv. Columbia Airport, Eastern Airlines Flight 216, at 3:43 p.m., Ar. O'Hare Airport, Chicago at 5:43 p.m. Reservation: Hyatt Regency Chicago (Guaranteed) (312) 565-1000
<u>Wednesday, March 19</u>	Meeting at the Hyatt from 9:30 a.m. to 5 p.m. with Ms Doris Lang, Mr. Howard Teeds, Mr. C. L. Kingston of Bellmont Glass Corporation about a possible acquisition. (Mr. Kingston, Chief Accountant for Bellmont, will bring a certified audit report to the meeting.) Dinner with Hal Parker, our sales representative in Chicago, at 8 p.m. at the Consort Room at the Westin Hotel--reservations have been made (North Michigan Avenue at Hancock Center)
<u>Thursday, March 20</u>	Lv. O'Hare Airport, United Airlines Flight 118, at 7:15 a.m., Ar. Philadelphia Airport at 10:02 a.m. Reservation: The Warwick Hotel (215) 735-6000 Dinner with Howard Curtis, Chief Executive Officer of Garden State China Corporation, in the hotel dining room
<u>Friday, March 21</u>	All-day meeting (annual corporate meeting) of our subsidiary, Garden State China Corporation, at the Warwick Hotel Main Ballroom

(Continued on the following page)

	Dinner at 8 p.m. at the home of Tim Day (Garden State China's President) at 3601 Crescent Park Drive, Cherry Hill, NJ (Drive to Cherry Hill with Mr. Day after the annual meeting)
Saturday, March 22	Lv. Philadelphia Airport, United Airlines Flight 1040, at 8:38 a.m., Ar. Cleveland Hopkins Airport 10 a.m.
	Reservations: Stouffer's Inn on the Square (216) 752-5600
	Attend Ohio Restaurant/Hotel Suppliers Convention at the hotel 3/23-3/25--Speak at Luncheon 3/24 at noon in the hotel ballroom
Tuesday, March 25	Lv. Cleveland Hopkins Airport, Delta Airlines Flight 1619, at 11:55 a.m., Ar. Atlanta Airport at 1:31 p.m.
	Lv. Atlanta Airport, Eastern Airlines Flight 360, at 3:41 p.m., Ar. Greensboro Airport at 4:38 p.m.

Fig. 170. A nine-day itinerary

FOR REVIEW AND DISCUSSION

1. What information does the **Official Airline Guide, Quick Reference, North American Edition** contain?
2. Explain the following airline codes:

Classes of Service Codes	**B**
F	**L**
Y	**D**
S	**S**
Meal Service Codes	

3. Explain the following jet aircraft codes:

DC8	747
L10	737
SSC	737

4. Explain the following airline travel terms:
   Direct Flight
   Connecting Flight
   Ticket Time Limit
   Connecting City
   Booking
5. What three types of information about hotels/motels are necessary in order to make satisfactory reservations?
6. When you are ready to book a specific hotel/motel reservation for an executive, what information must you have from him/her?
7. What information must you give a rental agent when you are reserving a rental car for someone?
8. After an executive has purchased traveler's checks, what steps should he/she take to protect himself/herself in case they are lost or stolen?
9. What is an itinerary? Who should have copies of an executive's travel itinerary?
10. What is the secretary's responsibility when the executive is out of town on business?

Turn to your workbook and complete Student Projects 26 through 29.

CHAPTER 19

Leadership

OBJECTIVE

After you have studied Chapter 19, you will understand:

- What leadership is
- The qualities leaders frequently exhibit
- The relationship between leadership and power
- Traits leaders frequently possess
- The function of a leader
- Behavior styles leaders frequently exhibit
- How to apply the qualities of leadership to a work situation

JOB-RELATED VOCABULARY

Leadership—The ability to cause others to follow willingly, usually in initiating change.

Relevant—Providing evidence that tends to prove or disprove the matter or issue under discussion.

Anxieties—Fearful concern or interest about something.

Authority—Power to influence or command thought, opinion, or behavior.

Consensus—General agreement.

Arbitrator—A person chosen to settle differences between two parties in controversy.

Authoritarian—Of, relating to, or favoring concentration of power in a leader who acts without the consent of the group.

Ambiguity—The quality or state of being doubtful or uncertain in meaning.

Autocratic—Characteristic of displaying undisputed influence or power.

Participative—To share (as to share in group decision making).

Interrelationships—The act of having the same feelings one for the other (such as having the same feelings for a person that he/she has for you).

Leadership skills are vital skills that every business person who aspires to have a role in business management must possess. An understanding of the skills that contribute to successful leadership will also help you to be a better member of a group. In recent years, researchers and social scientists have begun to realize that leadership is a quality that can be clearly defined and carefully developed.

Robert Durbin defined leadership as **the ability to cause others to follow willingly, usually in initiating change.**

Every group needs creative leadership to help reduce uncertainty and confusion. However, if a group is functioning fairly smoothly, very little leadership may be required. Since one of the chief goals of leadership is to keep the group focused on its goals, leadership can have an important effect on a group's morale. Leaders bring about change in a group either by making decisions or by encouraging members of the group to make them. Therefore, **a group's trust in its leader is affected by the quality of the leader's decisions.**

Being A Leader

It is important to realize that a group does not necessarily have only **one** leader. A group **can** have only one leader, but **every member** of the group can also be a leader. **All people are potential leaders;** and if they are given the desire and the opportunity, people can develop into effective leaders. Since all groups are made up of more people who can exercise leadership (at least temporarily) than there are positions of leadership to be filled, sometimes in a crisis situation, a person not previously known to possess leadership skills emerges as an extremely effective leader. This is one way that officials of an organization learn where potential leadership skills are to be found.

Since group goals and tasks change, new leaders emerge; and shifts of power occur. Therefore, leadership in a group depends on group standards and what leadership rules are acceptable at a given time. An effective leader is one who is able to understand a situation from the points of view of all (or most) of those involved. In addition, a leader must be aware of his/her impact on others and the impact of others on the leader. Leaders must be able to assess all relevant factors in a situation, including their own personal needs and anxieties.

Leadership And Power

While all leaders have authority (or power), not all people who have authority are leaders. Leaders derive their authority from the group.

Authority, or externally derived power, **usually stems from position or rank.** The heads of companies, the managers of departments, government officials, and the elected officers of organizations are examples of persons who have authority by virtue of the positions they hold. **Authority may also come from knowledge and expertise.** A group that is planning to purchase a computer, for example, might look to the most knowledgeable and experienced experts they can find in computer technology. Those experts will have authority by virtue of the knowledge and expertise they possess rather than by virtue of their position or rank. It is important to remember that leaders are **usually given power gradually by group consensus** because they have established trust and recognition with members of the group.

Remember, too, that there is an important distinction between leadership and power. **Power is conferred** on an individual by virtue of his/her position, rank, knowledge, or expertise. **Leadership is earned** by an individual who has the backing of the group. (It is a common practice to grant leadership to people who already have power.)

Leadership Traits

According to Murray Ross and Charles Hendry, co-authors of the book, NEW UNDERSTANDINGS OF LEADERSHIP, effective leaders:

- Are self-confident, well integrated, and emotionally stable
- Want to take leadership responsibility and are competent in handling new situations

- Identify with the goals and values of the groups they lead
- Are warm, sensitive, and sympathetic toward other people and give practical, helpful suggestions
- Are intelligent in relation to the other members of the group
- Can be relied on to perform leadership functions continuously
- In elected or public positions usually possess more enthusiasm and capacity for expression than other types of leaders do

It is also important to distinguish between social popularity and leadership and to recognize that **they are not the same thing.** A **socially popular person** is:

- Sought after in a social context within and outside the group.
- "Liked" during the decision making activities of the group.

A **popular leader** is:

- Effective in influencing the group's behavior.
- Sought after in the performance of other leadership functions (such as representing the group to others).

Considering the foregoing information, it is not unlikely that many groups will develop two types of leaders with very different goals, "the social leader" and "the task leader." These two very different types of leaders frequently complement each other and accomplish their goals with a minimum of conflict. The **task leader** contributes most to the achievement of the task at hand. In achieving the task, the task leader may anger people and damage the unity of the group. The **social leader** has the role of restoring and maintaining group unity and satisfaction. (In this way, the task leader and the social leader work together for the benefit of the group.) Sociologists indicate that it is a rarity when one person can be both an effective task leader and an effective social leader. For that reason, it is important for a task leader to recognize a social leader within the group and to form an alliance with him/her.

The Function Of A Leader

The functional concept of leadership stems from the underlying idea that leadership acts are those that help the group to achieve its objectives. Usually within a group there are many leadership roles, such as responsibility for: planning, informing, producing, evaluating, and rewarding. In applying the functional approach to leadership, an attempt is made to match personalities and styles with the type of leadership to be exercised.

Every leader has **three major functions** (or actions) as he/she works to keep the group unified and acting effectively:

- **Identifying Goals**—When a group creates goals, the group also creates bonds. When leaders are firmly identified with the group's goals, followers are more likely to identify with the leaders. For that reason, a leader must always help the group to attain its goals (whether or not he/she has helped to formulate the goals).
- **Making Decisions**—A leader's wishes certainly have weight in making decisions (depending on the leader's power within the group). An effective leader helps to clarify possible alternatives for action, and he/she can prevent the group from stalemating and fragmenting.
- **Resolving Differences**—In resolving group differences, the leader listens to all sides of the argument (in an uninvolved, neutral way), and he/she helps group members to arrive at a solution. If that is not possible, the leader must then arrive at a solution alone. In this situation, the leader is put in the role of arbitrator in order to prevent

group splintering. To help a group resolve its differences effectively, a leader must:

- Be aware of and in agreement with group goals
- Be aware of and in agreement with the standards by which the group operates
- Be aware of and in agreement with the sensitivities of group members

Social scientists indicate that groups and organizations are undergoing radical changes as they struggle to adapt to rapid changes in society. (You will be able to see this clearly by taking a careful look at the changes taking place in the groups to which you belong.) There is also a psychological threat to leaders and to others that stems from the movement toward more humanistic, democratic behavior from leaders. The "team approach" to leadership, which has been emerging in recent years, utilizes a variety of talents and creates an atmosphere of openness, trust, and cooperation.

Behavior Styles

Like leadership traits and functions, the **styles** by which leaders perform can also be described. Leadership styles are based on the type of **control** leaders exercise in the group and their **behavior toward** group members.

Behavior theorists do not dismiss the force of leaders' personalities, but they say leaders use leadership styles that are consistent with their personalities. A person who has trouble trusting other people's judgment, for example, will probably tend toward an authoritarian leadership style. Another person may choose to be authoritarian simply as a way to save time.

An examination of leadership behavior indicates strongly that people are not "born leaders" but that they can be trained in leadership techniques. Let us examine three popular leadership styles.

Autocratic Leaders—Autocratic leaders have no doubt about who is "in charge." They use the power they acquire (by their rank, knowledge, or skills) to reward and punish as they see fit within the group. Authoritarian (often called autocratic) leaders give orders and assume that people will respond obediently. (This posture of an autocratic leader does not necessarily imply hostility or negativity, but rather absolute sureness of will.) Because the directions given by an autocratic leader are often detailed, any ambiguity can be resolved easily; and some members of the group adapt well to this style of leadership. However, since autocratic communication is usually one to one, the lack of feedback can lead to misunderstandings and confusion within a group. Because of the lack of feedback, the leader does not always know what members of the group are thinking. Poor decisions frequently result when a leader makes decisions without first listening to the ideas and advice of other members of the group. Also, members of a group frequently resent and resist a leader who excludes them from involvement.

Participative Leaders—Participative leaders request and expect constant feedback from the group. This practice should provide them with the best available information. However, participative leaders do not disguise their power to make the final decision, particularly if they are faced with a crisis.

Most people demonstrate a high productivity when they are given a reasonable amount of freedom. In such situations, people usually discover their full potential, and their creativity and productivity increase. Therefore, they usually experience personal satisfaction and a sense of accomplishment.

On the other hand, participative leadership can be very time consuming; and it requires a great deal of energy. A participative leader must be certain that **real** participation occurs. Members of a group resent acts of bad faith. (If members of a group are asked for recommendations, they do not like to see those recommendations ignored and rejected without further discussion.)

Both the autocratic leader (who is task oriented) and the participative leader (who is people oriented) have important roles to play depending on the group, the time span, the problem, and the environment.

Free-Rein Leaders—Free-rein leaders (or group-centered leaders) are almost completely nondirective. Free-rein leaders communicate goals and guidelines, and they permit members of the group to meet those goals without further directions, unless further direction is specifically **requested.** One goal of this type of leader is to allow all members of the group to participate in a project as equally as possible. This leadership style offers the greatest use of time and resources because the highest possible degree of authority is vested in the group. The "hands off" atmosphere created by this type of leader can motivate people to initiate and carry out complex work plans efficiently and responsibly. This style of leadership is sometimes extremely effective in a group composed of professional persons who have a highly defined sense of personal motivation. It can be extremely **ineffective** if the members of the group are not highly motivated.

It is important to remember that group style dictates leadership style. As a group progresses (and grows), subtle changes in leadership style are required so that leadership is compatible with the needs of the group.

In general, the behavior styles of leaders may be summarized as follows:

- The autocratic leader **makes and announces** decisions (the benevolent autocratic leader presents a decision subject to changes, seeks ideas, and sells the decision).
- The participative leader **seeks ideas from members of the group before making a decision** (the democratic leader makes a decision with the group on a "one-person, one-vote" basis).
- The free-rein leader **asks the members of the group to make the decision.**

However, this is not to imply that these behavior styles are rigid and easily defined. Frequently leaders are a **combination of one or more of the leadership styles described in this chapter.**

Leadership needs change as leaders move from one level (or group) to another. For that reason, it is important to identify and include secondary leaders whose style and knowledge of the group will supplement the efforts of the main leader.

In business, leadership roles are expressed in such jobs as company officers, supervisors, group leaders, and members of the professional and management staffs.

An understanding of the qualities and traits that leaders usually possess and an understanding of the function of an effective leader coupled with an understanding of the behavior styles that are common to various types of leaders should help you to be more aware of what is required to lead a group successfully and productively.

FOR REVIEW AND DISCUSSION

1. Define the term leadership.
2. Describe what is required to "be a leader."
3. Explain how authority is derived.
4. Explain the relationship between leadership and power.
5. Describe the traits usually possessed by effective leaders.
6. Explain the difference between popularity and leadership.
7. Explain the differences between the **social leader** and the **task leader.**
8. Explain the three major functions (or actions) of a leader.
9. Explain the relationship between **leadership styles** and the **personalities of leaders.**
10. Describe the following popular leadership styles:
    Autocratic Leaders
    Participative Leaders
    Free-Rein Leaders

Turn to your workbook and complete Projects 30 through 32.

CHAPTER 20

Planning A Career As A Secretary

OBJECTIVE

After studying Chapter 20 you will understand:

- The duties a secretary performs
- The wide variety of career choices available to a secretary
- The skills a secretary must possess
- How a secretarial career can be an "open door" to advancement

JOB-RELATED VOCABULARY

Transcribing Dictation—Transferring symbol, ABC, or machine shorthand or machine dictation to typewritten form.

Initiative—Willingness to take the first step toward a goal without being prompted.

Flexible—Capable of responding to or conforming to changes in a positive manner.

Production—Making goods available to meet human wants and needs.

Marketing—The activities of buying and selling something.

In recent years, the secretarial position has made a complete departure from the traditional role of taking and transcribing dictation, typing letters and reports, and answering the office telephone to a management role. In these days when the pressure from business is so great and the demands on the executive's time and talents are almost beyond endurance, the secretary often fills the role of an executive assistant with special projects and responsibilities which he/she handles without constant supervision. By handling extensive projects independently, the secretary becomes a vital part of the management team that helps the company to plan for growth and to work toward continued development in its field.

THE ROLE OF THE SECRETARY

According to the approved definition of the term "secretary" from Professional Secretaries International (PSI), a secretary is "an **executive assistant** who possesses a mastery of office skills, demonstrates the ability to assume responsibility without direct supervision, exercises initiative and judgment, and makes decisions within the scope of assigned authority." (The words "executive assistant" are an important part of the definition of the term "secretary.")

The complete answer to the question, "What does a secretary do?" is almost endless! It is important to remember that there may be several levels of secretarial jobs within a single company. (One large, well-known company has 12 levels of secretarial jobs!) "Secretarial" jobs can range from typist to executive assistant. A secretary frequently performs the following activities:

- Answers incoming telephone calls and places outgoing calls.
- Takes handwritten or machine dictation.
- Transcribes handwritten or machine dictation.
- Acts as office receptionist and screens callers, directing them to whoever can best help them.
- Processes incoming and outgoing mail (including personal mail as directed).
- Writes routine correspondence on his/her own initiative.
- Makes appointments for the executive(s) for whom he/she works and reminds the executive(s) of the appointments.
- Performs general office work as required to relieve the executive(s) of some management and clerical duties.

In addition, some secretaries supervise clerical employees in the department or office, keep personnel records, and make travel arrangements for the executive(s) for whom they work.

One of the most attractive reasons for being a secretary is that a secretary works with little supervision and uses a great deal of initiative. After a secretary receives an assignment, he/she is expected to complete it using his/her own resources and creativity with little or no additional direction. Working with so much freedom permits one's creativity to blossom, and it is very satisfying to most people.

It has been said that secretarial work falls into three categories:

- Routine Duties—telephoning, filing, handling mail, typing reports and memorandums, stocking supplies—activities that are usually a part of each day's work.
- Assigned Tasks—those tasks that come about as the result of the day's work (transcribing letters, making travel arrangements, handling banking transactions, getting reference materials for the executive).
- Original, Creative Work—finding unassigned, nonroutine ways to assist the executive with his/her management role—an alert secretary develops this part of his/her work as a result of what is happening within the office during a particular time. (A secretary should try to find ways to aid the executive for whom he/she works with whatever projects are current **without being asked**.)

The very nature of the role he/she must fill requires a secretary to be **flexible** so he/she can shift from one type of activity to another as work in the office demands. A secretary who is creative, alert, and flexible and who is a skilled worker is an important asset in his/her role as a member of the management team of the company.

CAREER CHOICES FOR THE SECRETARY

Because the term "secretary" does not describe any one position but, rather, a great many different jobs all with a wide variety of duties and some individual specializations, there are a great variety of career choices for **well-trained** secretaries.

Private Secretary—A private secretary works for a particular executive and becomes involved in most phases of the work assigned to that executive. The private secretary's role usually requires him/her to get involved with every department within the company and to have a broad overall understanding of the total operation of the entire company.

Office Secretary—An office secretary performs secretarial functions for a number of people in one office area (usually a designated department). Even though the office secretary's base of operation is not so wide as a private secretary's base of operation, it is an excellent place for a new secretary to gain valuable experience and to learn about the operation of a company.

Executive Secretary (Administrative Assistant—In most instances, any secretary to a top executive is an executive secretary or an administrative assistant.) The executive secretary usually has specific responsibilities within the company which he/she handles on his/her own initiative, and he/she has the authority to make decisions regarding those responsibilities. In addition, an executive secretary usually has staff assistants (secretaries, typists, or clerks) reporting directly to him/her.

Government Secretary—Under the civil service system of Federal, state, and local governments, secretaries can obtain excellent secretarial jobs offering good job security without having to deal with the competitive environment of business and industry. Beginning government secretaries usually work for staff members in various departments, bureaus, and agencies of government. Frequently, these secretaries advance to the position of executive assistant.

Public Stenographer (Secretary)—A public stenographer is usually an experienced secretary who performs a wide variety of secretarial skills for various people who might require secretarial help at a particular time. (Business people who travel for their work sometimes hire a public stenographer.) A public stenographer usually has his/her office in a highly accessible public place (office building, hotel, airport) where business people who have need for secretarial services are likely to be. A public stenographer is paid on a fee basis that is determined by the services performed and the materials used. It is important for the public stenographer to be experienced as a secretary because he/she is likely to be called upon to perform a wide variety of duties (dictation, transcription, typing minutes of a meeting, typing manuscripts, duplicating, arranging meetings) within a short period of time.

Medical Secretary—A medical secretary has had specialized training in medical terminology, medical ethics, and in the methods of running a medical office (medical record-keeping, preparing insurance claims, managing financial records, booking appointments, and collecting fees) in addition to his/her basic secretarial training. A medical secretary is an important help in a doctor's office because he/she assists the doctor in keeping records and financial information in order that the doctor can devote himself/herself exclusively to practicing medicine.

Technical Secretary—In addition to performing the basic secretarial skills, the technical secretary must be able to recognize, spell, and use correctly an ever-increasing technical vocabulary. The technical secretary must also be able to recognize mathematical and engineering symbols, and he/she must understand the requirements for precision and accuracy. In addition, the technical secretary should be able to interpret technical data, and he/she should possess technical writing ability.

Legal Secretary—The legal secretary must be able to perform basic secretarial skills, must have a detailed understanding of the function, preparation, and execution of legal documents, and must understand legal terminology. The legal secretary must also understand legal ethics, and he/she must understand the need for complete accuracy in his/her work.

Corporation Secretary—The corporation secretary is **an officer of a corporation** rather than a secretary to a person. The corporation secretary is charged (by law) with the responsibility for keeping the legal and financial records of the business in good order. Ordinarily, a secretary in a business office does not reach the corporate secretary's level.

THE TRAINING OF A SECRETARY

The training a secretary receives for the complicated world of business he/she will enter will determine, to a great extent, how successful the secretary will be "on the job."

Skill Training

It is clear that a secretary must possess excellent business skills that will enable him/her to perform the following office functions:

- transcribe machine dictation
- operate a typewriter
- operate standard office machines
- understanding the advantages and costs of various duplicating processes
- maintain office records
- keep financial records
- make appointments
- answer the telephone
- place telephone calls for employer
- take telephone messages for employer
- process incoming and outgoing mail
- order office supplies
- write business letters
- address envelopes and packages
- prepare minutes of meetings
- make travel arrangements
- make meeting arrangements
- supervise other employees
- participate in management decisions

Understanding Of Business Practices And Business Organization

In addition to excellent skills, a secretary must possess a broad understanding of the following business functions in order to be able to understand business trends and changes:

- competition
- production
- profit

- finance
- marketing

A secretary must also understand how a business is organized and how the chain of command flows from one level to another in order to communicate effectively with everyone in a business.

Human Relations Techniques

Because the nature of his/her role requires constant communication of ideas and information, the secretary's training should include courses in speech, human relations, personality development, and wardrobe and grooming in addition to complete training in business and secretarial skills.

If a secretary's training includes complete training in each of the preceding areas, he/she should be prepared (at least by training) for success on the job.

A SECRETARIAL CAREER—THE OPEN DOOR

For a secretary who is interested in the work he/she is doing and who takes advantage of the opportunity to learn all he/she can each day about the operations, products, and services of the company for which he/she works, the opportunity for advancement can be unlimited. There are few people within a business who have as much information about the operations of the business as the secretary to a top executive. At the proper time, such information and background can provide a secretary with an excellent opportunity to move into a management position.

Many situations can be cited where a secretary, because of his/her background, understanding and insight, seemed to be the logical person to replace an executive who retired or who left the company.

FOR REVIEW AND DISCUSSION

1. Name the functions a secretary performs in an office.
2. Name and explain the three types of work a secretary does.
3. Name and explain at least eight different types of jobs a secretary can consider.
4. To be able to perform his/her role effectively, a secretary should have specialized training in three different types of duties—name and explain each one.
5. Why is a secretarial job sometimes said to be "an open door" to a management position with a company?

CHAPTER 21

The Secretary A Master Typist

OBJECTIVE

After studying this chapter you will understand:

- How to take care of a typewriter
- How to perform helpful typewriting techniques
- How to choose, order, and store stationery and supplies

JOB-RELATED VOCABULARY

Mechanism—The printing heads of the typewriter.

Paper Table (or Paper Rest)—The part of the typewriter behind the cylinder on which the paper rests.

Because a secretary spends so much of his/her time using the typewriter, he/she should to be able to produce copy at the typewriter with both **speed** and **accuracy.** The first step toward this goal is for the secretary to "know" his/her typewriter, to understand how the typewriter functions and what it is capable of doing. The second step is to give the typewriter the care it requires so it will function properly. The third step is to develop those typewriting techniques that will permit him/her to produce at the typewriter in the most efficient manner. By fulfilling each of these three steps, the secretary can be sure that the work he/she produces at the typewriter will represent the company for which he/she works in the best possible way.

Electronic Keyboarding

Electronic keyboards (such as the keyboards on computers and word processors) are being used more and more frequently in business offices. Data entered into a system through an electronic keyboard are often displayed on a television-like screen called a CRT (Cathode Ray Tube). Corrections, additions, and deletions can be made simply and easily **before a document is printed.** Certain functions such as centering, underscoring, tabulating and justifying margins are **automatic functions** that are **built into the system**, and, therefore, make entering data much easier. Data can be stored on electronic media (such as disks, cards, and tapes) and can be recalled for use and/or revision at a later time.

Some authorities are predicting that electronic keyboards attached to microcomputers will completely replace typewriters in the office of the future.

THE TYPEWRITER—AN EFFICIENT FRIEND

If a secretary expects his/her typewriter to function properly when he/she needs to use it, the secretary must expect to take proper care of the typewriter.

Most typewriter companies provide an instruction booklet with each new typewriter they sell. The booklet explains the special features the typewriter possesses, and it explains how the typewriter should be cared for to provide for the best operating results. If no booklet has been provided with the typewriter you are assigned to use, call the typewriter representative and ask him/her for one; or follow these suggestions:

THE CARE OF YOUR TYPEWRITER

1. Dust your typewriter daily.
   - Use a longhandled brush to dust hard-to-reach parts.
   - Be sure to dust **under** the machine.
2. To prevent excessive dust from accumulating:
   - If your typewriter has a movable carriage, move the carriage to the extreme right or the extreme left before you erase (unless you are using a typewriter with an element or a daisy wheel).
   - Always be sure the typewriter is covered when you leave at night. (This practice prevents excessive dust from settling on the typewriter.)
3. Periodically clean the typewriter keys as follows:
   - Roll a piece of chemically treated fiber surface paper into the typewriter; put the ribbon indicator in stencil position; and strike each key several times until the imprint on the paper is clean and sharp. (This is the cleanest method of cleaning typewriter keys.)
   - Press a plastic type cleaner firmly against the type and pull it away; then fold the soiled part into a ball. Repeat this process until the keys are clean.
   - Use a stiff, dry, short-bristled brush in a light tapping motion (not a gouging motion). To clean the brush, rub the bristles on a piece of scratch paper.

   (Most typewriter dealers do not recommend the use of a liquid cleaner to clean typewriter keys.)
4. Protect the cylinder (platen) and the paper-feed rolls as follows:
   - Clean the cylinder and the paper-feed rolls with a cloth lightly moistened with alcohol or a special liquid cleaner.
   - If the cylinder is removable, lift it out, and dust the trough.

   (If the cylinder becomes dirty from ink and dust collecting on it, it will become shiny and will lose its grip.)
5. Have the typewriter serviced periodically.
   - Arrange with a local typewriter service agency to check, oil, and service your typewriter so it will continue to provide reliable service. (It is not a good idea to oil your own typewriter; leave that for experienced service people who know what and where to oil!)

HELPFUL TYPEWRITING TECHNIQUES

The following techniques will help you to use your typewriter more efficiently. Be sure to practice these techniques so you can perform them efficiently and quickly.

To produce quality work at the typewriter, you must be able to make corrections that **are not detectable.**

Erasures

1. Unless you are using a typewriter with an element or a daisy wheel, move the carriage to the extreme right or left (depending on what side of the paper the error is on). Moving the carriage will prevent erasure

crumbs from clogging the mechanism. If the error is on the upper two thirds of the paper, **roll the paper up** before you erase. If the error is on the lower third of the paper, **roll the paper down** before you erase. (The latter procedure will prevent the paper from accidentally slipping while you are erasing.)

2. Use a typewriter eraser in light, up-and-down, oval motions. Blow lightly to remove grit as you erase.
3. Sometimes it may be desirable to "fade out" an erasure by rubbing the erased area with a piece of chalk, a correction pencil, or a touch-up stick before you type the correction.
4. Reposition the carriage and the paper, and type the correction (lightly).

Cover-Ups

1. Back space to the incorrect letter or letters.
2. Place the cover-up (a piece of chalk-coated paper), coated side down, and **retype the error.** Some of the chalk from the paper will transfer and cover the error.
3. Remove the chalk-coated paper, backspace, and type the correction. (You may have to go over the letter or word retyped several times so it will match the other typing on the page.)

Special correction paper is available for use on carbon copies and with carbon ribbons. Some typewriters are equipped with a correcting ribbon.

Correction Fluids

To make corrections using correction fluids (sometimes referred to as "white out"), follow these steps:

1. Roll the paper so the error is easy to reach.
2. Open the bottle of correction fluid and wipe the brush on the inside of the bottle opening to remove excess fluid.
3. With the **tip** of the brush, **dot** the correction fluid over the error. **Follow the outline** of the incorrect letter. Correct only **one letter at a time.**
4. Allow the fluid to **dry thoroughly before typing the correction.** (**Chemical-base** correction fluid dries in **eight to ten seconds. Water-base** correction may require **up to a full minute** to dry.)
5. Reposition the paper, and type the correction.

Squeezing And Spreading

To type a word containing **one letter more** than the error, follow these suggestions:

1. Erase the shorter word typed in error.
2. Move the carriage to the **space after** the word which precedes the erasure.
3. Depress and hold the half-space key (if your typewriter is so equipped), type the first letter of the word to be substituted, and release the key. If your typewriter does not have a half-space key, use the paper release and move the paper slightly.
4. Repeat step 3 for each letter of the correction.

```
Watch what you re doing!

Watch what you are doing!
```

Fig. 171. Squeezing

To type a word containing **one letter fewer** than the error, follow these suggestions:

1. Erase the word typed in error.
2. Move the carriage to the space where the **first letter of the erased word was.**
3. Depress and hold the half-space key (if your typewriter is so equipped), type the first letter of the word to be substituted, and release the key.
4. Repeat step 3 for each letter of correction.

```
Think what yoou are doing!

Think what  you  are doing!
```

Fig. 172. Spreading

Back-Feeding Envelopes

From time to time you may have a large number of envelopes or cards to type. Here are some suggestions that will help you to do the job more easily:

1. Feed the first envelope so that only about one-half inch of the envelope is free (against the paper table).
2. Place the top of the second envelope (flap toward you) between the cylinder and the bottom of the first envelope.
3. Type the first envelope.
4. As you turn the cylinder to remove the first envelope, the second envelope will be in position for typing. **Before you type** envelope number two, insert envelope number three using the procedure described in step 2.

Fig. 173. Back-feeding envelopes

Front-Feeding Small Cards

1. Make a pleat about a half-inch deep across the middle of a sheet of paper 8½ x 11 inches. (The depth of the pleat controls how far down you can type on the cards.) Tape the pleat down on the sides to hold it in place.
2. Feed the pleated sheet into the typewriter and align the fold of the pleat with the top of the alignment scale on the typewriter.
3. Place the first card into the pleat and position it for typing. (Before you type the first card, draw a line with a pencil on the paper along the outside left end of the card. This line will serve as a guide for the

placement of the cards, and it will permit you to type each card with consistent margins.)

4. Remove each card after it is typed.

Fig. 174. Front-feeding small cards

Justified Right Margins (On A Machine With Standard Spacing)

At some time during your secretarial career, you may be asked to type a manuscript or a report with justified (or even) right margins. Such a request might be made when a report is being prepared that will be given to a very special group—such as the Board of Directors of a company. To justify the right margin when you are typing on a machine with standard spacing, follow these steps:

1. Set the margins for the exact column width you want.
2. In order to be able to see more accurately where the right margin ends, draw a pencil line on the paper at the point where the right margin locks.
3. Type each line of copy (double spaced) **the full width of the writing line.** Fill in unused spaces at the end of a line with diagonals. (The diagonals indicate additional spaces that must be included in the final typing to bring the copy to the right margin.) NOTE: Careful planning is required here so words do not extend past the assigned right margin.
4. Remove the draft copy from the typewriter, and indicate with a penciled check mark the places in each line where you can add extra spaces (as indicated by the number of diagonals at the end of the line). As a general rule, do not leave an additional space after the first word in a line; and do not isolate a short word with a space on each side.
5. Retype the copy with **single** spacing and insert the extra spaces as indicated in the draft copy.
   NOTE: If your typewriter is equipped with proportional spacing, follow the directions in the manual explaining the operation of the typewriter.

```
Throughout the centuries, the most advantageous method for a//
person to sell his wares has been to exhibit them in such a///
manner that the prospective buyer is permitted a visual and///
tactile inspection of them.  This elementary principle of/////
merchandise presentation has persisted, intact, in Mexico,////
Africa, and India.  In our society merchandise presentation///
has experienced a dynamic evolution due to changes in the/////
culture, changes in the merchandise itself, and new merchan-//
dising philosophy as well as increased demands and sophistica-
tion on the part of the consumer.  From its humble beginnings/
in the open markets, visual merchandising has grown to be an//
integral and dominant part of the selling process.
```

Fig. 175. Copy marked for justifying

Throughout the centuries, the most advantageous method for a person to sell his wares has been to exhibit them in such a manner that the prospective buyer is permitted a visual and tactile inspection of them. This elementary principle of merchandise presentation has persisted, intact, in Mexico, Africa, and India. In our society merchandise presentation has experienced a dynamic evolution due to changes in the culture, changes in the merchandise itself, and new merchandising philosophy as well as increased demands and sophistication on the part of the consumer. From its humble beginnings in the open markets, visual merchandising has grown to be an integral and dominant part of the selling process.

Fig. 176. Final copy with a justified right margin

Realigning Copy

There are times when it will be necessary for you to reinsert a typewritten page to make a correction or an insertion in the copy. To make a perfect realignment takes considerable patience and skill, but it can be done. Here are some suggestions that will make it easier for you to realign copy:

1. As you type, study the exact distance between the bottom of the typed line and the aligning scale on your typewriter. This procedure will enable you to realign the **line position** more easily. Each typewriter is just a little different from the other, so it is important to use one typewriter all the time so that you can get accustomed to the exact distance on the machine you use.
2. If you always keep the paper guide on your typewriter set at one spot and if you are always careful to have your paper straight before you begin to type, you will have a much easier time aligning the letters. After you are sure the paper is straight, study the relationship of the letters to the **vertical lines** on the alignment scale. The letters may be exactly in line with the vertical lines or they may be a little to the left or a little to the right (each typewriter is different). If you use the same typewriter all the time, you will know it well; and realignment will be much easier.

By mastering the techniques suggested in this section of the chapter, you will be typing much more efficiently.

CHOOSING STATIONERY AND SUPPLIES

The choice of stationery and supplies is important because one of the ways a company projects its image is through the choice of high-quality stationery. For that reason, it is important for the secretary to understand what characteristics are a part of quality stationery and supplies.

Bond Paper

Bond paper (so called because it was originally used for bonds) can be made from all-cotton fiber (rag), from all-sulphite (wood pulp), or from any combination of the two. Bond made of a high-cotton fiber count is of excellent quality. It is long lasting, and it does not deteriorate with age. Bond paper with a high-cotton fiber count is hard to the pencil touch, and it is difficult to tear. Usually papers for business forms that must be kept for a long period of time are of cotton fiber bond; and paper for business forms that need to last only a few years are made of all-sulphite or high-sulphite bond.

When two or more pages are needed for a letter, the plain bond paper chosen for the second and succeeding pages should be **of the same quality** as the letterhead bond used for the first page. (Letterhead bond is usually 20-pound paper, although some companies use 16- or 24-pound bond for letterheads.)

Watermarks

If you hold a letterhead sheet up to the light, you will usually see a design or words embedded in the paper. The design is known as a **watermark.** The watermark can be the company seal, the company trademark, the company name, or it can be the brand name of the paper. Only the better grade of bond paper has a watermark. Therefore, the watermark is an indication of quality paper.

When watermarked paper is used, the watermark should be read across the paper from left to right in the same way the typing is read. Special care should be taken when you use plain sheets of watermarked paper to be sure the watermark is going in the proper direction.

Weight Of Paper

The weight of paper is described by **substance number.** The substance number is determined by the weight of a ream containing **500 sheets** of 17-by-22 inch paper. If a ream weighs 16 pounds, the paper is referred to as substance 16 or 16-pound weight. Paper is produced in a wide variety of weights. Letterheads and envelopes are **usually** of substance 16, 20 or 24. Airmail stationery is **usually** of substance 9 or 13.

Erasability

Some papers have a special erasability feature. Such paper has a special coating that barely allows ribbon ink or carbon to rest on the paper. While it is very easy to make an erasure on paper with the special erasability feature, it is equally easy to smear and smudge the type. Usually an erasure can be made without much difficulty on a 16-pound, high-cotton-fiber bond paper that does not have the special erasability feature. The most difficult paper on which to make neat, clean erasures is the all-sulphite paper (the type of paper usually used for typewriting assignments in school).

LETTERHEADS

Many companies have two types of letterheads:

- A general letterhead designed for general use that contains the company name, address, and telephone number; and it sometimes contains information about the company's products or the names of company trademarks.
- Top executives in many companies have a special "prestige" letterhead made of unusually fine-quality paper (such as 100 percent rag) using specialized printing techniques. The executive letterhead usually shows the company name and address and the executive's name and title. Executive letterheads usually **do not** contain a telephone number nor any mention of the company's products or trademarks.

Letterheads are usually ordered with matching envelopes and matching blank sheets for two-page letters.

Second Sheets

Thin sheets used for file copies of letters and for multicopy typing are referred to as second sheets, onionskin, tissue, or manifold. Second sheets are available in lightweight paper of substances 7 to 13 with smooth, glazed, or rippled finish. Second sheets with rippled finish slip less than the second sheets with smooth or glazed finish, and they **appear** to be of better quality. However, ripple finish second sheets create more bulk in the files and in storage drawers than the smooth finish second sheets do.

Carbon Paper

Typewriter carbon paper—a thin, dark-colored tissue coated on one side with carbon—is available in a variety of sizes, colors, weights, finishes, and qualities.

The top (non-carbon) side of most carbon paper is coated with a plastic, varnish, or metallic finish that makes the sheet curl-free; and it reduces wrinkling. High-quality carbon paper that is coated is smudge-free; it produces a neater carbon copy; and it lasts much longer than uncoated carbon paper.

Carbon Paper Finish

Generally speaking, a lightweight carbon paper with a hard finish produces the sharpest impressions. However, the carbon paper finish to be used depends upon many factors. Here are some guidelines for selecting the right carbon paper finish:

USE . . .

Soft Finish—

IF . . .

- The typewriter has a soft cylinder
- The typist has a soft touch

(NOTE: Do not use soft finish carbon if the typewriter has elite [or smaller] type.)

Hard Finish—

IF . . .

- The typewriter has a hard cylinder
- The typist has a heavy touch
- The typewriter has elite (or smaller) type

Medium Finish—

IF . . .

- The typing situation is not covered under the headings, soft and hard-finish carbon paper, above

Carbon Paper Weight

Carbon paper weight depends upon the weight of the copy paper being used and the number of carbon copies to be typed. Here is a chart to help you select the correct carbon paper weight:

Carbon Copies To Be Typed	Correct Weight of Carbon Paper	Copy Paper Weight (Substance)
Up to 3	standard or medium	13-, 16-, or 20-pound
4 or 5	medium	13- or 16-pound
6 to 10	medium or light	9- or 13-pound
11 to 15	light	9-pound

To save paper and avoid crowding files, **both sides** of the **copy sheet** should be used when you are typing a two-page letter.

When memory typewriters or microcomputers are used, it is not necessary to prepare carbon copies because the data are stored on electronic media (such as disks, cards, and tapes), and an extra copy can easily be "played out" if one is required.

Some office workers suggest that the use of carbon copies is no longer necessary because of the ready availability of photocopy machines in offices. It is important to remember, however, that the **cost** of a copy made on a photocopy machine is **considerably more** than the cost of preparing a carbon copy.

Ordering Office Supplies

If you expect office supplies to do the job for which they are intended, it is important to purchase quality materials. To get quality supplies at a fair price and to be sure that sound advice is available when you need to purchase something with which you have not had previous experience, it is important to establish a contact with a reputable office supply dealer serving your area. (The company for which you work will probably have a long-established relationship with such a dealer.) Usually an office supply dealer will have a salesman who will call on your firm periodically. Be sure to keep a list of office supplies that are getting low so they can be ordered when the salesman calls. (If you work for a large company, you will order office supplies from the Stock Room. The Stock Room will, in turn, order from the office supply dealer as necessary.)

Be extremely cautious about overbuying office supplies. Some supplies such as mimeograph stencils, carbon paper, and typewriter ribbons dry out or harden after a period of time. Whatever money was saved on buying in large quantities would soon be lost if the office supplies were not usable! However, to take advantage of a good price, some companies do plan their needs for paper a year in advance. Usually, the paper is ordered at one time, but it is delivered at three or four preset times during the year.

Storing Supplies

It is extremely important to store office supplies in an orderly manner. All supplies of the same type should be stored together, and the **oldest** supplies of each type should be toward the front (so they will be used first). Frequently used supplies should be stored so they are most accessible. Loose materials should be stored in marked boxes. It is also a good idea to put a list of the supplies to be stored on each shelf on the door of the storage cabinet next to the shelf. This procedure encourages everyone who uses the cabinet to help keep it neat.

FOR REVIEW AND DISCUSSION

1. How does electronic keyboarding differ from typewriting?
2. What are the three steps that will enable a secretary to produce at the typewriter with speed and accuracy?
3. Explain the five steps that should be taken to take proper care of a typewriter.
4. Explain the following typewriting techniques:
   A. Making Erasures
   B. Using Cover-Ups
   C. Squeezing and Spreading Copy
   D. Back-Feeding Envelopes
   E. Front-Feeding Small Cards
   F. Justified Right Margins (on a machine with standard spacing)
   G. Realigning Copy
5. Explain the following terms related to stationery:
   A. Bond Paper
   B. Watermarks
   C. Erasability
6. Explain the two types of letterheads used by many companies.
7. Describe the three types of carbon paper finish and the circumstances that govern their use.
8. Describe the circumstances that determine the weight of the carbon paper to be used.
9. Explain how office supplies should be stored.

Turn to your workbook and complete Student Projects 33 and 34.

CHAPTER 22

Dictation/Transcription And The Secretary

OBJECTIVE

After studying this chapter you will understand how to:
- Take dictation professionally
- Give dictation
- Produce high-quality shorthand and machine transcription
- Proofread transcripts with accuracy

JOB-RELATED VOCABULARY

Ambiguities—Statements or expressions that are unclear, indistinct, capable of being misunderstood.

Comprehensive Transcript—A transcript that explains and answers the situation completely.

Because a business executive spends a considerable amount of time communicating by means of letters, memorandums, and reports, it is extremely important that a secretary possess excellent dictation and transcription skills. In fact, almost all executives will say that they consider dictation, transcription, and typewriting (and keyboarding) skills to be of **primary** importance to a secretary even though other skills are also very important.

For best results, dictation must be a cooperative effort of the dictator and the secretary. The executive makes the decisions about content and priority of dictation. The secretary detects omissions, errors, and ambiguities; and he/she types a complete, comprehensive, well-organized transcript.

TAKING DICTATION

A number of executives still prefer to dictate directly to a secretary (rather than to a dictating machine). However, as the use of word processing (discussed in Chapter 10) continues to grow, it seems likely that machine dictation (particularly centralized dictation systems of the phone-in type) will become more and more popular.

Many executives have a particular time each day when they like to dictate (usually just after they have had an opportunity to study the contents of the morning mail). For that reason a secretary should plan his/her schedule to be free of other duties during the time the executive chooses for dictation. It is important, too, for the secretary to indicate to other office workers the time the executive usually chooses for dictation. Knowing this, they will take responsibility for answering the telephones so that the secretary and the executive will not be interrupted during dictation (except for emergencies or extremely urgent business). This procedure is important because interruptions often cause the person dictating to lose his/her train of thought, and valuable time is then wasted reviewing and getting started again.

Helpful Dictation Supplies

Here is a list of supplies you will need to have for dictation in order to do a more efficient job:

1. **A Stenographer's Notebook**—A notebook with green tinted pages is easiest on your eyes in fluorescent lighting. Choose a notebook with a spiral binding at the top so the pages will lie flat. A notebook with hard front and back covers will stand upright during transcription.
2. **A Pen**—A fineline pen with dark ink is best for taking dictation because the notes taken with it are easier to read. Always have a second pen in reserve.
3. **A Pointed Colored Pencil or Pen**—Usually a secretary uses a colored (red) pen or pencil for editing his/her shorthand notes.
4. **A File Folder**—In the file folder you can put any letters, memorandums, or notes that the person dictating gives to you. Put a few paper clips on the sides of the file folder in case you need them during dictation.
5. **A Rubber Finger Pad**—By placing a rubber finger pad on your left thumb, you will be able to turn the pages of your stenographic notebook more easily while you are taking dictation.

Good Dictation Practices

The following practices will make you seem to be more efficient as a secretary, and they will make it easier for you to take dictation:

1. Be available for dictation as soon as the executive indicates that he/she is ready. Have your dictation supplies together and ready to use so that all you have to do is get them and go to the executive's office when you are called. Be sure to have your stenographer's notebook open to a clean page with the current date at the top of the left-hand corner of the page or on the bottom line. (If you take dictation from more than one executive, write the executive's initials at the beginning of the dictation or use a different notebook for each executive.)
2. When you are in the executive's office, sit quietly without squirming and without talking. It is extremely important for the executive to be able to concentrate as he/she gives dictation in order to maintain his/her train of thought.

   Usually, you will not have difficulty adjusting your shorthand writing speed to the executive's dictation speed. The executive will soon understand how fast he/she can dictate without having to repeat, and he/she will dictate at that speed to keep his/her concentration at peak level. **(This fact, however, should not be used as an excuse for poor shorthand skill!)**

Sometimes young executives dictate very rapidly so as not to appear to be "too slow" in the eyes of the secretary. Usually they will reduce the rate of dictation to a more reasonable rate as they feel more confident.

3. If the executive is interrupted when he/she is dictating, use the time you are waiting to read your notes and mark punctuation and paragraphs in them using your red pen or pencil.
4. Leave three or four blank lines in your notebook between each item of dictation. In this space you can write insertions or special directions if they are required.
5. Avoid writing over or between notes in order to make insertions the executive dictates after he/she has completed the original dictation. Instead, use the blank lines at the end of the dictation and code the extra material into the original dictation by using a circled letter Ⓐ or number ① at the place in the original dictation where the new material should go.
6. If you have any idea you will not be able to transcribe proper names easily, write them in longhand. (Remember: it is better to be safe with longhand occasionally than unsure with shorthand!)
7. To remind yourself to clarify something (spelling or an ambiguity) put a large "X" or a "✓" in your notes at the point where the clarification is needed.
8. Do not interrupt the dictator to clarify a point. Wait until he/she has stopped dictating and then clarify. (The only time the secretary should interrupt the executive during dictation is when the executive is so far ahead that the secretary could never catch up.)
9. Number each item of dictation at the **beginning of the item** as follows:

This procedure will tell you when you have completed transcription of one item and are ready to begin another.

10. If the dictator gives you a letter or memorandum to accompany an item of dictation, number the letter or memorandum the same as the dictation that goes with it, and put it into the file folder you are carrying.
11. To help turn a notebook page more easily during dictation, use **one** of the following methods:
    A. Wear a rubber finger pad on your left thumb to help grasp the page.
    B. Bend the lower left-hand corner of the notebook pages upward so the pages will separate, making them easier to grasp and turn.
    C. Move the notebook page up continuously as you write. By doing this, your hand stays in the same writing position instead of moving up and down on the page; and the page is separated from the other pages in the notebook, making it easier to turn.
12. Date the front cover of the new stenographer's notebook with the date you started using it. When you have filled the notebook, add the date of the last dictation in the notebook to the front cover also. File filled notebooks (latest dates on top) for a period of time—depending upon the nature of the dictation in the notebooks and company policy.

Informal Dictation

In addition to the formal dictation given in the executive's office, there is also the matter of dictation given over the telephone and dictation given at the typewriter.

Telephone Dictation—Since the dictator cannot watch you while he/she is dictating to you over the telephone, it is helpful if you say "yes" after you have completed each phrase. Do not hesitate to ask to have a phrase repeated if you didn't understand. When you have completed the dictation, read the entire set of notes to the dictator so he/she can check them for accuracy.

Dictation at the Typewriter—Occasionally, an executive may ask you to type something as he/she dictates it. Before you begin to type, ask whether it will be long or short so you can determine the margins that should be used.

To be successful in taking dictation at the typewriter, you must concentrate completely on what you are doing. Do not stop to correct errors as you make them; wait until the dictator has completed his/her dictation. Frequently, it is necessary to go back and retype the entire dictation because the placement is not correct and because errors need to be corrected and insertions need to be made.

More than likely you will not encounter a large amount of informal dictation, but you should practice so you can be ready if you are asked to take dictation over the telephone or at the typewriter.

GIVING DICTATION

Because many secretaries have administrative responsibilities, they have reason to dictate correspondence as well as to take dictation. Secretaries understand the dictation process completely, and they should develop dictation skills quickly. These suggestions will enable you to dictate letters more efficiently:

1. Take a few minutes before you begin to dictate to organize your thoughts about the dictation you will give.
2. Speak clearly and distinctly. Be especially careful to pronounce proper names, technical terms, and numbers carefully. (Spell proper names and technical terms if they are difficult.)
3. As you start to dictate, mention what you are dictating—letter, memorandum, report—first.
4. Indicate the number of copies you will need (if more than one) and to whom they are to be sent at the beginning of your dictation.
5. Dictate "rush" items first.
6. If the item is to be transcribed in a form that is different from what is usually done, give instructions at the time you dictate the item.
7. If the person taking or transcribing the dictation has a question, be gracious when you answer.
8. Proofread finished transcripts carefully to be sure they are accurate. (Take the opportunity to praise work that is well done. It is a great source of encouragement.)

Following these suggestions will help you to develop a more satisfactory (and a more efficient) dictating procedure.

QUALITY SHORTHAND TRANSCRIPTION

The desirable end product of all dictated material is a **mailable** transcript of that material; that is, a transcript that the dictator of the material will accept. The secretary's primary tools for efficient transcription are spelling, punctuation, word usage, typewriting skill, ability to use reference books, and logical thinking. The combination of these skills along with the ability to take shorthand efficiently and to read the notes enables a secretary to produce a mailable transcript.

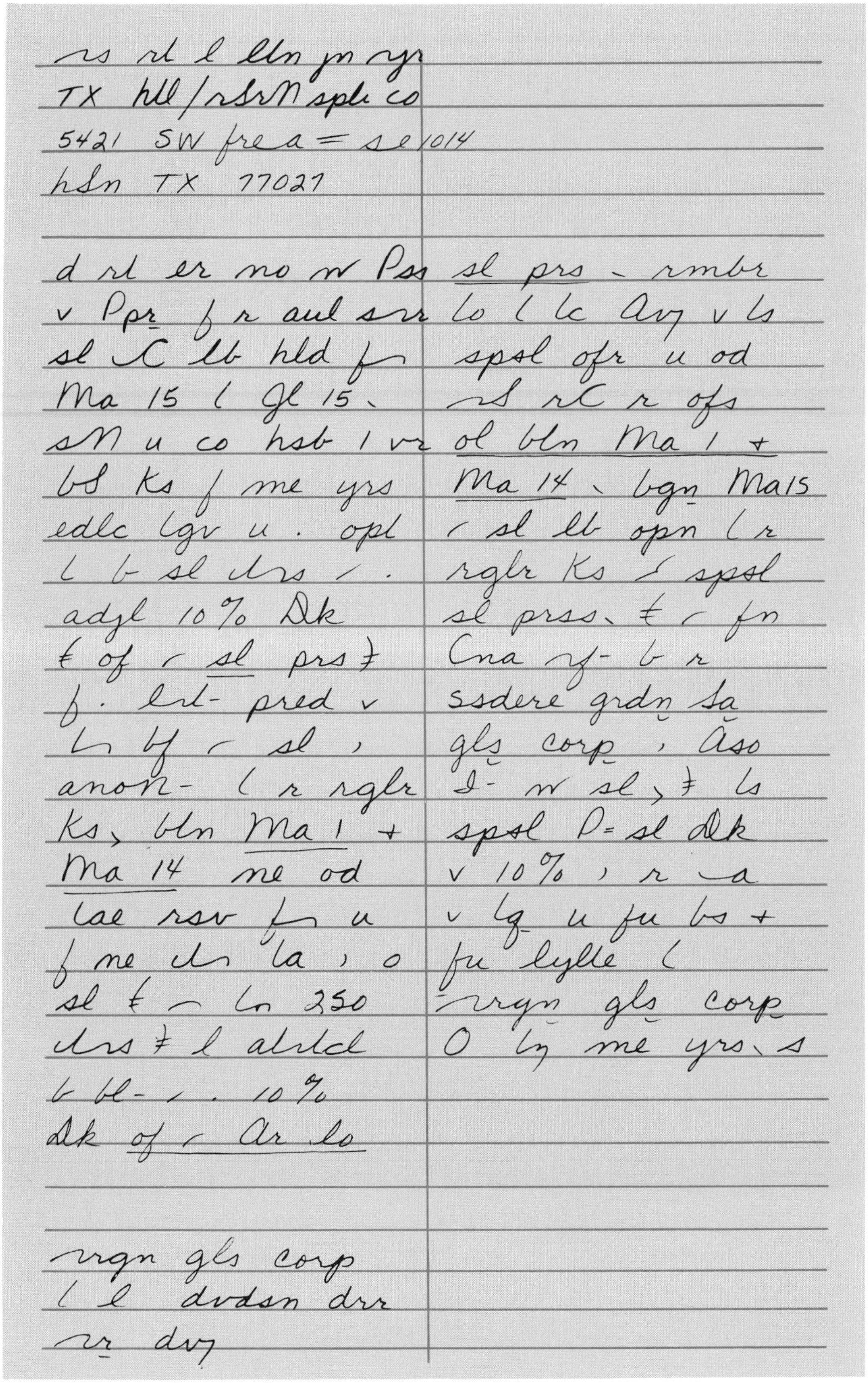

rs rl l lln jn ryr
TX hll/rSrN spl co
5421 SW fre a = se 1014
hsn TX 77027

d rl er no w Pss
v Ppr f r aul ssr
sl C lb hld f
Ma 15 l Jl 15.
sN u co hsb l vr
bS Ks f me yrs
edlc lgv u . opl
l b sl drs / .
adjl 10% Dk
€ of sl prs ‡
f . lrl- pred v
Ls bf sl ,
anoN- l r rglr
Ks, bln Ma 1 +
Ma 14 me od
lae rsv f u
f me drs la , o
sl € ln 250
drs ‡ l alrlcl
b bl- / . 10%
Dk of Ar lo

sl prs - rmbr
lo l lc Avj v ls
spsl ofr u od
rS rC r ofs
ol bln Ma 1 +
Ma 14 . bgn Ma 15
sl lb opn l r
rglr Ks & spsl
sl prss. € fn
Cna rf- b r
ssdere grdn Sa
gls corp , Aso
I- w sl , ‡ ls
spsl D=sl Dk
v 10% , r a
v lg u fu bs +
fu lylle l
rrgn gls corp
O lg me yrs. s

rrgn gls corp
l l dvdsn drr
rr dvj

*Fig. 177. Notes written in **Speedwriting** Shorthand*

MGC **MORGAN GLASS CORPORATION**
4675 West Market Street
Greensboro, NC 27408-1925

April 12, 19--

Ms Ruth L. Lawton, General Manager
Texas Hotel/Restaurant Supply Company
5421 Southwest Freeway - Suite 1014
Houston, TX 77027

Dear Ruth:

We are now in the process of preparing for our annual summer sale, which will be held from May 15 to July 15. Since your company has been one of our best customers for many years, we would like to give you an opportunity to buy sale items at an additional 10 percent discount (off the <u>sale</u> price) for a limited period of time before the sale is announced to our regular customers.

Between <u>May 1</u> and <u>May 14</u> any order that we receive from you for any item that is on sale (more than 250 items) will automatically be billed at a 10 percent discount <u>off the already low sale price</u>. Remember, though, to take advantage of this special offer, your order must reach our office <u>only between May 1 and May 14</u>. Beginning May 15, the sale will be open to our regular customers at the special sale prices. (The fine china manufactured by our subsidiary, Garden State Glass Corporation, is also included in the sale.)

This special pre-sale discount of 10 percent is our way of thanking you for your business and for your loyalty to Morgan Glass Corporation over these many years.

Sincerely,

MORGAN GLASS CORPORATION

T. L. Davidson

T. L. Davidson, Director
Marketing Division

em

Fig. 178. Letter transcribed from the shorthand notes on the previous page

Steps In The Transcription Process

Here are the steps you will want to follow to produce a mailable transcript of the shorthand notes you have taken:

1. Plan your time so you can transcribe your notes soon after the dictation period is over. By doing this, you will be working with your notes while the dictation is still fresh in your mind. Regardless of the order of the notes, transcribe the items marked RUSH first. (Transcribing RUSH items first will make you appear to be more efficient.)
2. Before you begin to type, read your notes and mark capitalization, punctuation, and paragraphing to be inserted during the transcribing. This process is called "editing" your notes. It is a good practice to use a red pen or pencil to edit your notes so the punctuation, capitalization, and paragraphing stand out as you transcribe.
3. When you insert the papers in the typewriter, be sure to include the correct number of carbon copies.
4. Place your stenographer's notebook in the "stand-up" position to the left of your typewriter, so it will be easier to see your notes as you transcribe.
5. The margins on your typewriter will need to be set after determining whether the item to be transcribed is short, medium, or long. The chart that follows will help you to determine the correct margin settings for a short, medium, or long item:

Number of Words		**Margins** Pica Type	Elite Type	**Lines Between Date and Inside Address on Letters**
Short	up to 100	22-62	27-75	8
Medium	125 to 175	17-67	21-81	6
Long	200 to 300	12-72	15-87	4

6. Read a complete sentence from your shorthand notes; be sure it makes sense; then type it. Follow this procedure until the entire item has been transcribed.
7. **Before** you remove the transcript from the typewriter, proofread it carefully. Doing so will enable you to make necessary corrections without having to reinsert and realign the paper in the typewriter.
8. If the item that has been transcribed requires an envelope, type the envelope (review "Envelopes" on pages 29 to 31 of this textbook).

Fig. 179. Transcribing machine dictation

Here are some additional suggestions that will help you to transcribe more efficiently:

Correcting the Dictator's Errors—Usually the dictator will expect you to correct errors in names, dates, amounts, or grammar without checking with him/her first. As you make corrections, be careful not to change the emphasis or meaning of a sentence. If you cannot make a correction without rewording a sentence, consult the dictator before you make the change.

Verifying Confusing Items—If certain words, figures, dates, or times do not make sense to you or if they seem to be out of place or in a misarranged order, check with the dictator before you transcribe them. NEVER TRANSCRIBE ANYTHING THAT IS NOT CLEAR AND LOGICAL.

Canceling Shorthand Notes—As soon as you have transcribed an item of dictation, draw a diagonal line or an "X" through your shorthand notes for that item. Canceling transcribed items helps you to see at a glance what dictation has not been transcribed. Since shorthand notes are not always transcribed in the order in which they are dictated, the canceling procedure is important.

Presenting Transcribed Items for Signature—Once dictated items have been typed, they should be presented to the person who will sign them. Present a letter for signature by inserting the original, the copy, and the enclosures (if any) under the flap of the envelope with the addressed side of the envelope at the back. After the letters have been signed, they should be returned to the secretary, who will fold them, insert them in envelopes, and place them in the outgoing mail basket. The carbon copies will be put in the file basket, or they will be prepared for distribution.

QUALITY MACHINE TRANSCRIPTION

There are many times when it is more convenient for an executive to use a dictating machine to prepare his/her dictation than it is to dictate to a secretary. These times might include the following:

- Answering correspondence while traveling
- Preparing dictation during the evening
- Preparing dictation during weekends
- Drafting a report or a memorandum

For these reasons, it is important for a secretary to be skilled at operating the transcribing unit of the standard dictating machines.

Each dictating/transcribing system has certain features that are distinctive. Those features can be determined by studying the operator's manual that comes with the system. If you cannot find the operator's manual for the dictating/transcribing system in your office, call the dealer from whom it was purchased. The dealer will be happy to supply you with a copy of the operator's manual, and he/she might even send a salesperson to your office to demonstrate the operation of the system.

Mailable Transcripts And Machine Transcription

Unless the dictator specifically requests a "draft copy," you will be expected to produce a **mailable transcript** directly from the transcribing unit with no retyping. Producing a mailable transcript directly from the transcribing unit is made much easier if the dictator follows the suggestions listed under the heading, GIVING DICTATION, on page 232 in this chapter. Here are a few additional techniques that will help make you a skilled transcriber of machine dictation:

1. Study the indicator slip (or dial) in the transcribing machine you are using. It will help you to:

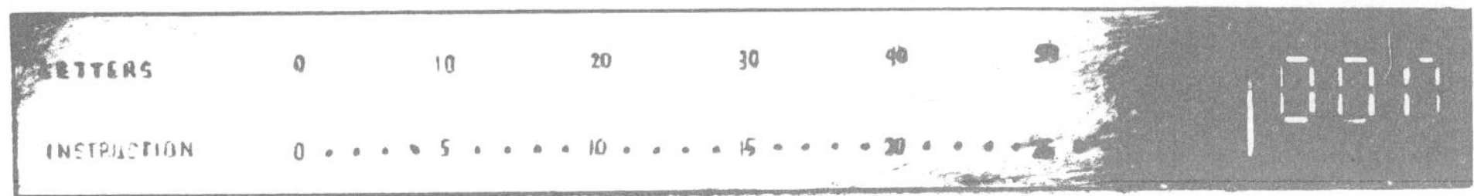

Fig. 180. Indicator slip from a dictating/transcribing system

   A. Determine the length of the items you will transcribe so you can set the margins of your typewriter properly.
   B. Know where the dictator made corrections as he/she dictated so you can preview the corrections and make notes about them in order to be prepared to transcribe efficiently.

2. Follow the suggested transcribing rhythm:
   A. **Listen** to the dictation in phrases or word groups.
   B. **Stop** the transcribing unit.
   C. **Type** the dictation.
   Just before you finish typing the final word in the phrase or word group, start the rhythm again—Listen, Stop, Type.

3. When the entire item has been transcribed, proofread it carefully **before** you remove the paper from the typewriter.

4. Present the transcribed items to the person who will sign them; then follow up by preparing the signed items for mailing or distribution. (See page 33 for procedures for presenting items for signature and preparing them for mailing or distribution.)

With practice you should be able to operate accurately any transcribing unit to which you are assigned; and you should be able to produce an accurate, mailable transcript directly from the transcribing unit (without retyping it).

FOR REVIEW AND DISCUSSION

1. Explain the roles of the executive and the secretary in giving and transcribing dictation.
2. How can a secretary plan his/her time to be ready for dictation as he/she is needed?
3. What supplies does a secretary need to take dictation efficiently?
4. Explain the "Good Dictation Practices" described in this chapter.
5. Explain the term, "Informal Dictation."
6. Explain the eight steps to **giving** effective dictation.
7. Explain the eight steps in the transcription process.
8. What is the correct procedure for presenting transcribed items for signature?
9. When might a dictator want to use a dictating machine rather than have you take a letter in shorthand?
10. Explain the **first two steps** in the machine transcription process.

Turn to your workbook and complete Student Projects 35 and 36.

CHAPTER 23

Public Relations And The Secretary

OBJECTIVE

After studying this chapter you will understand:

- The secretary's role in public relations
- How to make appointments for an executive
- How to receive office callers
- How the secretary "sets the pace" for other office workers

JOB-RELATED VOCABULARY

Precise Word—A word expressing the exact meaning required.

Productivity—The condition of bringing about positive results or benefits as the result of effort or work.

Today a company must employ successful public relations in order to grow and develop. It is not enough for a company to produce a product and to service that product well in order to make sales and create a profit. First, public relations tell a company how and what its "publics"—customers, employees, stockholders, government, suppliers—are thinking and how their attitudes change. Second, public relations tell a company how its actions (or lack of actions) are accepted by its "publics," and they indicate how the public is likely to react to what the company plans to do.

THE SECRETARY'S ROLE

All the good work done by expensive public relations specialists who are hired to advise a company about the best ways to project a strong, positive image can be destroyed by company employees who are curt and abrasive as they deal with the public (in person, through letters and memorandums, or over the telephone). The secretary plays a vital role in public relations each time he/she greets a caller. By being polite, gracious, and efficient, the secretary can increase the caller's confidence in the company. A secretary who understands that creating a friendly atmosphere and a feeling of respect for the company is a vital part of his/her public relations goal is a valuable asset to his/her company.

Psychologists state that our initial contacts with people and with situations are the ones that make vivid impressions on them. For that reason, the secretary needs to be particularly aware of his/her role in the public relations of the company so he/she will "set the stage" for positive, productive meetings and business transactions through the initial contact he/she has with company callers.

The following suggestions tell you what you can do to create an atmosphere for positive public relations:

1. Smile—A pleasant, friendly smile is a reassuring way to put people at ease.
2. Listen carefully—Learn to concentrate on what other people are saying; shut out all distractions. (Concentrating on what a person is saying is a sincere form of flattery.)
3. Keep an open mind—Genuinely respect other people's ideas and judgments. Show consideration for a point of view different from your own.
4. Display good manners—Good manners indicate thoughtful consideration of other people.
5. Speak distinctly—By using the precise word that expresses the idea or condition best and by making your requests concise and to the point, you will be showing concern for other people's time.
6. Be prepared—Learn all you can about your company, its products, and its services; and develop a thorough understanding of the requirements of your own job so you can make the best possible effort to help others.
7. Converse pleasantly—A limited amount of light, social conversation on topics of mutual interest with customers, colleagues, and superiors can help create a relaxed, friendly atmosphere for important business dealings.
8. Be punctual—Few things do more to damage good relationships with others than being late for appointments and meetings and failing to contain meetings within the specified time periods.

MAKING APPOINTMENTS

One of the ways a secretary can help with public relations is keeping the appointment calendar in good order. Few situations are as annoying to an executive and to a person calling on an executive (or to a secretary!) as finding out at the last minute that appointments have been jumbled and that the executive must be somewhere else. Such confusion and annoyance can be avoided if the secretary follows a few simple rules concerning appointments:

1. Keep two separate appointment books or appointment calendars, one for yourself and one for the executive(s) for whom you work. Be sure to **check daily** to see that the information in your appointment book or calendar and the executive's are exactly the same.
2. Never make a firm appointment for the executive(s) for whom you work without consulting with him/her. (It could happen that the executive has made an appointment for that exact time that he/she forgot to tell you about.)

3. When you make an appointment, be sure to get the following details:
   A. Who is requesting the appointment?
   What is his/her business affiliation?
   B. What date and what length of time does the person making the appointment request?
   C. What will be discussed during the appointment?
   D. Where will the meeting take place?
4. As soon as a firm appointment has been made, be sure to **write the details** in your appointment book or calendar and in the executive's. (Never try to keep the details of appointments in your mind.)
5. Check with the executive for whom you work **daily** to determine if he/she has made appointments that have not been brought to your attention, and be sure to put them into both appointment books immediately.
6. Find out your employer's preferences about appointments. For example, some executives do not like to make appointments in the morning (the time when they usually handle mail and dictation). Most executives do not like to have appointments on the day before they leave on a business trip (because of last-minute arrangements and preparations) or on the first day they return to the office from a business trip (because of the press of business problems and heavy mail).

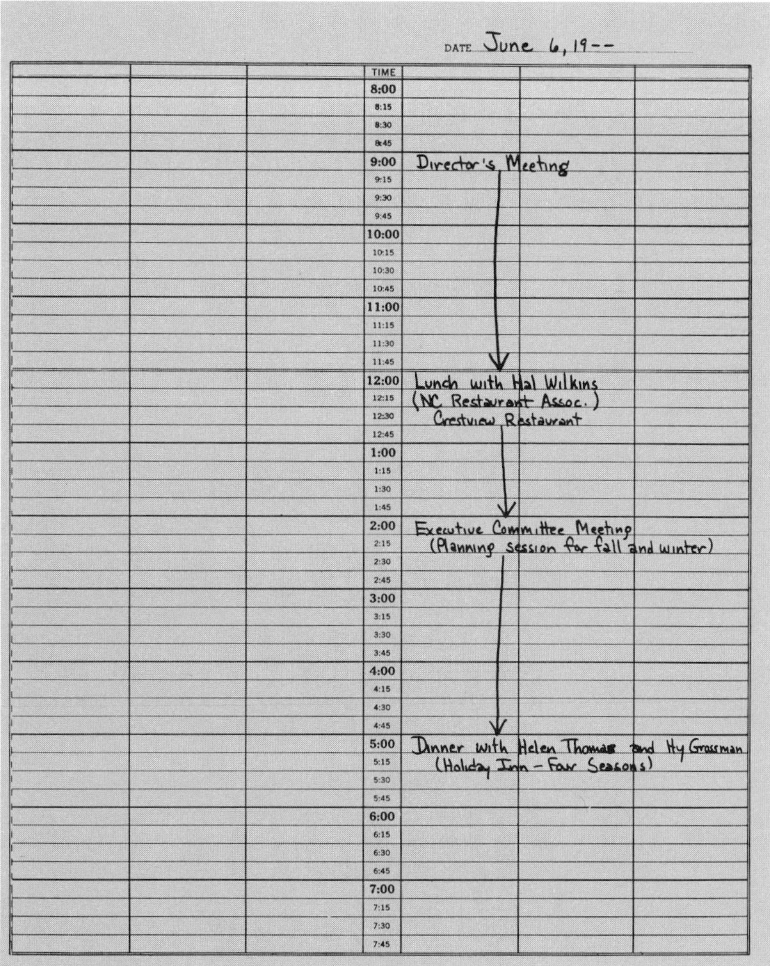

Fig. 181. Completed appointment book

7. If illness or unexpected business interruptions make it impossible for the executive for whom you work to keep his/her appoinments, get in touch with the expected callers well in advance of the time they are due for the appointments and cancel them. Simpy state the situation without making excuses. Offer to reschedule the most urgent appointments soon, and assure the others that they will be notified when your employer has time available.

Receiving Office Callers

By greeting office callers with a warm friendly smile and by calling them by name, the secretary helps callers to feel welcome; and he/she puts them in a relaxed frame of mind. Here are some additional steps a secretary can take to make the office visitor comfortable:

1. If the caller is wearing a topcoat and a hat, offer to take them and hang them. In bad weather, have a special place (near the door) for overshoes and umbrellas.
2. Provide a comfortable chair for the caller to sit in if he/she has to wait, and provide current magazines and newspapers for him/her to read.
3. If the company for which you work serves coffee, offer to get the caller a cup of coffee.
4. Notify the executive for whom you work that the caller has arrived.
5. When the executive for whom you work indicates that he/she is ready to see the caller, ask the caller to accompany you to the executive's office. Unless your employer and the caller are already well acquainted (ask your employer if you are not sure), you will need to introduce **the caller to your employer.** Example: "Mr. Thomas (your employer), this is Howard Nelson (the caller) of Perkins Restaurant Supply Company in Louisville." As soon as the two people have greeted one another, you should leave the room, close the door, and return to your work.
6. On the way out, most callers will stop at your desk to say "thank you." A gracious gesture and a friendly smile will send the caller on his/her way with positive businesslike thoughts about your company.

KEEPING ORDER/SETTING THE PACE

The secretary to an executive has the responsibility to keep his/her office in order and to plan and execute his/her work carefully and accurately. Many of the other employees within a company watch carefully what is going on within the executive offices, and they decide by what they see there how much (or how little) work they should be expected to do. From that point of view, the secretary to an executive is "setting the pace" that other employees in the company will follow. The secretary must always be certain that the pace he/she sets will add to and not detract from the efficiency and productivity of the company.

FOR REVIEW AND DISCUSSION

1. What two functions does public relations perform for a company?
2. What is the secretary's role in public relations?
3. Explain the eight steps a secretary can take to create an atmosphere of positive public relations.
4. Explain the seven basic rules for making and keeping a record of appointments.
5. Explain the six basic rules for receiving office callers.
6. How does the secretary "keep order and set the pace" in an office?

Turn to your workbook and complete Student Project 37.

CHAPTER 24

Reference Sources And Their Uses

OBJECTIVE

After studying this chapter you will understand:

- The contents of the basic reference sources that are used **frequently** in an office
- The contents of additional reference sources that are used **periodically** in an office
- How to use reference sources
- How to use the library
- How to list reference sources
- How to take notes from reference sources

JOB-RELATED VOCABULARY

Unabridged Dictionary—A dictionary that is complete in and of itself; one that is not based on a larger work.

Synonyms—Words having the same or nearly the same meanings.

Antonyms—Words having opposite meanings.

Prefixes—Sounds or a series of sounds or letters coming before the main syllable of a word.

Suffixes—Sounds or a series of sounds or letters attached to (coming after) the main syllable of a word.

Biennially—Happening every two years.

Consecutively—One after the other in order without gaps.

Every secretary needs a collection of reference sources that will enable him/her to find needed information quickly. Certain basic reference sources should be kept in the office for instant reference. Others, less frequently used, can be listed in a card file under the types of information they contain for ready reference when they are needed.

BASIC REFERENCE SOURCES

As essential desk-side references, every secretary needs:
- Secretarial handbook
- Dictionary
- Almanac
- Telephone directory

Secretarial Handbook

In order to cope with the seemingly endless questions that arise about grammar, punctuation, capitalization, abbreviations, writing style, letter-writing procedures, and other problems that are encountered by a secretary, it is essential to have a good secretarial handbook.

Some companies prepare an office procedures manual of their own explaining how things should be done for the sake of uniformity (which is considered to be very important to the "image" being created by the company). If you go to work for a company that has an office procedures manual, study it carefully so you will understand the procedures you should follow. If the company does not have an office procedures manual, perhaps you will want to prepare your own reference notebook containing information about company procedures, important people within the company, and other data. Such a notebook should be kept in loose-leaf form (to make revisions and additions easier) and should be properly indexed to make the information it contains instantly available.

Here is a list of some good secretarial handbooks from which you can choose:
- REFERENCE MANUAL FOR STENOGRAPHERS AND TYPISTS by William Sabin
- STANDARD HANDBOOK FOR SECRETARIES by Lois Hutchinson
- YOU CAN BE AN EXECUTIVE SECRETARY by Lucy Graves Mayo
- COMPLETE SECRETARY'S HANDBOOK by Doris L. Miller and B. M. Miller
- PRIVATE SECRETARY'S ENCYCLOPEDIA DICTIONARY by Bessie May Miller
- GUIDE TO TRANSCRIPTION (Reference Manual) by Lois E. Frazier and Harry R. Moon

Dictionary

Keep in mind that dictionaries can (and do) go out of date. It is important to have a dictionary that is not more than three or four years old. (The English language can change drastically in that time!)

Here is a list of good desk-size dictionaries:
- THE RANDOM HOUSE DICTIONARY OF THE ENGLISH LANGUAGE
- THE AMERICAN HERITAGE DICTIONARY OF THE ENGLISH LANGUAGE
- WEBSTER'S NEW COLLEGIATE DICTIONARY
- FUNK & WAGNALL'S STANDARD COLLEGE DICTIONARY

Although you will probably use the dictionary most often to check spelling, to verify pronunciation, and to find definitions, you will occasionally need to consult an unabridged dictionary if you do an extensive amount of writing and editing as a part of your job. Here are two widely used unabridged dictionaries:
- FUNK & WAGNALL'S NEW STANDARD DICTIONARY OF THE ENGLISH LANGUAGE
- WEBSTER'S NEW INTERNATIONAL DICTIONARY

In addition to providing spellings, pronunciations, and definitions, dictionaries also contain such **basic** information as:

- Synonyms and antonyms
- Grammar
- Origins of words listed (etymology)
- Prefixes and suffixes
- Commonly used foreign words and phrases

Dictionaries usually contain the following **supplementary** information (either as a part of the body of the dictionary or in a separate section):

- Biographical names
- Vocabulary of rhymes
- Punctuation
- Spelling
- Compounds
- Tables of: weights and measures, money, the metric system, and standard time
- Italicization
- Proofreaders' marks
- Colleges of the United States and Canada
- Capitalization
- Abbreviations
- Common English given names
- Forms of address
- Pronouncing gazetteer

Another dictionary-type book that is valuable to a secretary is 20,000 WORDS by Louis A. Leslie. In this book 20,000 commonly used words are correctly spelled, divided, and accented for quick reference.

Almanac

Almanacs are a compilation of vital statistics, important dates, and other important information covering such topics as: history, geography, business, politics, science, celebrities, literature, and religion. Almanacs are published annually. Three well-known, frequently used almanacs are:

- THE WORLD ALMANAC AND BOOK OF FACTS
- READER'S DIGEST ALMANAC AND YEARBOOK
- INFORMATION PLEASE ALMANAC

Get a copy of a current almanac and study it carefully in order to understand the types of information it contains.

Telephone Directory

The alphabetical and classified pages of telephone directories have already been thoroughly discussed in Chapter 8, THE TELEPHONE. Go back and review the information on pages 79-81 if you need to do so. In addition to providing telephone numbers, the telephone directory is also useful in determining the correct spelling of firm and personal names and for determining correct addresses.

OTHER REFERENCE SOURCES

In addition to having the essential desk-side references, every secretary should be aware of the following reference sources that he/she may need to consult in the course of his/her work:

- HOTEL RED BOOK
- POSTAL MANUAL and NATIONAL ZIP CODE DIRECTORY
- City directories
- Thesaurus
- Biographical information

- Governmental information
- Published material
- Encyclopedia

HOTEL RED BOOK

The HOTEL RED BOOK, published annually by the American Hotel Directory Corporation, lists hotels and motels alphabetically by city and state. It also contains information about hotels in many foreign countries. In addition to the names, addresses, and telephone numbers of hotels, the Red Book provides information about room rates, dining facilities, rooms available for meetings, and transportation carriers serving the area. This reference is extremely valuable to a secretary who has to arrange business travel and/or meeting facilities for his/her company.

POSTAL MANUAL

As stated in Chapter 7, the POSTAL MANUAL, available through the Superintendent of Documents in Washington, DC, is the final authority on all matters concerning the United States mail. When special mailing situations arise, the POSTAL MANUAL is a valuable reference.

In addition to the POSTAL MANUAL, every office should have a copy of the NATIONAL ZIP CODE DIRECTORY, also available through the Superintendent of Documents. The NATIONAL ZIP CODE DIRECTORY lists the correct zip codes for mailing addresses within the United States. The zip codes are listed by state name, then by city (town/village) name, then by sections within the larger cities.

City Directories

City directories usually have two sections: alphabetic and classified. In the alphabetic section, residents of a city are listed alphabetically by name, street addresses, and occupations. In the classified section, names of business concerns and professional people are arranged **alphabetically by type of business or profession.** City directories are published by independent publishing companies, not by city governments. To be valuable, a city directory (like any other directory) must be up to date.

Thesaurus

In a thesaurus, you check an idea (or word) in an alphabetic index first. The idea is followed by a list of synonyms (words having **approximately** the same meaning). Each group of synonyms is followed by numbered references to a specific section of the thesaurus. Then you turn to the appropriate section of the thesaurus to find the word or words to express exactly what you mean. The thesaurus is an extremely valuable reference to anyone who does creative writing. Probably the thesaurus most commonly used today is ROGET'S INTERNATIONAL THESAURUS.

Biographical Information

WHO'S WHO IN AMERICA, published biennially, contains information such as background, age, parentage, education, degrees, occupation, affiliations, honors, and marital information for prominent **living** Americans in every field. Other biographic-type reference books include:

- WHO **WAS** WHO IN AMERICA
- WHO'S WHO OF AMERICAN WOMEN
- WHO'S WHO IN FINANCE AND INDUSTRY
- WHO'S WHO (Worldwide—mostly British entries)

Certain biographic-type reference books list data for prominent **deceased** Americans. Among those references are:

- CONCISE DICTIONARY OF AMERICAN BIOGRAPHY
- DICTIONARY OF AMERICAN BIOGRAPHY

Major cities throughout the United States have a Social Register that is published annually. The Social Register gives a brief biographical sketch of socially prominent people in the city. The NATIONAL SOCIAL DIRECTORY lists socially prominent persons in the entire United States.

Governmental Information

Usually local governments (city, town, village, county) prepare a directory of persons holding various positions within the government and list various departments and agencies of the government. A secretary can usually obtain such a directory at the following places:

City, town, village—At the municipal building or from the clerk of the local court

County—At the county courthouse or from the clerk of the county court

For information about state governments, consult the BOOK OF THE STATES, which is published annually. For information about the structure of the Federal Government and about the specific agencies and bureaus within the Federal Government, consult the UNITED STATES GOVERNMENT ORGANIZATION MANUAL (published annually), which is available through the United States Government Printing Office in Washington, DC.

Accurate statistical information on population, labor, climate, roads, and income can be obtained from an annual publication called STATISTICAL ABSTRACT OF THE UNITED STATES, which is published by the Bureau of the Census, United States Department of Commerce.

Published Material

BOOKS IN PRINT is a reference source that contains over 275,000 books available from more than 2,000 publishers. Volume I contains an **alphabetic listing of books by author.** Volume II contains an **alphabetic listing of books by title** and an **alphabetic index of publishers.**

The UNITED STATES CATALOG is an index of all **American** books in print as of January 1, 1928. The Catalog is kept up to date by the CUMULATIVE BOOK INDEX, which is published monthly. The Index now includes all books in print in the English language regardless of their country of origin. The following information is provided for each book listed:

- Author
- Title
- Subject
- Price
- Publisher
- Type of binding
- Number of pages
- Date of publication
- Library of Congress card number

READERS' GUIDE TO PERIODICAL LITERATURE, published semimonthly from September through June and monthly in July and August, contains a listing of **articles** published in leading magazines. Articles are listed under the following headings:

- Name of the author
- Title
- Subject

Special indexes are also available that list articles in periodicals devoted to specific fields, such as the BUSINESS PERIODICALS INDEX for business publications.

Encyclopedias

Many encyclopedias contain essay-type articles about subjects significant to mankind or of important information pertinent to a specific field. Articles are usually enhanced with bibliographies, pictures, diagrams, and maps. Encyclopedia entries are usually arranged alphabetically, and encyclopedias are often published in sets of several volumes. Several encyclopedias keep articles up to date by issuing an annual yearbook. A good one-volume encyclopedia is the COLUMBIA ENCYCLOPEDIA.

USING REFERENCE SOURCES

When you are ready to study various reference sources for data, be sure you organize your search for materials by limiting it to the best sources available for the information you are seeking. Here are some questions you will need to answer for each reference source you are considering:

1. Is the material authoritative?
2. Is the material up to date?
3. What scope do you need for your data, an essay-type article or just the essential facts? (The answer to this question will determine the **type of reference** you will use.)

Using The Library

The library card catalogue is the key to the vast storehouse of information the library contains. Each book in the library is listed in the card catalogue as follows:

- By author
- By title
- By subject (under one or more headings)

Each card in the card catalogue is coded with a Library of Congress number (or some other numbering system). By finding the area in the book stacks where the number you are seeking appears, you can find the book stacked alphabetically by author within that decimal number.

The library also has a Vertical File Service Catalogue. This catalogue lists pamphlets, booklets, and leaflets by subjects. The references are not listed in the card catalogue, and they are stored in vertical file drawers instead of the library shelves.

Many libraries provide photocopying service so patrons can make copies of reference materials in the library. Ordinarily, a small charge is made for this service.

Most libraries make use of microfilming for newspapers and periodicals because it makes material more easily available to library patrons and because it drastically reduces the amount of storage space required. Library patrons can get permission to use microfilm viewing equipment, usually in a place where they can take notes on what they are viewing.

TIPS ON USING THE LIBRARY

- Be quiet, be courteous, be brief.
- Check out only as much material as you can use at one time.
- Bring materials back to the library on or before the day they are due. (Other library patrons may be waiting for them.)
- Ask the librarian for help as you need it.

Listing Reference Sources

When you are researching a subject, you will first need to find the reference sources containing the information you need. As you find a listing for a reference that contains the information you need, prepare a 3 by 5 card for the reference. (See Figs. 182 and 183.) The following information should be provided for each reference listed:

- Author's name (last name first)
- Title and edition
- Publisher's name and location
- Date of copyright
- Inclusive (from/to) pages for the information you need
- Library number for the reference
- Number the cards consecutively in the upper right-hand corner

Taking Notes

After you have selected the references you intend to use in your study, obtain the books, magazines or articles you need, and begin to take notes. For your notes use notebook-size sheets of paper, starting a new sheet for each new reference. Follow these procedures as you take notes:

1. Number your notes to correspond with the number on the card listing the reference source.
2. Take notes on only the material that is **directly related** to what you are studying.
3. Enclose direct quotations from the reference source in quotation marks, and show the page from which the quotation was copied.
4. List a page reference for each item of information in your notes (even if it is not a direct quotation).

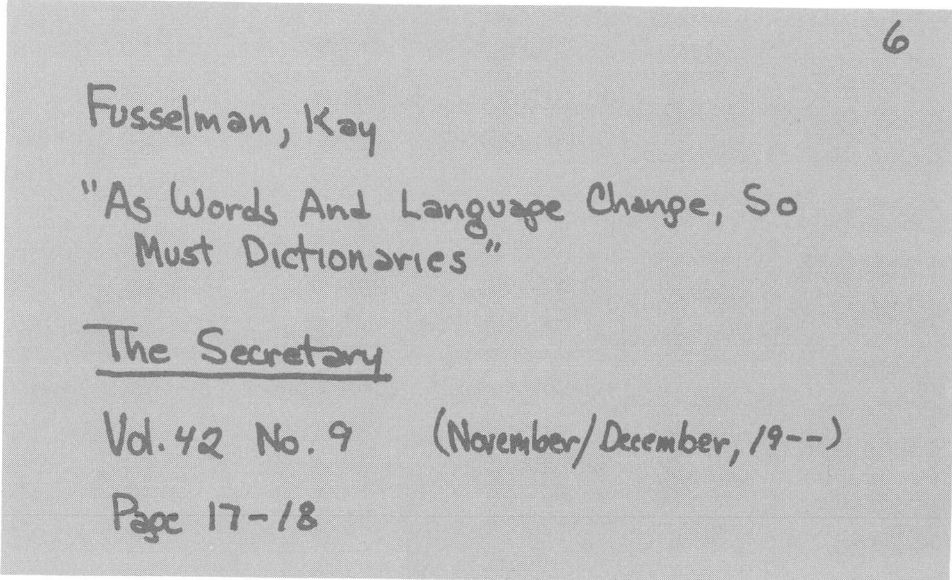

Fig. 182. A magazine listed as a reference source

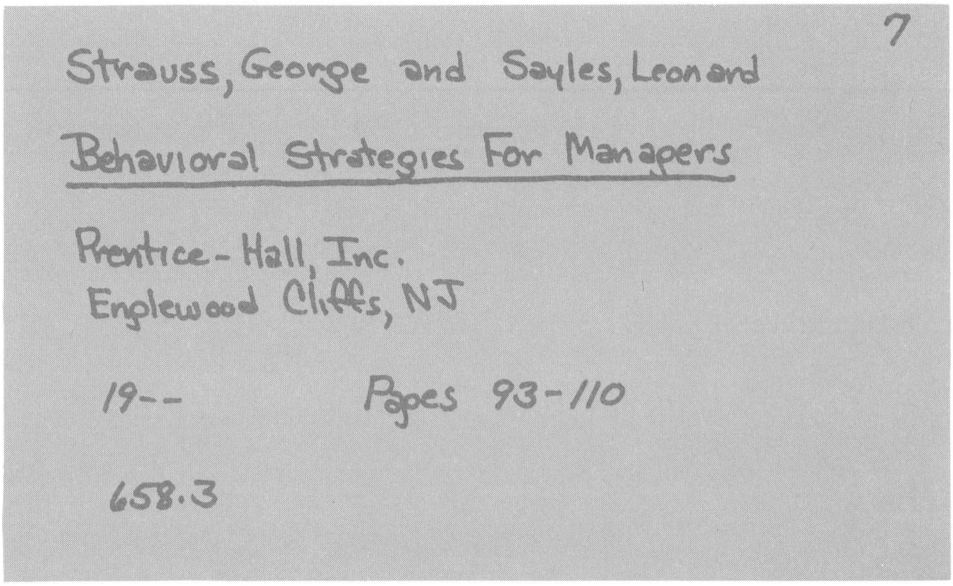

7

Strauss, George and Sayles, Leonard

Behavioral Strategies For Managers

Prentice-Hall, Inc.
Englewood Cliffs, NJ

19-- Pages 93-110

658.3

Fig. 183. A book listed as a reference source

Some people prefer to use cards for their notes instead of a notebook. If you use cards, limit each card to only one subject so you can add new material easily. Notes on cards can be arranged and rearranged more easily than notes in a notebook, and cards can be rehandled without smudging the notes because they are sturdier than notebook paper.

FOR REVIEW AND DISCUSSION

1. Name and explain the contents of the essential desk-side references that every secretary should have.
2. Explain the contents of the following additional reference sources:
   NATIONAL ZIP CODE DIRECTORY
   HOTEL RED BOOK
   Thesaurus
   City Directories
   NATIONAL SOCIAL DIRECTORY
   BOOKS IN PRINT
3. What questions should be answered about a reference source to determine whether or not it is suitable?
4. How are books listed in a library card catalog?
5. What is the function of the Vertical File Service Catalogue?
6. What information should be given when you are **listing** a reference source?
7. What are the procedures to be followed when you are **taking notes** from a reference source already listed?

Turn to your workbook and complete Student Project 38.

CHAPTER 25

Management And Supervision

OBJECTIVE

After you have studied Chapter 25, you will understand:

- The differences between management and supervision
- Methods of designing effective management strategies
- The characteristics of successful managers in a practical management system
- The earmarks of successful supervisors
- Ways a person acquires management skills
- The overall characteristics of successful managers
- The importance of communications in management and a plan for successful communications
- The importance of cost control in management
- Ways to deal with difficult situations

JOB-RELATED VOCABULARY

Management—The act or art of handling or directing with a degree of skill the affairs of a business firm or other organization. (Management requires a higher level of skill than does supervision.)

Supervision—A critical observing and directing (overseeing), such as watching and directing the activities of employees on a day-to-day basis in order to accomplish objectives through the efforts of others.

Diverse—Differing from one another; unlike.

Rationale—The underlying reason for something.

Strategies—Carefully made plans or methods.

Dissipated—Spread out or spread thin to the point of vanishing or becoming ineffective.

Catalyst—The means by which something takes place or is pulled together. (The supervisor or manager can serve as one who pulls things together.)

Acquire—To get as one's own.

Integrator—Person who blends or unites the varying thoughts and ideas of a group.

Credibility—Believability.

Productively—Effectively completing a measured amount of usable work.

Demotivating—Causing to **lose interest in** taking action.

Rapport—A relationship marked by harmony, conformity, accord, and affinity (attraction to or likeness for).

Abruptly—Occurring without warning.

Cynical—Being contemptuously (despising or disdaining) distrustful of human nature and motives.

Irascible—Angry, frequently marked by a quick temper.

Vulnerable—Open to attack, personal hurt, or damage; capable of being physically wounded.

Condescending—Having a patronizing attitude, an attitude of voluntarily lowering one's position or rank in order to deal with a person considered to be an inferior.

The overall management and the day-by-day supervision of employees are **vital factors** in the success of every business. Because the goal of many employees of a business is to earn an important role in the supervision and management of the business, they need a clear understanding of the duties and responsibilities of effective managers and supervisors. Since the role of the secretary is changing very rapidly, there is ample evidence that the new role of the secretary includes making management-level decisions and supervising other employees. In order to feel secure in this role, secretaries and other office support personnel should have an understanding of the roles of management and supervision in business.

THE ROLES OF MANAGERS AND SUPERVISORS

The **management group** of a company selects goals and sets the overall company policies and procedures. To do this, the management group must deal with such diverse concepts as budgeting, marketing, production, service, advertising, research and development, and finances. The **supervisory group** has the responsibility to see that the policies and procedures established by the management group are carried out on a day-to-day basis. To do this, the supervisory group must work with the individual personalities within the group being supervised; they must communicate clearly and directly to the members of that group (and **encourage open communications within each group**); and they must cultivate leadership styles that will motivate and stimulate members of the group to grow within the framework of their jobs and to work together creatively and effectively.

While the duties and responsibilities of managers and supervisors are somewhat easy to describe, the day-to-day tasks of successful managers and supervisors require knowledge and carefully developed skills. In dealing with people, these skills must be applied sensitively and creatively.

MANAGERS

Experts in management usually agree that the best management strategies are those that are **designed cooperatively** by members of the management group (as opposed to strategies that are "handed down" to the management group from top management). The rationale behind this thinking is the fact that the members of a management group will be committed to the success of a plan they have helped to design.

Successful managers have a sensitivity to the drives, anxieties, and reactions of people within the management group, to employees of the company in general, and to those (such as stockholders, customers, competitors, and government officials) who are beyond the sphere of control of company management. While the importance of good human relations must not be taken lightly in the management role, it must be remembered that an important overall objective of all management is **to get a job done correctly in the shortest time possible with minimum resources.** To this end, **it is important for management to help people to be organized, motivated and productive.**

The four basic functions of management are: planning, organizing, leading, and controlling. Most workers will find job satisfaction by virtue of doing a good job, serving others, and sharing the rewards of improved productivity. If too much emphasis is put on human relations without proper emphasis on organization and production, energies are dissipated; and the task at hand will not be accomplished. It is clear then that successful management must include a **realistic balance** of organization, motivation (or human relations), and production.

Practical Management

Many management specialists believe that a simple, uncomplicated management concept used to achieve success with work needs is extremely practical. The following are the characteristics of a successful manager in a practical management system, according to management specialist, Thomas T. Samaras. To be a successful manager:

- Keep in touch with overall company objectives, plans, and needs and communicate them to your staff.
- Focus the attention of supervisors and staff on tasks, ideas, and products (or services) that will provide the company and its customers with the greatest benefit.
- Help people to work efficiently by providing proper facilities, tools, and staff and by removing roadblocks when they occur.
- Provide realistic leadership by choosing (or by helping your staff choose) the right things to work on and the best methods to use to accomplish the work.
- Provide discipline. (Even highly motivated people need to have some framework, rules, or system within which to work—although they may not want to admit it!)
- Be a catalyst for **worthwhile** innovations in operations and production.
- Solve people problems (and problems of unfair employee reward) **effectively and quickly.**

Acquiring Effective Management Skills

The next question that needs to be asked is: "How does a person acquire effective management skills?" Mr. Samaras suggests the following practical 13-step plan:

1. Acquire a thorough understanding about the company and its operations, the industry of which the company is a part, and the products (or services) of the company.
2. Follow the examples of other successful managers. (If a manager is not available who has superior overall management skills, follow the examples of people who excel in a specific area of management, such as organization, planning, leadership, and decision making.)
3. Begin immediately to practice management skills you acquire from successful managers.
4. Acquire management skills gradually through a step-by-step growth process that will evolve from simple to more complex management tasks.
5. Maintain a desire to grow in your understanding of management skills and a desire to find and use new and better methods.
6. Be consistent in your application of management skills, and work hard at developing and refining them.
7. Learn from the **mistakes and the successes of other managers.** Consciously practice the successes, and avoid the mistakes.

8. Follow the Golden Rule. (In today's business world, anyone who steps on or abuses another person is bound for failure.) Managers who are fair usually get similar treatment from other managers, supervisors, and staff members; their promotions are based on job performance.
9. Learn from **your own mistakes and experiences.**
10. Through a genuine interest in and openness to people, develop an understanding of human strengths and weaknesses. Listen carefully as people talk about how they have been wronged or hurt by other people so you can avoid those problems.
11. Prepare a management plan, and follow that plan.
12. Keep up with new developments in your industry, with your competitors, and in management theory. Also keep up with changes in laws and in society's standards, directions, and expectations.
13. Constantly evaluate the results of your decisions, and take proper (and immediate) corrective steps as they are indicated.

Characteristics Of Successful Managers

Social scientists indicate that successful managers are leaders, followers, compromisers, and doers and that they get projects or work **done to specifications within budget and time allocations.** While personalities may interfere with the success of a potentially effective manager, successful managers usually possess the following characteristics:

- **Leadership ability**—is able to set goals and to motivate people to achieve those goals
- **Integrator**—has the ability to bring groups with varying points of view together to get a task accomplished
- **Achievement Oriented**—exhibits a strong drive to achieve objectives
- **Decision Maker**—makes decisions based on adequate information and makes the right decision most of the time on routine matters and almost all of the time on critical decisions
- **Rapport with Higher Management, Peers, and Staff**—has trust of upper management and negotiates well with them; has open, cooperative relationship with other managers; has ability to understand needs, problems, and anxieties of supervisors and staff and communicates that understanding well
- **Knowledgeable**—knows the business without getting entangled in minute details
- **Good Planner**—understands the principles of planning, budgeting, and scheduling a project and has ability to see that a plan is carried out
- **Recognizes Important Projects**—and works on those projects and sees that staff members do too; doesn't get diverted to wasting time on low priority (or low payoff) activities
- **Loyalty**—inspires people to do what is best for their boss and for the company—even when they are working in an unsupervised situation
- **Helps Others to Grow**—provides challenging job assignments that "stretch" the abilities of workers
- **Shares the Glory**—shares credit for successes with members of his/her staff (but is quick to take the blame when things go wrong)
- **Determination**—goes "to bat" for his/her ideas and employees when they are right (but knows when to back off so as not to become personally offensive)—doesn't let circumstances, criticism, or other people's opinions deter his/her course or plan
- **Confidence (based on ability)**—a powerful quality in getting things done and in obtaining the support of higher management supervisors and staff

- **Good Staffer**—is able to identify and select "doers" rather than "talkers"
- **Sense of Humor**—which helps to promote a good group spirit and to relieve tension—a depressed or worried manager projects an unsettling image to his/her staff which can lower staff morale and productivity

Communications And Management

Communication in business is defined as a message sent, received, understood, and acted upon in an appropriate manner. When workers are left out of the communication network, they often feel unwanted, hurt, and angry. Including workers, no matter what their level on the management tree, in important information about their company, helps them to feel that they have a part in the company's plans; and it helps them to feel accepted.

When management has made a decision to provide new information to members of the staff, the information should be provided **immediately.** If the management group waits too long to present important information, the informal information network within the company (gossip) will take over and spread the word before management does. When that happens, the management (or **official**) communication system will look foolish presenting information everybody already knows. Some management specialists insist that very little information is really secret in an organization once it has been exchanged between two people, especially if it is written. Therefore, tight security is needed to keep confidential information from being circulated by the grapevine (the **informal** communication network).

The National Industrial Council reports that workers usually want to know some of the following types of information:

- The history and organizational structure of the company
- The products and services provided, how they are provided, why they are needed, and who uses them
- New products, services, and operating systems that are being planned
- What the company expects from workers and how well workers measure up to those expectations
- Ways workers fit into the organization and their opportunities for advancement
- Company income and profitability
- Advanced warning about changes in job status (why the changes are necessary and who will be affected)

Here are some suggestions that will help you to communicate with your workers more effectively when you have management responsibility:

- **Plan** what you will say and determine the best way to say it.
- **Explain** what you mean using short, familiar words and sentences.
- **Individualize** your message by focusing on as many individuals as practical.
- **Appeal to as many senses** as feasible.
- **Listen** to what workers are saying so you can understand what they are thinking and feeling.
- **Repeat** key points—people frequently don't get the message the first time. Don't mistake silence on the part of workers to indicate understanding.
- **Act on** what you say (failure to do so reduces your credibility and the effectiveness of future communications).
- **Evaluate** the effectiveness of your communications to see that actions requested are being carried out or check to see that a sampling of listeners indicates an understanding of the message.

Cost Control And Management

The **prime objective** of a business organization is to **earn a profit.** Productivity and efficiency on the part of workers are key factors in earning a profit. Cost consciousness is a needed quality in all business organizations, even at those times when the money supply seems endless. An effective manager instills in his/her workers a respect for money and a determination to keep costs down so that frills, unneeded purchases, poor maintenance of equipment, and wasted labor and material are considered a **serious** breach of company policy. It is vitally important, too, that middle management personnel keep upper-level management informed about the steps being taken to reduce costs. (Otherwise, a middle management person could get caught in a bind if a directive to cut costs to the bone comes down from top management and, because of already efficient management, the middle manager has very little room to cut.)

SUPERVISION

Apart from the various levels of management within a company, the company supervisors have the specific responsibility to see that the policies and procedures established by the management group are carried out by the workers on a day-by-day basis.

Since the day-by-day tasks within a company are performed by **people,** it is essential for supervisors to be skilled at working with other people in a manner that will help workers to grow and develop within the framework of their jobs and to find satisfaction in their job functions. (Failure to do this can have disastrous results in terms of company morale and worker productivity!)

Here are some time-tested suggestions that will help you to supervise other workers efficiently and productively when the time comes for you to do so:

1. **Maintain a "You" Point of View**
   Since many people are primarily interested in themselves, an effective supervisor makes his/her presentations focus on showing how workers can get what they want by doing what the supervisor wants them to do. Try to show the people you supervise how your ideas or procedures will meet **their objectives,** increase **their influence, power, or status,** or perhaps **get them a promotion.** Focusing on the "you" point of view will cause the workers you supervise to be more friendly and cooperative, and it will help you to get things done in your department or organization.
2. **Help People to Feel Important and Worthwhile**
   Most people have a strong need to feel that they are important and to be recognized for their contributions to the company. Studies show that recognition is a key factor in motivating people to work harder. (From the opposite point of view, talking down to people and ignoring them are powerful methods of **demotivating** them.) Here are some ways you can help to make people feel important and worthwhile:
   - **Listen** to them.
   - Give **deserved** compliments.
   - **Acknowledge people** who are waiting to see you.
   - Pay attention to **each person** in a group.
   - **Use people's names.**
   - Show **genuine interest** in people's achievements.
3. **Criticize Constructively**
   When it is necessary to criticize an employee, do it in a **positive, helpful** way that will encourage the employee to respond in a constructive way. Here are some suggestions about criticizing constructively:

- Criticize in **absolute privacy.**
- When possible, precede criticism with a **deserved** compliment or a kind word.
- Criticize the **act, not the person.**
- Show the employee how to correct the situation.
- **Ask** for the employee's cooperation in correcting the situation (**don't demand** it).
- End the criticism with a positive or friendly remark (for example, "Let's work this out together.").

4. **Listen Carefully**

If a supervisor is to be successful in developing a rapport with the people he/she supervises and in improving communication and motivating people, the supervisor must acquire information about workers' needs, interests, problems, and experiences. Some of this information can be obtained from records, but the art of listening is the **prime source** of useful information. (This means **really listening,** not just remaining silent while someone is talking so you can develop an answer to his/her argument or thinking!) Here are some ideas that will help you to cultivate effective listening habits:

- Listen for **ideas** and **facts.**
- Listen to gain a better understanding of the situation.
- Don't end a conversation abruptly because you heard something you didn't like.
- Try to see how much information you can gather from what people say (this technique will help you to learn to listen better).
- Make a **conscious effort to remember** what people say.

5. **Thank People**

A **sincere** expression of appreciation that is **based on real accomplishments** from a supervisor can give an employee a big lift.

6. **Don't Tease People**

Few people enjoy being the center of jokes or funny remarks; but most people, because they want to be considered to be "good sports," will not show their true feelings. However, if the teaser hits a sensitive spot, the person teased may resent the teaser for a long time. (If the teaser is a supervisor, his/her rapport with the other person may be badly damaged!) Take great care to avoid teasing other people, particularly about the following:

- Weight
- Age
- Height
- Baldness
- Eyeglasses
- Speech
- Religion
- Clothes
- Mannerisms
- Race (or nationality)
- Lifestyle
- Relatives

7. **Use an Open Performance Appraisal System**

In an open performance appraisal system (or performance by objectives), **an employee's performance is measured against a set of preestablished goals or against his/her own performance from the year before** (rather than measuring an employee's performance by comparing him/her to his/her peers). The open performance appraisal system implies that virtually everyone can do well if he/she wants to (regardless of the performance of peers). Through an open performance appraisal system, a much healthier climate is created **for the employee and the company.**

8. **Don't Expect Perfection**

If you expect employees to be errorless, you will constantly be disappointed; and you will become cynical and irascible. When this happens, anxiety is created, productivity decreases, and errors frequently increase. If **you** set realistic expectations for your employees but

encourage them to produce their very best, you will frequently be pleasantly surprised by the quality of work produced.

9. **Answer Your Telephone Calls**
   Great care should be taken to answer telephone calls (from employees or customers) promptly. Failure to answer calls may mean that an **employee** can't go on with a project because he/she doesn't have necessary information, or it may mean that **you** won't get information that would be helpful to you in making a decision or avoiding a costly mistake. In addition, an unanswered telephone call might imply to an employee or customer that you feel that he/she is not important. That implication can cause anger and resentment.
10. **Remove Roadblocks to Motivation**
    Many experts in management and supervision feel that it is a sound approach to assume that most employees want to do a good job and then to work at removing obstacles that tend to demotivate them. Six major roadblocks to employee motivation have been identified:
    A. Failure to state expectations clearly
    B. Demanding high productivity without identifying objectives clearly; then responding in an exacting, hostile, judgmental, punitive way because objectives are not achieved
    C. Failure to acknowledge good performance
    D. Approving wrong or misdirected projects for long periods of time, then criticizing severely for consistently poor performance
    E. Failure to tie pay, recognition, bonuses, praise, and promotion to achievement
    F. Failure to provide proper resources and equipment to get a job done
11. **Avoid Constant Nit-Picking**
    Nit-picking is criticizing minor details that do not contribute to the effectiveness or quality of the task at hand. Besides damaging the morale of employees, the supervisor who indulges in nit-picking is wasting valuable time and diverting energy from meaningful business activities. **Save critical comments for important business-related issues.**
12. **Avoid Hiring Friends or Relatives**
    Unless friends or relatives who are hired have **very special talents** that are readily apparent to other members of the staff and unless other members of the staff have a clear understanding of how the friend's or relative's talents can help them (members of the staff) to accomplish their own goals, loss of motivation, hostility, and even transfers and resignations may result. A number of problems exist when a supervisor hires friends or relatives:
    - Existing staff members feel more vulnerable because their comments, errors, and shortcomings may be reported to the supervisor when he/she is visiting with his/her friend or relative.
    - Staff members feel that good job openings will go to friends or relatives even if they are not qualified.
    - Staff members feel that raises and performance ratings will be affected by the personal relationship that exists between the supervisor and his/her friend or relative.
    - Staff members feel that friends and relatives are permitted to do things (such as leaving early for lunch or returning late) that aren't tolerated from other employees.
    - Staff members feel that if a cutback of staff is required, friends and relatives will be the last to go even if other employees perform their job functions better.

A wise supervisor avoids hiring friends and relatives and saves himself/herself many problems.

13. **Prepare a Policy and Procedures Manual**
It is a time-saving, cost-saving move for supervisors to prepare a departmental policy and procedures manual. Whenever a question about policy or procedures occurs, departmental employees will have an instant source to which they can refer. To be usable, a policy/procedures manual must meet the following tests:
    - The manual must provide information about policies and procedures in a **clearly stated, uncomplicated** manner. (Otherwise, employees will not use it!)
    - The manual must be revised periodically so it is up to date and in line with the current goals and objectives of the company and the department.
    - It must have the approval of top management. Otherwise, confusion, frustration, and working at cross purposes could harm the company and damage employees' morale.

DEALING WITH DIFFICULT SITUATIONS

Anyone who is going to manage or supervise other people must acquire skills to deal with difficult circumstances that may develop. Here are some suggestions that will help you to be effective when you are dealing with unpleasant or difficult people and difficult situations:

1. Learn to be a good listener. By listening carefully, you will be able to determine what the problem is and the extent to which the problem "has control" of the people involved. Also, by being a good listener, you will give the troubled individual(s) an opportunity to vent his/her feelings about the situation, which frequently helps to eliminate some of the anger and frustration.
2. Concentrate on a solution; don't constantly restate the problem. Once the problem has been defined, concentrate on what can be done to correct the situation or to eliminate the factors that caused the problem. Constantly restating the problem enhances anger and frustration and adds "more fuel to the fire."
3. Remain polite, calm, and businesslike no matter what happens. **Under all circumstances,** a manager or supervisor must remain polite and businesslike. Sarcastic remarks, angry statements, and a condescending tone of voice do not serve a positive purpose, and they can add more problems (some with legal implications) to an already inflamed situation. Work diligently to develop a calm, businesslike manner.
4. Evaluate the justification for the problem the person is stating. If you determine that some (or all) of the problem being expressed is justified, begin **immediate** action to solve the problem so that the solution will be satisfactory to everyone. As a part of the solution phase, ask the person(s) who is expressing the problem what he/she would consider a satisfactory solution. The closer the final solution comes to the solution suggested by the person(s) expressing the problem, the more he/she will feel that his/her needs and point of view have been understood and acted upon.

    Most people are fair enough to realize that compromises frequently must be made in order to arrive at a workable solution to a problem. When they are consulted, workers are usually more committed to the workability of the solution agreed upon.

If you develop a thorough understanding of the concepts of management and supervision presented in this chapter and if you make an effort to practice those concepts in your day-to-day business life, you should be ready to accept a promotion to a job in supervision or management when the opportunity comes.

FOR REVIEW AND DISCUSSION

1. Describe the role of the **management** group of a company.
2. Describe the role of the **supervisory** group of a company.
3. What three skills must members of the supervisory group of a company develop to supervise effectively?
4. What types of management strategies do experts in management usually consider to be most effective? Why?
5. What is the overall objective of all management?
6. What are the earmarks of a practical management system?
7. Explain how a person acquires effective management skills.
8. Name and explain at least five characteristics of successful managers.
9. Define communication in business.
10. Explain why it is important for managers to provide workers with important information about the company for which they work.
11. According to the National Industrial Council, what types of information about the company do workers usually want?
12. Explain the eight steps managers can take to communicate effectively with workers.
13. Explain the importance of cost control to management.
14. Name and describe at least six techniques that will help a person to supervise efficiently.
15. Explain four suggestions for dealing with difficult situations.

Turn to your workbook and complete Student Project 39.

CHAPTER 26

Finding A Job

OBJECTIVE

After you have studied Chapter 26, you will understand the correct procedures for presenting your personal and job skills to a prospective employer in a professional manner, including:

- Taking a personal inventory
- Taking a job-skill inventory
- Finding job information
- Preparing a resumé
- Preparing an application letter
- Interviewing
- Following up an interview

JOB-RELATED VOCABULARY

"Marketing"—Presenting your personal and job skills to an employer in the hope that the employer will hire you (buy your skills).

Personal Needs—Those factors necessary for satisfying desires and personal longings.

Introvert—A person who concentrates on himself/herself.

Extrovert—A person who concentrates on what is outside himself/herself (opposite of introvert).

Resume—A short account of a person's career and qualifications (usually prepared by an applicant for a position).

Detectable—Easily noticed.

Stability—The condition of being constant without great fluctuations in personality.

Maturity—Development at an advanced level; the quality of making judgments that are based on slow, careful considerations (not hurried or impulsive).

Perseverance—The ability to continue in spite of opposition or negative forces.

Scope—Range or depth of activity.

Responsive—Quick to react.

Pertinent—Relevant or applicable to the matter being considered.

Optimum—The most favorable condition under implied or specific circumstances.

Now that you have developed your skills and your understanding of business to a high level, you are ready to look for a job. Actually, you will be "marketing" your job skills to a prospective employer. You will need to **prepare yourself** for job hunting so you will present your credentials to prospective employers in a professional way. You will also want to think seriously about your personal needs, your skills, and the type of job that will be the best for you. Then, by planning thoroughly and preparing carefully, you should be able to match your skills with a job that will be "right" for you. The following **six** steps will help you to present yourself to prospective employers in a professional way:

STEP 1—TAKING A PERSONAL INVENTORY

Long before you begin to think about a **specific** job with a specific company, you will need to take an inventory of your personal needs. Ask yourself the following questions:

- Am I an introvert or an extrovert?
- Do I prefer a job with a wide variety of duties or do I prefer a job with very specialized (limited in number and scope) duties?
- Do I prefer to work for a large company or a small company?
- Do I prefer to work in a large city or a smaller community?
- Do I prefer a center-city working location or a suburban working location?
- Do I work well under pressure?

The honest answers to these questions will help you to understand your personality as it relates to work. The answers to these questions should also help you to plan your job hunting activities so you will be able to find the kind of job with which you will be happy.

STEP 2—MAKING A JOB-SKILL INVENTORY

After you have considered your personal needs, make a list of the **specific** job skills you have to offer an employer. It is essential for you to be absolutely honest with yourself as you list the specific skills you possess. If you are not totally honest with yourself, you could find yourself applying for jobs for which you are not qualified.

Next, make a list of all the business experience you have had that is related to the type of work for which you are applying. Give a brief description of each job and the specific duties you have performed. By completing this step thoughtfully, you should be able to match your skills and experience to a specific job description when the time comes to do so.

STEP 3—OBTAINING SOURCES OF JOB INFORMATION

After you have taken an inventory of your personal needs and the specific job skills (and experience) that you possess, you will be ready to look for a **specific** job with a specific company. To do this effectively, you will need to be aware of a number of sources of job information. Be sure that you consider all of the following sources of job information as you search for jobs for which you are qualified:

- Friends and members of your family
  (One recent survey of employers even indicates that this was the **most frequent** method by which applicants learned of job openings.)
- Your school placement office
- Newspaper advertisements
- Specialized publications, such as company house organs (newspapers)
- Civil service announcements
  (Federal, state, and sometimes city government job openings are frequently announced this way.)

- Employment agencies
  (Federal, state, and city governments frequently operate employment services. Usually there is no placement charge to either the employee or the employer for placements by these agencies. Private employment agencies match people with jobs **for a fee.** The fee, usually based on a percentage of the first month's wages, can be paid by either the employee or by the employer. Before signing an agreement with a private employment agency, be sure you understand **exactly what the agency will do for you and exactly what you will be responsible to do.)**
- Company Personnel Department
  Usually this source of job information has been considered the least productive, especially if the applicant does not know a job is available. However, in the survey of employers to which reference was made previously, the employers found this to be the second most popular source of job applicants—following "word of mouth."

After you have studied all the sources of job information carefully, you will want to select two or three jobs for which you have the qualifications. (It is never a good idea to limit yourself to only one job prospect.) Then you will need to learn all you can about the companies you select **before** you actually begin applying for a job. Here are some questions that will help you with your study of the companies you select:

- What is the company's major line of business?
- How old is the company?
- Is the company locally owned or is it part of a larger corporation?
- How is the company viewed by its employees and by the community?
- Are in-company training programs available to employees?
- Does the company follow a "promote-from-within" policy?
- What is the company's outlook for continued growth and expansion?
- How does the company rate as a leader in the industry of which it is a part?

Some of this information can be obtained from employees of the company. Frequently, the local chamber of commerce and local banks can give you information (not specific financial information) about companies within the trading area they serve. (Whatever you do, don't make it appear that you are "finding out" about the company to determine if they are "worthy" of you!)

By knowing the answers to these questions, you will be able to make a more effective application for employment, and you will be more informed during the interview. In addition, you will be making a more intelligent job judgment by knowing all you can about a prospective employer.

STEP 4—PREPARING A RESUMÉ AND AN APPLICATION LETTER

After you have selected two or three jobs for which you have the qualifications and after you have learned all you can about the companies where those jobs are available, you will be ready to prepare a resumé and an application letter to go with it.

Resume

Keep in mind that there is no "right" design for a resumé. As long as it is neatly arranged and attractive to see, a resumé can and should be as individual as you want to make it (without going to extremes) because it is your sales representative. The experts usually agree that a one-page resumé (see Fig. 184) is sufficient for a person who is seeking his/her first full-time job after graduating from school. However, a person who has had considerable work experience might require a two-(or more) page resume (see Fig. 185). Remember that a new resumé should be written to meet the particular needs of the job for which you are applying.

While the form that a resumé takes may vary considerably from person to person, certain basic information should be included in all resumés. That information includes the following:

A. **Heading**—Include your name, your complete address, your telephone number (including the area code), the date of the resumé, and the type of job(s) you are seeking.
   Provide your date of birth (optional since Federal law prohibits employers from **requiring** you to give this information) and your social security number.
B. **Education**—List your education beginning with your most recent training and work backward to your high school training. Give the following information: name of school and address, dates attended, date of graduation, diploma or degree earned, course specialization, listing of significant courses related to the type of job you are seeking. (There is more and more evidence that a one-page resumé is desirable. If that is the situation, the listing of significant courses would probably need to be eliminated.)
C. **Activities and Awards**—They indicate something about your personality—whether you are introverted or extroverted—and they indicate how well you would "fit in" with the other employees and how you would "get along" on the job.
D. **Experience**—List all work experience—both full time and part time—that suggests that you are an industrious, mature, stable person. (Be sure that no gaps are evident in dates from the time you finished high school to the present time.) Under experience, give the following data for each employer:
   - Name
   - Complete address
   - Telephone number
   - Dates of employment (from/to)
   - Job title
   - Name of your immediate supervisor
   - A **brief** description of the duties you performed on the job.

   It is not necessary to list the salary you earned at each job, but you should be prepared to discuss your previous salary at an interview if you are asked about it. Meaningful statements and accurate facts about your previous work experience will help to influence a prospective employer in a positive way.
E. **References**—It is important to select references very carefully and to get permission before you use a person's name as a reference. Give a minimum of three references. Try to give the names of two people who will be able to give information about your work habits and accomplishments (preferably not your teachers). Give one person who will be able to give information about your ethical and moral values (preferably someone who has known you for at least five years). Do not use relatives as references.

   The reference section of a resumé should contain the following information:
   - Name and title of each reference
   - Complete business address
   - Business telephone number

   It is usually agreed that a person applying for an entry-level job **should** include references on his/her resumé. Some personnel experts suggest that references should be omitted from other resumés, and a statement indicating that references are "available on request" should be added to the resumé.

RESUMÉ OF:

William C. Malone
462 Trent Road
Boise, ID 83706

Date of Birth: 3/8/-- (optional)

Telephone: (208) 344-4973

Social Security: 421-74-3971

Date: August 15, 19--

Position Sought: Management training position with an opportunity to apply my business administration training to a challenging management job with growth potential.

EDUCATION:

University of California at Los Angeles, Los Angeles, CA 19-- to 19--, Graduated, June, 19--: BS (business administration) Specialization: Economics and Finance

Central High School, Boise, ID, 83706; Graduated (with highest honors) June, 19--; Major: College Preparatory Course

ACTIVITIES:

University

. Finance Club (three years)
. Sigma Chi Fraternity (President, senior year)
. Basketball Team (four years)
. Men's Glee Club (two years)
. University Student Council (two years)
. Newman Club (President, junior year)

High School

. Senior Valedictory Award
. Basketball Team (four years)
. Drama Club (two years)
. Men's Chorus (two years)
. Y Teens (two years)

EXPERIENCE:

Dalton Associates (CPA Firm), 1212 Century Boulevard, Los Angeles, CA 90057--Part-time accountant during junior and senior years at UCLA and during summers of 19--, 19--, and 19--.

I handled clients' monthly accounting records and prepared quarterly statements and annual tax returns.

REFERENCES: (with permission)

1. Ms Helen C. Thomas, Accountant, Dalton Associates, 1212 Century Boulevard, Los Angeles, CA 90057 Telephone (213) 484-1484

2. Dr. T. R. Kohn, Dentist, 308 West Market Street, Suite 1100, Los Angeles, CA 90057 Telephone (213) 485-8000

3. Mr. George E. Morse, Attorney, 1121 Hopewell Avenue, Room 516, Boise, ID 83706 Telephone (208) 344-1761

Fig. 184. One-page resumé

RESUMÉ OF:

Elaine C. Wilson
414 Montgomery Road
Syracuse, NY 13202

Telephone: (315) 774-5681

Social Security: 164-82-6014

Date: June 28, 19--

Position Sought: A professional secretarial position with growth potential

EDUCATION:

Cazenovia College, Cazenovia, NY 13021; Graduated, June, 19--, Associate Degree, Secretarial Science; Specialization: Secretarial Science Program; Significant Courses:

. Typewriting/Keyboarding--70 net words a minute
. Machine Transcription
. Secretarial Procedures--filing, communications, mail, telephone usage, financial records, business travel
. Business Statistics--methods of representing and interpreting business trends
. Economics--concepts and understanding of prices, wages, credit, interest rates, taxes, and insurance
. Business Law--contracts, sales, installment sales, employer and employee rights and duties, principal and agent, negotiable instruments, and business organization
. English composition
. Fundamentals of business psychology
. Word processing
. Records management

East Side High School, Syracuse, NY
Graduated with honors, June 19--
Major: College preparatory

ACTIVITIES AND AWARDS:

. Drama Club (high school)
. Staff of high school yearbook
. Substitute organist at Christ Episcopal Church in Syracuse
. Member Future Secretaries of America (FSA) (high school)

EXPERIENCE:

. Century Insurance Company, 84 Towne Road, Cazenovia, NY 13035, June to September, 10--; Summer secretary for three insurance underwriters; Anne C. Thomas, Supervisor

Answered the telephone and learned to deal with many types of people. Had responsibility for processing loss estimates and summaries. Filed correspondence and loss reports, and transcribed from the dictating/transcribing machine.

. Assistant Managing Editor of college yearbook, 19--/19-- school year

REFERENCES: (with permission)

1. Ms Louise Kanton, Manager, Trust Department, Empire Trust Bank, 738 Monroe Avenue, Syracuse, NY 13203 Telephone: (315) 228-6141

2. Mr. R. D. Thomas, Adviser for Student Publications, Cazenovia College, 816 Walton Avenue, Cazenovia, NY 13021 Telephone: (315) 387-9080 Ext. 116

3. Ms Helen C. Thompson, President, First National City Bank, 2811 State Street, Syracuse, NY 13200 Telephone: (315) 281-8965 Ext. 660

Fig. 185. Two-page resumé

F. **Picture**—A picture may or may not be used. (Discrimination laws forbid employers from requiring you to provide a picture.) Some personnel specialists say that a clear, attractive picture that presents you "as you are" is an added advantage. However, other personnel experts complain that pictures on resumés have caused embarrassing situations for them. For that reason, it is probably better **not to include a picture** on a resumé.

Application Letter

It is **never** appropriate to mail a resumé to a prospective employer without an application letter. The letter will help you to express your personality and your ability to communicate in writing to a prospective employer. The letter will also help you to "sell" your job skills to a prospective employer and to call his/her attention to your resumé, which will be enclosed. Keep in mind that an application letter is in reality a SALES letter. Therefore, it must be personal in tone; and it will, of necessity, contain a number of personal pronouns. An application letter should contain the following information:

A. It should indicate the position for which you are applying and how you learned that the position is available.
B. It should indicate to the prospective employer how your training, experience, and personality relate to the position for which you are applying. Be specific here. Relate your background to the particular needs of the prospective employer. (This is one reason why you should learn all you can about a company to which you plan to apply for work.)
C. It should refer the prospective employer to the enclosed resumé.
D. The application letter should close with a request for an interview.

Figures 186 and 187 are examples of well-written application letters that follow the suggested outline presented here. The objective of an application letter is to secure a personal interview where the applicant can discuss in detail information highlighted in the resumé and application letter.

Both the application letter and the resumé should be typewritten on **good quality** bond paper **without** any **detectable corrections.** Remember, to sell your professional skills to a prospective employer, they must be presented in a **professional** manner.

STEP 5—THE JOB INTERVIEW

Everything that you have done up to this point is in preparation for the job interview itself. If you have prepared properly and presented your credentials well in your resumé and your application letter, you already have created a favorable impression. However, you will need to give careful thought and preparation to the job interview itself if you are to get the position you are seeking. Here are some suggestions:

A. Be prepared for the interview:

- Plan well in advance what you will wear. Tailored, well-coordinated, understated (yet fashionable) business clothes are always in good taste for either men or women. Your hair should be attractively (but not exotically) styled. Clothes should be neatly pressed so they have a crisp, clean appearance. Everyone (either man or woman) should wear only a minimum of jewelry to accent clothes. Women should be sure that makeup is tastefully applied and natural looking. Perfume or cologne should be used in moderation. Men should be clean shaven. Men who wear beards or mustaches should keep them carefully groomed and neatly trimmed. After-shave lotion and talcum powder should be used

ELAINE C. WILSON
414 Montgomery Street
Syracuse, NY 13202

July 1, 19--

Mr. Sterling P. Hayden, Director
Personnel Department
Empire Publishing Corporation
2451 Lakeshore Drive
Syracuse, NY 13200

Dear Mr. Hayden:

My brother-in-law, Howard Lewis, who works for your company, has suggested that I apply for the position of secretary in the Personnel Department of your firm, which I have been told is now available. I have always been fascinated by the publishing industry, and I am sure I would find it an exciting, challenging place in which to work.

My training in secretarial techniques has equipped me to do a "first-rate" job as a secretary. I enjoy meeting people--both in person and on the telephone--and I work well with others. I am comfortable when meeting deadlines, and I work fast and accurately under pressure. My machine transcription and typewriting skills are excellent, and I have a high production rate in both of these areas.

The enclosed resumé outlines my training and my experience. I hope you will be sufficiently impressed with my ability and my sincerity to grant me a job interview.

Very truly yours,

Elaine C. Wilson

(Miss) Elaine C. Wilson

Enclosure: Resumé

Fig. 186. Application letter (short form)

WILLIAM C. MALONE
462 Trent Road
Boise, ID 83706

August 12, 19--

Mr. John D. Tatro
Personnel Department
Bank of California
3700 El Cajon Boulevard
San Diego, CA 92115

Dear Mr. Tatro:

Dr. Mary C. Hines, Professor of Business at UCLA, has mentioned an employment opportunity in your Management Training Program. Please consider me an applicant for this position.

Can you use a young man with a working knowledge of statistics, a background in accounting and economics, and an ability to prepare effective reports and analyses?

In June 19--, I was graduated from UCLA's College of Business Administration with a major in economics and finance. My related courses were in accounting, budgeting, marketing, industrial psychology, statistics, and business law.

During my last three years of college, I worked part time (full time summers) in the offices of Dalton Associates, a CPA firm in Los Angeles. Through that job, I gained valuable practical experience in monthly accounting procedures, preparing quarterly statements, and preparing annual income tax returns for clients. A very important part of that job was developing a working relationship with clients. This experience--together with being an active part of several college organizations--has provided valuable administrative experience and the opportunity to get along with many different types of personalities. The enclosed resumé lists additional information and provides references.

May I have an interview at your convenience? You may telephone me at (208) 344-4973 or reach me by mail at the address given above.

Sincerely yours,

William C. Malone

William C. Malone

Enclosure

Fig. 187. Application letter (long form)

sparingly. (One recent study indicates that personal appearance plays an important part in the employee selection process.)

- Plan what you will take to the interview with you, so you won't forget anything essential. Here are some suggestions:
  —Several ballpoint pens that work and two well-sharpened pencils
  —Pocket dictionary
  —A copy of your resumē (for information and dates)
  —Your social security card
  —Stenographer's notebook (if you are applying for a job requiring dictation)
  —Typewriter eraser and erasing shield or other correcting devices (if you are applying for a job requiring typewriting)
- Get a good night's sleep the night before the interview. Plan your time so you will arrive at the interview at least 15 minutes before the time of your appointment. **Nothing** makes a worse impression than arriving late for a job interview. Go to the job interview ALONE. Do not take friends or relatives with you **for any reason!**

B. During the interview:
When you arrive for the interview, you will probably be greeted by a receptionist or secretary in the Personnel Department. Be courteous and cooperate with these people. (They may have been asked to evaluate their overall impressions of you!)

1. Ordinarily, you will be asked to complete an application form before you talk with the employment interviewer. (If you are applying for a civil service job, you will be sent an application blank in the mail to complete and return before the time of the interview. This procedure is also followed by some private companies.) The application form in Fig. 188 has been completed properly, using the information from the resumē in Fig. 185. Notice that the information requested has been printed so it is easy to read. Also notice that every item has been carefully completed. When an item does not apply to the situation, it is marked "N/A" (not applicable). After you have completed the application form, take it to the person who gave it to you; and sit quietly until you are called by the interviewer.
2. When you are called to talk with the interviewer, he/she will have studied your application carefully; and he/she will probably have come to some general impressions about your acceptability as a candidate for the job opening.

   When you go into the interviewer's office, go in a confident, self-assured manner. A secretary or receptionist will probably introduce you to the interviewer. Be friendly and courteous. Smile. Experienced interviewers know that people are usually a little bit nervous at job interviews. However, excessive nervousness can be an indication that you feel unsure of your ability; and that implication can hurt your chances of getting the job.

   During a traditional interview, the interviewer will try to evaluate your interests, your ability to adjust to ever-changing circumstances, and your potential for future growth and development. This will be done through questioning and conversation. The following is a listing of the questions you might expect to answer during the interview. Be sure that you have given careful thought to the answers to all of these questions before you go to the job interview.

APPLICATION FOR EMPLOYMENT

MORGAN GLASS CORPORATION
Greensboro, NC

PERSONAL INFORMATION

Date: June 30, 19-- Social Security Number: 164-82-6014

Name: Wilson (Last) Elaine (First) C (Middle)

Present Address: 414 Montgomery Street (Street) Syracuse (City) N.Y 13202 (State)

Permanent Address: Same as above (Street) (City) (State)

Phone No.: (315) 774-5681

If related to anyone in our employ, state name and department: none Referred by: Ms. Helen Thomas-friend

EMPLOYMENT DESIRED

Position: Professional Secretarial Date you can start: July 1, 19--

Are you employed now? No If so may we inquire of your present employer: N/A

Ever applied to this company before? No Where: N/A When: N/A

EDUCATION

	Name and Location of School	Years Completed	Subjects Studied
Elementary School	Eastland School, Syracuse, N.Y.	8	N/A
High School	Palmerton High School, Syracuse, N.Y.	4	College Prep.
College	Utica College, Utica, N.Y.	2	Secretarial Science

Subject of special study or research work: Word Processing

What foreign languages do you speak fluently? None Read: None Write: None

U.S. Military or Naval service: None Rank: N/A Present membership in National Guard or Reserves: No

Activities other than religious (civic, athletic, fraternal, etc.): Drama Club, Yearbook Staff (High School)

Exclude organizations the name or character of which indicates the race, creed, color or national origin of its members

(CONTINUED ON OTHER SIDE)

Fig. 188. Application for employment

FORMER EMPLOYERS List below last four employers, starting with last one first

Date Month and Year	Name and Address of Employer	Position	Reason for Leaving
From 6/-- To 9/--	State Farm Insurance Co. 378 Burton Road Syracuse, N.Y. 13200	Stenographer	Summer Employment
From School Year 19-- To	Palmerton High School Yearbook Staff	Assistant Managing Editor	Project Completed
From To			
From To			

REFERENCES Give below the names of three persons not related to you, whom you have known at least one year.

Name	Address	Business	Years Acquainted
1 Ms. Louise Kanton	Trust Department National City Bank 378 Monroe Avenue Syracuse, N.Y. 13203	Banking	3
2 Mr. R. I. Thomas	Utica College 1186 Fourth Avenue Utica, N.Y. 13302	Student Publications Advisor	3
3 Ms. Helen C. Thompson	President Franklin National Bank 4483 Wilson Street Syracuse, N.Y. 13200	Banking	6

PHYSICAL RECORD

Have you any defects in hearing, vision or speech which might affect your job performance? No

In case of emergency notify Doris E. Wilson (mother), 414 Montgomery Ave., Syracuse, N.Y. 13202 (315) 774-5681
Name Address Phone No.

I authorize investigation of all statements contained in this application. I understand that misrepresentation or omission of facts called for is cause for dismissal.

Date 6/30/-- Signature Elaine C. Wilson

- What is your education?
- What **special** training have you had for this job?
- What business experience have you had? By what firms have you been employed?
- Why do you want to work for this company?
- What do you consider your strong points to be?
- What salary do you expect? (Do your homework; have a **realistic** answer!)
- What have you learned from some of the previous positions you have held?
- What are your special interests?
- Do you feel that you are flexible in your thinking and open to suggestions?
- What types of job duties do you like best?
- What are your plans for the future?

It is generally agreed by personal experts that job success is related to eight specific areas of behavior. They are:

- Stability
- Industry
- Maturity
- Self-Reliance
- Competitiveness
- Loyalty
- Motivation
- Perseverance

It will also be possible for you to ask questions during the interview. If the following questions are not answered specifically during the interview, you might want to ask them before the interview is concluded:

- What will be the scope of the work in this job?
- With whom would I be working in this job?
- Does this position provide opportunities for advancement? If so, what type of advancement?
- Does this company have a "promote-from-within" policy?
- Does the company have a training program for which I would be eligible?
- Does this company reimburse employees for job-related courses they take?

If the interviewer is really interested in you as a prospective employee, he/she may ask you to talk with someone else in the company (perhaps the head of the department where the job opening exists). You may also be asked to take some tests (both psychological and skill) if the interviewer is seriously interested in you as a prospective employee. Be gracious and cooperative with these requests even though they produce additional stress. They are necessary procedures that help the prospective employer to determine your suitability for the job opening.

Do not make it appear that you are trying to control the interview. Avoid any discussion of vacations, coffee breaks, clubs, and sick leave. You will be told about these things after you are hired. Be alert, interested, and responsive; but let the interviewer conduct the interview. When the interviewer indicates that the interview is over, rise, thank him/her for granting you an interview, and leave. On the way out, take time to thank the receptionist and/or secretary and anyone else who helped you during the interview.

In addition to the traditional interview (an interview which is directed by an interviewer) described here, two other types of interviews, the **open-ended interview** and the **highly structured interview,** are being used more and more frequently.

During an **open-ended interview,** the interviewer instructs the applicant to "tell me about yourself." The applicant should then give the interviewer appropriate information about his/her training and experience that relate to the job for which the applicant is applying. (The information on the applicant's resumē is the essential information that should be presented to the interviewer.) After the applicant has presented the appropriate information to the interviewer, the interviewer may have some additional questions to ask.

The **highly structured interview** is one in which a **panel** of interviewers (usually three persons) ask a series of questions that the panel has selected in advance of the interview. (Interviewers on the panel take turns asking questions.) Usually the applicant is given a list of questions that are to be asked during the interview to read before the interview begins. As the applicant answers questions that are asked by panel members during the interview, his/her responses to each question are recorded (on paper) for future reference by the interviewers. (Frequently a sex equity officer from the company conducting the interview observes the entire interview procedure.)

STEP 6—THE FOLLOW-UP

As soon as you get home from the interview, evaluate everything that happened. Analyze the discussion that took place and the questions that were asked. Take a small card and write on it the date of the interview, the name and address of the company, the title of the job for which you applied, and the name of the interviewer. Jot down any pertinent information that will be helpful to you at your next interview.

A. How did the interview go?

—What points did I make that seemed to interest the employer?
—Did I present my qualifications well? Did I overlook any that are pertinent to the job?
—Did I pass up clues to the best way to "sell" myself?
—Did I learn all I need to know about the job? Did I forget or hesitate to ask about factors that are important to me?
—Did I talk too much? Too little?
—Did I permit the interviewer to control the interview (during a traditional interview)?
—Was I too tense?
—Was I too aggressive? Not aggressive enough?

B. How can I improve my next interview?

If you are really interested in the job, you should follow up the interview with a letter to the interviewer. (Even if you aren't particularly interested in the job, this is a courteous gesture.) A follow-up letter should do the following:

- Express appreciation for the interview
- Express your desire to obtain the job—if you really want it
- Add an additional selling point—try to capitalize on something to which the interviewer responded favorably during the interview. (Figure 189 is an example of a follow-up letter that has been properly written.)

Finally, remember that interviewing for a job can be tiring (emotionally and physically). For that reason, limit yourself to two interviews a day. Try to allow **several hours** between interview appointments. By doing this, you will have time to "freshen up" between interviews and to evaluate the first interview before you go to the second one. Also, you will not have to be nervous and upset if the first interview runs longer than you anticipated.

By following the suggestions in this chapter about presenting your job skills to a prospective employer; by developing your job skills to optimum level; by projecting a positive, enthusiastic personality with concern for other people; and by working industriously and cooperatively to help the company for which you work to grow and prosper —you should find a full measure of satisfaction in your work. GOOD LUCK!

414 Montgomery Street
Syracuse, NY 13202

July 1, 19--

Mr. Sterling P. Hayden, Director
Personnel Department
Empire Publishing Corporation
2541 Lakeshore Drive
Syracuse, NY 13200

Dear Mr. Hayden:

I enjoyed meeting you yesterday and discussing the position of secretary that is open at Empire Publishing. I was especially happy to learn that you are a friend of my former boss, Ms Louise Kanton. I really enjoyed working with her.

After talking with you and after touring your lovely office, I feel more convinced than ever that I would like to work for Empire Publishing. The job in your Editorial Department particularly interests me, because I enjoy doing detailed work and following a project to completion.

If you wish to telephone me, I can be reached at home for the remainder of this week, (315) 774-5681.

Sincerely yours,

Elaine C. Wilson

(Miss) Elaine C. Wilson

Fig. 189. Follow-up letter

FOR REVIEW AND DISCUSSION

1. What factors should be considered in taking a "personal inventory"?
2. What factors should be considered in taking a "job-skill inventory"?
3. List the major sources of job information.
4. After you select two or more companies to which you intend to apply for a job, what facts should you learn about those companies? Why?
5. What information should be contained in a resume? What is the "right form" in which to prepare a resume? Should a resume ever be more than one page in length?
6. What information should be contained in an application letter?
7. How should a job applicant dress for an interview?
8. What types of questions is the **interviewer** likely to ask during a job interview? What types of questions might the **job applicant** ask during an interview?
9. Describe the following types of interviews:
   Traditional Interview
   Open-ended Interview
   Highly Structured Interview
10. How should a job interview be evaluated?
11. What information should be contained in a follow-up letter?

Turn to your workbook and complete Student Projects 40 and 41.

Cross-Referenced Index

C

D

E

R

S

T